WINE

Wine
A Cultural History

John Varriano

REAKTION BOOKS

For Marianne, Rachel and Wendy

Published by
Reaktion Books Ltd
33 Great Sutton Street
London EC1V 0DX, UK

www.reaktionbooks.co.uk

First published 2010

This book was published to accompany the exhibition *Wine and Spirit: Rituals, Remedies, and Revelry* organized by the Mount Holyoke College Art Museum.

> Mount Holyoke College Art Museum,
> South Hadley, Massachusetts, USA: 2 September–12 December 2010
>
> Memorial Art Gallery of the University of Rochester,
> Rochester, New York, USA: 30 January–10 April 2011

Printed and bound in Singapore by Craft Print International Ltd

British Library Cataloguing in Publication Data
Varriano, John L.
    Wine : a cultural history.
    1. Wine – Social aspects. 2. Wine and wine making – History.
    3. Wine in art. 4. Wine in literature. 5. Wine – Physiological effect.
    I. Title
    394.1'3-DC22

ISBN: 9 781 86189 790 9

Contents

Introduction

Wine is unique in the cultural history of food and drink. Its mystique has meandered from pre-historic times through the civilizations of ancient Greece and Rome, the perilous early years of Christianity and its later Reformation, and eventually into our own age. In nearly every period and every part of the world, it has captured the creative imaginations of the religious and the philosophical, the artistic and poetic, and even those in the healing professions. A source of meditation and metaphor, wine has sparked revelations and free associations wherever it has been consumed. The challenge of comparing its seemingly incomparable taste or colour with other types of experience has also been ubiquitous. When a respected contemporary philosopher compares a chablis to a Jane Austen novel, a Calliore to a sculpture by Maillol and a rare American varietal to 'the sound of a deep organ note beneath the choir of summer perfumes', he is only following a rhetorical practice that began with Homer's 'wine-dark sea'.[1]

The flow of wine narratives has remained continuous, but it has also been diverted by its natural potential for both raising the spirits and spurring disorderly conduct. Because it is so closely associated with immoderation and inebriation, wine has inspired more justifications for its pleasurable effects than any other intoxicant. The conflicting attitudes held towards its influence on behaviour have made the beverage a paradigm for expressions of moral ambivalence, a claim that cannot be made for beer, tobacco or hallucinatory drugs.[2] Indeed, no other food or drink carries the same 'halo of significance'.[3]

Wine: A Cultural History focuses mainly on Western civilizations where the beverage is made from *Vitis vinifera*, a species native to Eurasia that over time spread throughout Europe and eventually

Frontispiece:
Detail from illus. 66
(David Ryckaert III,
*Temptation of
St Anthony*, 1649,
oil on copper).

7

to the New World.⁴ For the sake of coherence, I do not discuss cultures in those parts of the world where wines were traditionally made from rice, fruits or other substances.

The grapevine itself was the source of wine's mystique. Vegetation cults celebrating the earth's fecundity are the oldest and most deeply embedded in human consciousness. The cycle of death and renewal that is so much a part of the natural order lay at the heart of the rituals they embraced, and the later resurrection myths of deities like Osiris, Dionysus and eventually Christ ultimately sprang from the same soil.⁵ Not surprisingly, religion has been the locus of some of the most enduring beliefs, practices and rationalizations involving wine. Faith in its ability to raise one's spirit above and beyond natural biological constraints began very early in human history, flourished in Greco-Roman cults of Dionysus and Bacchus and, metaphorically transformed, became central to the Judeo-Christian tradition, where in the Bible it is taken as a gift from God, and eucharistically as the blood of the Saviour.

From the beginning, wine has played a central role in secular rituals as well. Herodotus speaks of its importance in early Egyptian dinner parties, Xenophon in Athenian *symposia*, and Pliny in Roman banquets. Reminders of death – memento mori – often accompanied ancient feasts, not so much to moralize on the transience of life as to spur drinkers to indulge in its pleasures before it was too late. The idea of *carpe diem* originated before Horace popularized the term more than two thousand years ago, and even today the expression lives on. Wine's association with memento mori has been less constant, however, and in the seventeenth century the hedonistic message of *carpe diem* evolved to the darker one of *vanitas* with its fearsome reminders of death itself. Both *carpe diem* and *vanitas* placed the emphasis on the drinker's personal, even existential, state of mind while another Latin phrase, *in vino veritas* (in wine there is truth), denoted the unintended social disclosures that can accompany drinking. This, too, was a notion with a Greek pedigree that justified consuming wine in excess.⁶

Through the ages, wine-drinking has been a marker of social class, especially in places where other alcoholic beverages were readily available. Beer traditionally has been the most popular alternative, but deprecations levelled against it began in ancient Greece and continued until the Middle Ages, only to be resumed in the Renaissance.

8

The price differential between the two beverages was surely a factor, but wine drinkers have traditionally postulated class distinctions as well. Beer production may have been more technologically complex, but wine consumption has always been considered more sophisticated.[7] Nowhere has this been more evident than in early modern England where mature cultures of beer and wine existed side by side. The engraved frontispiece of a 1617 treatise on British drinking habits (illus. 86) presents a vivid contrast between the two worlds: the setting for the gentlemanly wine drinkers offers the comfort and beauty of a classical loggia and landscape, while the rowdy ale swillers live in a far less civilized environment.

The third recurring theme in wine's cultural history pertains to its real or imagined medicinal effects. This, too, is a story rooted in ancient times that has continued without interruption to the modern day. The raising of one's glass to toast the health of companions has evolved into a purely symbolic gesture, but the origins of the practice came from the desire to assure one's guests of the salutary nature of the wine itself.[8] Intrinsically, wine was long believed to have three therapeutic applications: as a topical treatment for wounds (a remedy known from both Homer's *Iliad* and the New Testament parable of the Good Samaritan); taken internally for its own presumed benefits; or as the liquid vehicle for other medications. Ancient humoral theories underlay most assumptions about wine therapy before the modern period, but even after these were discredited, the treatments remained surprisingly persistent. And no sooner did most of the world's pharmacopoeias eliminate prescriptions for wine or wine-based medications in the 1960s, but studies began to appear that indicated a low rate of cardiovascular disease among the wine-drinking French, known for their rich national diet. This 'French Paradox', as it has come to be called, put wine back on the table as a topic of medical discourse. Research on wine and health is now at an all-time high, although little attention is paid to the psychic benefits the beverage has always provided.[9]

The strength of wine's association with sacred ritual and secular revelry is indisputably linked to its liberating psychotropic effects. The modern philosopher William James captured the essence of this phenomenon in *The Varieties of Religious Experience* when, speaking of the pathology of human consciousness, he wrote:

The sway of alcohol . . . is due to its power to stimulate the mystical faculties of human nature, usually crushed to earth by the cold facts and dry criticisms of the sober hour. Sobriety diminishes, discriminates, and says no; drunkenness expands, unites, and says yes. It is in fact the great exciter of the *Yes* function in man. It brings its votary from the chill periphery of things to the radiant core. It makes him for the moment one with truth.[10]

James goes on to suggest that drink can be the poor man's substitute for the symphony and the unlettered man's literature. Karl Marx declared religion to be the opiate of the people, but, in truth, alcohol has probably played a more significant role in fostering escape, apathy, or a general sense of well-being. Surely there is some truth to the old Italian proverb, 'one barrel of wine works more miracles than a church full of saints'.

Drinking wine is not the same as imbibing other alcoholic beverages. Its unique 'soul-transforming effect' is more intimate, in the words of Roger Scruton (who goes on to compare it with an erotic kiss), 'more *face to face* than whisky's *in your face* demeanor'.[11] Moreover, the potential of wine to spark a deep sensory appreciation of colour, aroma and flavour has always set it apart from other intoxicants. The subtleties engendered by *terroir* and vintage come into play as well, a circumstance already acknowledged in notations on Egyptian wine jars from as early as the second millennium BC.

In the end, the capacity of wine to transform the spirit has been the basis of one of mankind's most enduring narratives. As the following chapters make clear, wine has supported and justified a variety of religious and secular expressions, consistently sustaining the hopes and fears, aspirations and delusions of those who throughout history have adapted its unique potential to needs of their own.[12]

one

The Origins of Wine

Wine has been around since the dawn of civilization. Its origins were most likely accidental, for the fermentation of yeast in a container of grapes is a natural process that requires no human intervention. This may have occurred as early as the Paleolithic period, although the first substantial evidence is from Neolithic sites in the near east. Mythic accounts of the unintended fermentation of grape juice have long circulated, but wine's beginnings can now be explored with a measure of accuracy through the advances of modern archaeology, archeobotany, and paleontology. More than any ancient text or artifact, radiocarbon dating, high-resolution microscopy, and DNA analysis reveal a better understanding of the origins of early viniculture.[1]

From such evidence, we learn that *Vitis vinifera*, the wild Eurasian grapevine, was first turned into wine at some time between about 8500 BC at the earliest, and 4000 BC at the latest. But the means by which this occurred involved more than simple cultivation of the grape. In addition to horticultural know-how, wine-making required vats for pressing the fruit, airtight containers for storing the juices and a basic understanding of the processes of fermentation. Where this first happened remains a matter of some debate, since Neolithic pottery vessels containing wine residue have been identified in both Egypt and Persia, while grapes themselves are known to have been cultivated around the same time in the Transcaucasus. The earliest wine jars known to us today were excavated in Hajji Firuz Tepe in northwestern Iran and date to 5400–5000 BC (illus. 1). Like the modern Greek wine retsina, their deposits consist of the juice of fermented grapes mixed with tree resins.

But what motivated our distant ancestors to make wine in the first place? Some evidence suggests that it served medicinal purposes

1 Neolithic wine jar from Hajji Firuz Tepe, *c.* 5400–5000 BC, clay.

of the kind Hippocrates and Galen would describe several millennia later, but its links to early – if uncertain – ceremonies imply a ritual role as well. The association is found in any number of works of art. To take but one splendid example, a Mesopotamian cylinder seal of *c.* 2400 BC from the Royal Cemetery at Ur (Iraq), depicts some revellers raising cups that have been poured from a spouted jar while others sip from straws inserted into larger, wide-mouth jars. The cups presumably contained wine, the other vessels beer, and the ceremony itself is clearly a banquet. Compositionally, later depictions of Greek symposia come to mind, yet the occasion commemorated here is not self evident. Because the seal was found in the tomb of Queen Puabi, its imagery most likely related to her death, depicting either her funeral banquet or the pleasures that awaited her in the afterlife.[2]

By the second millennium, wine was known throughout the ancient near east, although a distinction between viticulture (the growing of grapes), viniculture (the making of wine) and a true wine culture should be made. Sumerians and their successors in southern Mesopotamia, for example, are known to have cultivated grapes, but seem not to have had a taste for wine.[3] The earliest evidence for a true wine culture stems from Hittite texts that speak of libations and supplications offered to the gods, as when Ullikummi is offered 'sweet wine', and Illuyanka, the serpent, becomes inebriated after drinking too much of it.[4]

While a few Anatolian representations of wine-drinking are known, the pictorial record really begins in ancient Egypt, where tomb paintings, sculpture and papyri attest to the popularity of wine making, its consumption by priests and the social elite, and its offering to the dead. Wine offerings appear on the walls of temples, on stelae and obelisks, and in royal tombs from the earliest times to the Ptolemaic period.[5] The phenomenon is especially apparent during the New Kingdom (1570–1070 BC) in scenes like that depicted in the tomb of Nakht, an eighteenth-dynasty astronomer and priest in Thebes who is accompanied to the afterlife with a bounty of poultry and wine (illus. 3). Such offerings have been interpreted as gifts to the deities or blessings expected from them.[6]

Jars of the type represented in such images sometimes told a story of their own, with inked labels and seal impressions identifying the contents. The tomb of Tutankhamun is the most informative in this respect since 26 of the jars buried with the pharaoh are labeled with his regnal year, the location and proprietorship of the vineyard

2 Mesopotamian *Banquet Scene*, lapis lazuli cylinder seal and cast from the 'Queen's Grave' at Ur, *c.* 2600 BC.

3 *Men making wine, plucking poultry, and bringing offerings to the dead*, detail of Egyptian 18th Dynasty (16th–14th century BC) wall painting in the tomb of Nakht, Thebes.

and the name of the winemaker.[7] Thus the modern notion of 'vintage year' and 'appellation contrôlée' originates here. Tut's vintages were clearly the best to be had, but lesser wines were available to ordinary mortals as well. We know of one instance, for example, of a daily ration of wine being provided to men working in a quarry.[8]

Several minor deities like Shesmu, Thoth and Hapy contributed to the mythology of wine by overseeing its making or offering.[9] Because of the difficulty of cultivating grapes in the Egyptian climate and the greater importance attached to the waters of the Nile, their prominence was limited, however, and it was Ousir (later known as Osiris), the god of nature and agriculture, who ultimately left more of a legacy to the culture of wine.[10] Ousir not only symbolized the vine as one of the earthly bounties, but he was revered in the Egyptian cosmogony as the chief deity of death. After he was drowned in the Nile by his brother Seth, and restored to life by his wife, Isis, Ousir also became the god of resurrection, and it was in these uniquely conjoined roles that, along with Ra, he reigned supreme. As Herodotus later informs us, Egyptian gods were taken as prototypes for Greek ones, and legends of Ousir were appropriated for the myths of Dionysus.[11] It was through such 'correspondences' that the cults and rituals associated with wine would endure, with Dionysus going on to engender Bacchus, and Bacchus, in turn, becoming a prototype for representations of Christ.

Egyptians apparently were also the first to leave records attesting to the medicinal benefits of wine. Various medical papyri prescribe wine or wine-based medications for symptoms ranging from asthma to epilepsy, fevers, jaundice and loss of appetite.[12] Wine was recommended in salves, enemas and in bandaging, all treatments that, like Osiris's resurrection, would reverberate in succeeding eras.

One of the most captivating legends of early antiquity was King Midas's ability to turn everything he touched into gold. The alchemical gift may have been fabulous, and ultimately tragic, but Midas was in fact a real person whose life is recounted in contemporary Assyrian sources and later in the *Histories* of Herodotus and the *Fabulae* of Hyginus. He reigned as king of Phrygia in the eighth century BC and is believed to have been buried in a mound in Gordion on the central Anatolian plateau. The so-called Midas Mound was first excavated in 1957, but it was not until forty years later that the organic residues inside the burial chamber were examined by a second set of investigators. The 157 bronze vessels found among the tomb furnishings contained food and drink that presumably was consumed by mourners at a feast offered to Matar, the mother goddess, as part of the funeral ceremony. As such, these vessels tell us something of Midas's gastronomic preferences if not of his alchemical wizardry. One vessel found in the tomb, a ram-headed *situla* or drinking bucket, exemplifies the imaginative skills and high level of workmanship that marked the creation of such early objects.

Despite the biodegradation of the contents, a combination of infrared spectroscopy, liquid and gas chromatography and mass spectrometry of the remaining evidence allowed for a detailed reconstruction of the Midas feast. From this analysis, the main dish has been identified as a stew of spicy lentils and barbecued sheep or goat, while the beverage was a grog fashioned from grape wine, barley beer and honey mead. The residues were also intensely yellow in colour, suggesting that an untraceable herb or spice like fenugreek, safflower, coriander or saffron had been added to the brew. Such heady mixtures were not uncommon in pre-classical times, although by the fifth century BC varietal wines had replaced them in all but the most esoteric religious ceremonies. Beer, on the other hand, would eventually be dismissed by Greek writers and gourmands as a barbarian drink.[13]

4 Ram-headed Situla from the Midas Mound at Gordion, 8th century BC, watercolour by Piet de Jong of bronze vessel.

The Legend of Noah

The Old Testament has its own story to tell concerning the origins of viniculture. The book of Genesis, which presumably was written sometime after the tenth century BC, recounts the part Noah played in this: after building his ark and weathering the Great Deluge in the company of 'seven pairs' of animals and birds, he eventually saw the waters recede and landed the craft 'on the mountains of Ararat'.[14] Once ashore, Genesis continues, 'Noah, a man of the soil, was the first to plant a vineyard', a remark leading to the hypothesis that the biblical patriarch was also the world's first vintner. Genesis further reports that he 'drank some of the wine and became drunk, and lay naked in his tent'. Despite the shame that followed his discovery by his sons, Noah's transformation of grapes into wine remained a momentous achievement.

Genesis is on chronologically shaky ground when it first informs us (5:1–30) that Noah was born in the tenth generation after Adam, and later (9:28–9), that he died 350 years after the Flood, at the age of 950. Dates for the Great Flood itself have been independently estimated, however. Deep-water radar and borings, as well as radiocarbon dating of mollusc shells found in the area, have recently led two Columbia University geologists to conclude that there was a major climate change around 5600 BC that resulted in a precipitous rise of waters in the Black Sea.[15] Mount Ararat is, of course, a real place, not far from the Black Sea in the northeast corner of modern Turkey. Even more intriguing is its proximity to the Neolithic settlements in northwestern Iran where the earliest known wine vessels were made in the years 5400–5000 BC.

Noah's personal chronology may be implausible, but the scientific and archaeological evidence for the dating and the geography of the flood tends to support the biblical account of the origins of viniculture despite its having been written some 5,000 years after the event. Biblical 'minimalists' – those who find no reliable evidence in scripture – put little faith in the apparent coincidence between the subsiding of the flood and the earliest wine, but literalists or creationists will doubtless be heartened by the recent discoveries.[16]

Wine in Ancient Hebrew Texts

Judaism, like Christianity and Islam, was founded on monotheistic principles that disallowed the creation of supplementary gods. But while there was no deity like Dionysus/Bacchus, wine did play a significant role in early Hebrew religion, if not so miraculously as in later Christianity. For Moses and his followers, the bounty of the Promised Land was exemplified by a cluster of grapes so large that it took two men to carry it on a pole.[17] Wine figures prominently in any number of Old Testament rituals and celebrations ranging from circumcisions to weddings, with the Passover seder being the most common of festive banquets. In real life, Jews of the land of Israel adopted Hellenistic and Roman dining customs, although their celebrations were typically more family-centred, with the Torah being the main topic of conversation.[18] At the same time, rabbinic sources reveal some practices that were unique to Hebrew wine culture.

Early texts like the Derekh Eretz Rabbah and the Tosefta Berakhot tended to be proscriptive, offering advice such as 'a man shall not drink from a cup and place it on the table, but hold it until the servant arrives and hand it to him' (Rabbah, 9); 'a man shall not drink from a cup and hand it to his neighbour, since people are uncomfortable with one another' (Berakhot 5:9); and 'a man shall not drink all of [the contents of] his cup at once; if he does he is a bibber and a glutton' (Rabbah, 6).[19]

Most Old Testament narratives tend to be ambivalent about wine and its associations. On one hand, the Hebrew Bible speaks of it as one of the gifts God lavishes upon mankind.[20] Thus in Genesis (27:28) we read that Isaac blessed his son Jacob with the words

> May God give you of the dew of heaven
> And of the fatness of the earth,
> And plenty of grain and wine.

More than other earthly bounties, wine is singled out in scripture for its spiritual benefits. The Book of Psalms (104:14–15) thanks the Lord for bread 'to strengthen' the body, and oil 'to make the face shine,' but wine alone is credited with the capacity 'to gladden the human heart'. The Book of Solomon even goes so far as to use wine as an erotic metaphor when in 7:8–9 the lover imagines

O may your breasts be like clusters of the vine,
And the scent of your breath like apples,
And your kisses like the best wine
That goes down smoothly, gliding over lips and teeth.

All this assumes that the beverage is drunk in moderation. Excess consumption, by contrast, is condemned for its association with confusion (Proverbs: 20:1), violence (Proverbs 4:17), poverty (Proverbs 21:17; 23:20–21), arrogance (Habakkuk 2:5), and abuse of the poor (Amos 6:6). The stories of Lot and possibly Noah exemplify how inebriation can even lead to improper sexual relationships (Genesis 19:30–38; 9:21–7). Drunkenness is also used as a metaphor for God's Judgment, as in the case of the 'horror and desolation' forecast in the Babylonian prophecy (Ezekiel 23:30–34). With no benevolent Bacchus or Dionysus to guide them to higher spiritual realms, ancient Israelites were wary of the transformative effects of any wine set before them.

The Book of Proverbs (23:29–35) paints a colourful picture of the inebriated state of mind:

Who has woe? Who has sorrow?
Who has strife? Who has complaining?
Who has wounds without cause?
Who has redness of eyes?
Those who linger late over wine,
Those who keep trying mixed wines.
Do not look at wine when it is red,
When it sparkles in the cup
And goes down smoothly.
At the last it bites like a serpent,
And stings like an adder.
Your eyes will see strange things,
And your mind utter perverse things.
You will be like one who lies down in
the midst of the sea,
like one who lies on top of a mast.
'They struck me,' you will say,
'but I was not hurt;
they beat me, but I did not feel it.

When shall I awake?
I will seek another drink.'

Disapproving as that might sound, rabbinic sources routinely endorse the consumption of wine for medicinal purposes. The Talmud states that if a sick man has a cask of wine in his home, he has no need of drugs, for the wine will heal him (Gittin 69b). Even the prudent Berakhot (51a) recommends wine as 'beneficial for the heart and good for the eyes, and even better for the bowels; when one is accustomed to it, it is good for the entire body.' The Talmud also advises that those suffering from impotence drink 'three-quarters of a *log* of wine [about 25 fluid ounces] cooked with ground forest saffron', a remedy that seems to have worked for the Rabbi Yohanan who claimed 'these [treatments] have restored my youth' (Gittin 70a). Among other Talmudic prescriptions are the taking of wine to treat ear and eye infections, to replace body fluids lost in bloodletting, and when mixed with honey and pepper, to cure intestinal problems, and with bay leaves to rid the body of parasites.[21]

The Hebrew sages even addressed the problem of the poor who could not afford to buy medicinal wines. In such a case, the Talmud (Shabbat 129a) proposes that the man whose physician told him to drink a quarter *log* of wine, 'take a worn coin and visit seven wine shops. At each shop he should taste the wine, pretending to be interested in purchasing it. After the shopkeeper refuses to accept his worn currency, he should move on to the next shop, until he had consumed the necessary amount.'[22]

two

Wine in Ancient Greece

After water, wine was the most widely consumed beverage in ancient Greece. While beer was already available, it was dismissed as an 'effeminate' drink by Aeschylus and viewed with suspicion by most Greeks.[1] Wine, the more manly beverage, came in three types according to Mnesitheus: black, white and *kirrhos*, or amber.[2] The white and amber wines could be either sweet or dry, with the black being somewhere in between. Hippocrates made further distinctions among dark and white, harsh and soft, and sweet and dry wines. In his essay *On Diet*, he went on to characterize them as fragrant or odourless, slender or fat, and strong or weak. Nearly all Greek texts that have come down to us confirm that wine was typically diluted with water, and sometimes mixed with aromatic herbs or honey to disguise the taste of the pitch or resins used to seal the amphoras or preserve their contents.[3] By and large, early Greeks seem to have had little appreciation of regional varieties or particular vintages although they did recognize the benefits of ageing. A rare glimpse into wine tasting in ancient Greece appears on a fifth-century kylix that depicts a young man in a wine shop using a sponge to test the taste and bouquet of the contents of a krater.

Dionysus

Although Dionysus, the god of wine, is first mentioned by name on Mycenaean Linear-B tablets from around 1200 BC, it was not until the eighth century that the personality of this rural deity fully emerged.[4] From the *Homeric Hymns* we learn that he was born of Zeus and Semele although his place of birth remains uncertain.[5] Uncertainty proved to be a constant in Dionysiac mythology as the identity of the

5 *Youth in a Wineshop*, red-figure kylix attributed to Douris, *c.* 480 BC.

23

god was subject to a bewildering number of variations. Classical literary sources reveal him to possess a savage and violent temperament (the *Orphic Hymns* calls him one 'who delights in the sword and bloodshed' and Plutarch 'an eater of raw flesh'); a nurturing manner whose gift of wine removes all sorrow and care ('the delight of mortals' for Homer and 'god of many joys' for Hesiod); and the skills of a dancer, ecstatic lover and bestower of riches (*Greek Scholia*).[6] He was at home in both the depths of the sea and on dry land.

No other deity supported a more unstable legend than Dionysus. At various times embodying terror and ecstasy, wildness, ritual madness, theatrical performance and deliverance, his mythic presence was both a paradox and a collection of irreconcilable contradictions. Even his age and gender orientation were ambiguous. Early incarnations envisioned him as older and ruggedly masculine, a bearded figure cut in the mould of Zeus, while later ones portray him as younger and more androgynous.[7] Perhaps his conflicted character resulted from his having been born twice – first from the womb of his mother and then from the thigh of his father. Unlike other Olympians such as Zeus or Apollo, he was not particularly promiscuous despite having the phallus as his emblem when he was evoked as the god of fertility.

Given his free-wheeling nature, it is not surprising that Dionysus attracted an enormous following in the ancient world. Numerous cults devoted to his worship sprang up across Greece and Asia Minor, most of them overlooking the violent side of his personality as they celebrated the delights that came from drinking his wine. These festivities typically took place in wine-producing regions in the autumn or early spring at the time when the grapes were harvested or the wine released. Like modern All Souls' commemorations, some festivals such as the Athenian Anthesteria were closely linked to the dead. In these, it was believed that the deceased came back to visit the living and remained with them until a ceremonial pronouncement was made that signified the time had come for them to take their leave.[8] Given the number of drinking vessels found in tombs, wine was closely associated in Greek religious belief with the needs of the afterlife in general.[9]

Tens of thousands of lines of Greek and Latin poetry and countless works of art attest to the irresistible attraction of Dionysiac myths and cults in the ancient world. He and his circle of maenads, nymphs,

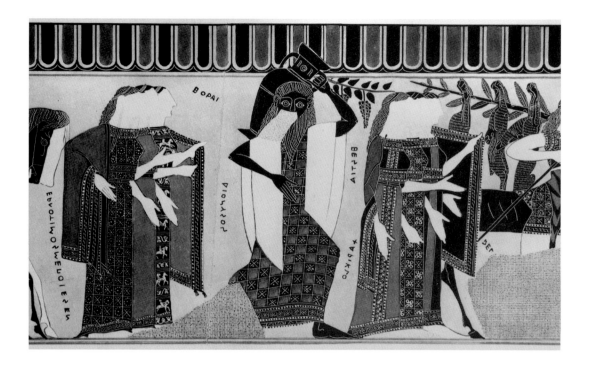

6 *Dionysus and his
Entourage*, detail
from the François
Vase, *c.* 570 BC,
from A. Furtwängler,
Griechische Vasenmalerei.

satyrs and sileni were among the most colourful and frequently represented figures in all of classical art and literature.[10] The earliest depictions were made in the sixth century BC, most commonly on black-figure vases where Dionysus tends to be rendered in an iconic, rather than narrative fashion. The François Vase, a large volute krater painted around 570 BC and now in the National Archeological Museum in Florence, was in many respects prototypical.[11] On one side of this vase, Dionysus stands among the pantheon of Olympian gods attending the wedding of Peleus and Thetis. The deity is shown as a massive bearded figure dressed in a boldly patterned chiton (tunic), his face turned toward the viewer with mesmerizing wide-open eyes. Although his anatomy and costume are highly stylized, we recognize the figure as Dionysus from the accompanying inscription and from his attributes of the amphora and grape branch.

The François Vase is itself a krater that would have been used to mix wine and water, but the amphora carried by the god was made to hold undiluted wine. A comparable black-figure amphora of a slightly later date (illus. 7), now in the Worcester Art Museum, depicts Dionysus holding a horn-shaped cup, a primitive form of drinking vessel.[12] By the mid-sixth century, this simple object would give way to

7 *Dionysus and his Entourage*, black-figure amphora by the Rycroft Painter, *c.* 530–520 BC.

OPPOSITE ABOVE:
8 Side view of red-figure kylix, with *Dancing Maenad* attributed to Oltos, *c.* 525–500 BC (see interior view, illus. 10).

BELOW: 9 Black-figure skyphos with Herakles, Athena and Hermes, attributed to the Theseus Painter, *c.* 500 BC.

a variety of pottery vessels whose shapes were more refined. The most common of these were the kylix for drinking and the skyphos for storage, each of which was provided with a base and a pair of handles.

Dionysus appears for a second time on the François Vase leading a procession of figures who accompany the god Hephaistos on his return to Olympus. These companions, as immobile as those attending the wedding of Peleus and Thetis, are identified by inscriptions as satyrs and nymphs. The role these creatures play in later Dionysiac imagery was destined to grow, and by the time the Worcester amphora

with flying feet', 'frisking like fillies' and 'mad, stark mad, possessed by Bacchus'.[18]

The capacity of wine to raise one's spirits was an idea that appealed to Greeks on more than one level, encompassing cultic ritual and theatrical performance along with the simple pleasures of the table. In the case of this kylix, the gradual emergence of the dancing figure at the bottom of the cup could only have enhanced the liberating effects of the wine upon the drinker.

By the middle of the sixth century, images of Dionysus had gained in complexity. If his earlier incarnations did little more than symbolize the promise of wine, his depictions in later Greek art increasingly disclosed the mythic dimensions of his literary persona. Conventional representations of him with maenads and satyrs by no means disappeared, but the iconographical repertory expanded to include more detailed narrative scenes that portray the god from the

10 *Dancing Maenad*, interior of kylix, 525–500 BC (see side view, illus. 8).

30

13 *Dionysus and his Entourage*, red-figure hydria in the manner of the Meidias Painter, *c.* 400–390 BC.

clothed wooden pole flanked by two female attendants who mix the wine. Walter Otto, in *Dionysus: Myth and Cult*, describes the ritual:

> Before the citizens drank it, the wine was mixed for Dionysus . . . A priestess, perhaps the wife of the Archon Basileus himself, took over the mixing of the wine and the fourteen *gerarai*, whom she would initiate, probably assisted in this rite. The celebrants lined up and had their pitchers filled by these priestesses. Then to the accompaniment of trumpet blasts, the famous drinking bout began in which the crowd joined together to honor the drunken god. Finally, each celebrant placed his wreath around the wine jar, handed it to the priestess who had

33

mixed it for him, and poured the wine that remained in the jar as a libation to the god.[20]

Dionysiac religious rituals were not the only occasions at which large quantities of wine were consumed in ancient Greece. Wine was central to upper-class sociability, and both weddings and funerals were awash in libations offered to newlyweds and the deceased.[21] Identifying the specific context for early depictions of drunken revelry is seldom easy given the multitude of social settings in which they occur. Because of the categorical confusion, the generic label *komoi* has been applied to those scenes in which the underlying motive remains unclear. One late fifth-century kylix is typical of the numerous works in which neither Dionysus nor his followers appear, and few if any iconographical clues are provided to help identify the

14 *Women Ladling Wine before Dionysus*, red-figure stamnos by the Dinos Painter, late 5th century BC.

15 *Reveller*, red-figure
kylix attributed to
Douris, *c.* 480 BC.

partygoers. In the interior of this vase, a nude *komast* (as such revellers are known) does a sideways step over his own kylix, while on
the cup's reverse a dozen male companions dance and play music.
The abundance of wine vessels depicted on the vase leaves little
doubt as to the inspiration behind their uninhibited behaviour.

Wine and Death

Although the all too familiar Latin expression *carpe diem* (seize the day) is rightly associated with Roman Epicureanism – a corruption of the philosophy of Epicurus himself – even earlier, Greeks embraced the notion of tasting the pleasures of life before death in poetry, plays and epitaphs of their own. Herodotus claimed the practice originated in ancient Egypt where at dinner parties wooden corpses 'carved and painted to resemble nature as nearly as possible' would be passed among guests with the exhortation to 'gaze here, and drink and be merry, for when you die, such will be you'.[22] If Herodotus was correct, this would constitute our earliest knowledge of the presence of *carpe diem* and memento mori (reminders of death) at the same table.

By the sixth century BC, the Greek poet Theognis of Megara endorsed the 'drink and be merry' philosophy – if not always the accompanying memento mori – in verses addressed to readers of all ages.[23] For those still in 'mid-career', he offered this advice:

> Let us prepare to dine; and eat and drink
> The best of everything that heart can think;
> And let the shapely Spartan damsel fair
> Bring with a rounded arm and graceful air
> Water to wash, and garlands for our hair;
> In spite of all the systems and the rules,
> Let us be brave, and resolutely drink;
> Not minding if the Dog-star rise or sink.[24]

But for the older reader, he suggests:

> Enjoy your time, my soul! another race
> Will shortly fill the world, and take your place,
> With their own hopes and fears, sorrow and mirth;
> I shall be dust the while and crumbled earth.
> But think not of it! Drink the racy wine
> Of rich Taygetus, press'd from the vine
> Which Theotinus, in the sunny glen
> (old Theotinus loved by gods and men),
> Planted and watered from a plenteous source,

Teaching the wayward stream a better course;
Drink it, and cheer your heart, and banish care;
A *load* of wine will *lighten* your despair.[25]

An identical chord was struck in lines from a fourth-century play by the comic poet Amphis. 'Drink! Have fun!', the audience is told, 'Life is mortal, and our time on earth limited; whereas death is immortal, once you're dead.'[26]

Greek tombstones offered a ready site for even more mordant messages, their inspiration supposedly derived from an inscription on the sarcophagus of Sardanapalus, last of the Assyrian kings. According to Athenaeus (quoting Chrysippus), this epitaph read: 'Keep in mind that you are mortal, and make yourself happy by enjoying feasts, nothing is of any use to you after you are dead.'[27] Greek tomb epigraphy frequently conveyed a similar message by bidding farewell to passersby with either a reminder to partake in the pleasures of sex and wine – with wine being the favourite of the two – or the deceased declaring that he had done so himself. Among the epitaphs, one finds:

Drink and eat and wear flowers, suddenly we are dead.
Drink, you see the end while you live, drink.
The man was a satisfactory follower of the muses and an agreeable fellow over his cups.
Bacchus was always my friend.[28]

The Symposium

In addition to the many cultic rituals and philosophical attitudes linked to wine, one secular event stands out in Greek wine culture and that is the symposium (*symposion* in Greek). This was a social gathering of men who drank and talked, often about specified topics, in a convivial setting removed from the constraints of everyday life.[29] Because they were conversational, symposia provided authors with an ideal discursive structure to follow for ruminations of their own. Plato, Aristotle, Xenophon, Epicurus, Aristoxenus and Heraclides were among those who exploited the genre in pursuit of the play of ideas. For Plato the topic was love, for Aristoxenus, music, and for Heraclides, the medicinal effects of food and drink. Of all the *Symposium* authors, Xenophon was the most descriptive of the atmosphere of the gathering. His little book was written around 380 BC, but it claims to record the conversation and entertainments of an event that occurred almost forty years earlier.

Like all classical symposia, this one took place after a banquet when 'the tables had been removed and the guests poured a libation'. Wine was critical to a symposium's success because of its capacity, in Xenophon's words, to 'moisten the soul' and when consumed in 'small cups . . . by gentle persuasion [induce] a more sportive mood'. While disquisitions on various subjects remained central to the occasion, entertainments provided by 'a fine flute-girl' and 'a very handsome boy' added significantly to the evening's merriment. This attractive pair, we are told, were brought by a visitor from Syracuse who 'made money by exhibiting their performances as a spectacle'. One infers from this that the duo were professional entertainers and their acts depended, at least in part, upon conventions of the theatre.[30]

Among the entertainments that accompanied the words and wine at Xenophon's symposium were an abundance of music and song, gymnastic exercises, the balancing and juggling of wineskins or winecups, wine-flinging contests and finally – with the late arrival of Dionysus and Ariadne – lovemaking. Unlike their literary peers, vase painters often ignored the discursive aspects of the evening to focus on the entertainments.

One of the entertainments that Xenophon failed to mention was the offering of trick drinking vessels to unsuspecting guests.[31] These appeared to be ordinary kylixes or bowls but were intended as practical jokes or deceptions for the recipient. One fourth-century amphora was constructed in such a way that even when it appeared to be empty, a plentiful supply of wine could still be poured from its hidden cavities.[32] Only by inverting the vessel and holding one's finger over a hidden hole in its bottom was one able to drink from it. In the hands of a practised server, it has been estimated that ten refillings might be poured for baffled symposiasts before all the wine in the secret chamber was consumed.

Other drinking vessels were intended to surprise or embarrass their users by proving impossible to drink from, by dribbling wine all over one's front or by making unexpected rattling noises. The earliest surviving of these, dating from the eighth century BC, appears to be a stacked set of geometric skyphoi but is, in fact, a single vase. 'Dribble cups' were probably the most disconcerting to those already in the throes of inebriation, for these could commence their unwanted flow at any time. In one kylix from the sixth century BC, the presence of tiny holes in the bowl and the base would have allowed a joker to tug on a string that dislodged a pin and stopper that kept the vessel from leaking.[33] Then, without warning, the soaking would begin.

Archaeological reconstructions of ancient banqueting halls reveal that seven to fifteen participants reclined – one or two to a couch – in a small and sparsely furnished room.[34] Because the settings tended to be so minimal, it is sometimes as difficult to recognize a proper symposium as it is to identify a Dionysiac ritual among the numerous drinking scenes that appear in Greek art.

A sixth-century black figure amphora (illus. 16) suggests how depictions of the symposium may have originated in the world of Dionysiac imagery. On one side of this vase, the deity himself reclines on a couch accompanied by a bare-breasted woman – presumably Ariadne – a flute player and two nude bearded dancers. This congenial grouping would seem to anticipate the deities' appearance at the end of an evening like the one Xenophon described in his *Symposium*. Myth gives way to reality on the reverse of the vase, however, as six ordinary mortals – three men and three women (probably *hetaerai*, or courtesans) – stand around or embrace one another. Clearly this is a drinking party, its conflation of the human and the divine facilitated by the deity's gift of wine. Nowhere in Greek ritual are the boundaries between higher and lower states of being more fluid than in the rites of Dionysus.[35] The spirit of the symposium seems to have been born of the instability of the myth itself.

The kylix, the most common of Attic drinking cups, was a natural site for illustrating the effects of wine consumption. A red-figure example from around 480 BC (illus. 17) portrays the progress of a symposium in graphic detail. This, we see, is not Plato's drinking party where Socrates lectures Diotima on the nature of love and beauty, but a scene of post-prandial debauchery. The painter Makron spared no indiscretion as he portrayed what Xenophon called the 'sportive' effects of wine on the six male participants, each of whom is attended by a compliant *hetaera*. Reading the vignettes clockwise from the wine krater set beneath one of the cup's handles, we find women disrobing, making love, spinning winecups from the ends of a finger, playing the flute and holding the head of a man who is caught in the act of vomiting.

16 *A Symposium*, black-figure amphora attributed to the circle of the Affecter Painter, *c.* 550–525 BC.

17 *A Symposium*, red-figure kylix attributed to Makron, signed by Hieronas potter, *c.* 480 BC.

18 *Erotic Scene*, red-figure kylix, attributed to Douris, *c.* 480 BC.

Scenes of boorish behavior were by no means uncommon on symposium vases – another kylix in New York shows a man urinating into a presumably empty *oinochoe* – but depictions of sexual abandon were even more popular. A kylix in Boston with unpainted sides features a copulating couple in the interior. The symposium context is suggested by the presence of the leg of a couch at the left.[36] As if further clarification of the subject was needed, two faintly rendered inscriptions have been included, the one above informing us that 'the girl is beautiful' while the other circles her waist with the directive 'hold still'.

The Greek appreciation of homosociality – and even homoeroticism – flourished in the permissive atmosphere of the symposium.[37] Plato condemned sexual intercourse among men as unnatural in his *Laws*, yet in some of the earlier speeches of the *Symposium* recognized that homosexual love was also capable of

19 *Two Youths at a
Symposium*, red-figure
kylix by the Colmar
Painter, *c.* 500–490 BC.

20 Drawing of a detail
of a *Symposium* vase
with woman drinking
from phallic-footed
kylix, *c.* 510 BC.

rising from the crudest passion to become a marriage of noble minds.[38] A kylix in the Louvre whose interior emphasizes the physicality of the friendship between two half-clothed youths explicitly acknowledges the role that wine has played in furthering their intimacy. Some vases were even more graphic in representing homoerotic activity while still others took the form of the male sexual organ itself. By raising such a vessel to one's mouth, the drinker would have entered an erotic zone before even tasting the wine.[39]

Drunkenness

Greek authors agreed on the revelatory effects of drinking wine when taken in moderation. For Alcaeus, 'wine reveals truth'; for Theognis, wine 'banishes care'; for Aeschylus, wine is the 'mirror of the mind'.[40] Plato concurred with the view that wine 'confers a sense of happiness, power, and freedom', and goes on to suggest guidelines for its consumption: children under the age of eighteen, he advises, should avoid it so as not to 'pour fire on the fire already in their souls'; young men under thirty may drink it in moderation, 'but must stop short of drunkenness and bibulous excess'; thereafter, they 'should summon Dionysus' to 'cure the crabbiness of old age' and 'soften their hard cast of mind'. Under its influence, an older man can shed his inhibitions and be moved to 'sing his songs with more enthusiasm and less embarrassment'.[41]

The highest state of mind associated with drunkenness in the Greek world was 'divine madness', a condition Plato associates with Dionysus, who, alone of the inspirational deities – which included Apollo and Aphrodite – was capable of inspiring 'mystical release from normally accepted behavior'.[42] 'The best things we have come from madness, when it is given as a gift of the god', Plato writes. In company of the Muses,

> Madness takes a tender virgin soul and awakens it to a Bacchic frenzy of songs and poetry . . . If anyone comes to the gates of poetry and expects to become an adequate poet by acquiring expert knowledge of the subject without the Muses's madness, he will fail, and his self-controlled verses will be eclipsed by the poetry of men who have been driven out of their minds.[43]

43

Plato's contemporary, the so-called Pseudo-Aristotle, went further in one of his *Problems* by positing links between creative madness, the intoxification of wine and the melancholic temperament which he (like everyone at the time) attributed to humoral imbalance.[44] To this way of thinking, wine was an artificial catalyst capable of inspiring 'divine madness' in those predisposed to its effects. The timeless trope of the boozy melancholic genius thus was born in fifth-century Greece.

However, too much wine also led to unruly behaviour. Evidence of the phenomenon appears much earlier,[45] but even in the decorous context of Plato's *Symposium*, we find Alcibiades stumbling into the party with a wreath of ivy and violets on his head, announcing that he was 'already drunk, utterly drunk'. Alcibiades somehow managed to keep the conversation on track until the appearance of yet another group of revellers prompted a 'general uproar [in which] all order was abolished, and deep drinking became the rule'.[46] Shortly thereafter, most of Plato's party either fell asleep or drifted away.

A comic verse by the fourth-century BC poet, Eubulus, plots the course from sobriety to drunkenness with respect to the number of kraters consumed by a group of symposiasts.

> Three kraters do I mix for the temperate;
> One for health, which they empty first,
> The second for love and pleasure,
> The third for sleep.
> When this krater has been drained,
> Wise guests go home.
> The fourth krater is ours no longer,
> but belongs to hubris,
> the fifth to uproar,
> the sixth to prancing about,
> the seventh to black eyes,
> the eighth brings the police,
> the ninth belongs to vomiting,
> and the tenth to madness
> and the hurling of furniture.[47]

The recommended threshold was three kraters for a group that typically numbered eleven drinkers.[48] Because of its high alcohol

21 *Seated Silenus*, vase, 4th century BC, terracotta.

content, Greek wine was usually diluted with water from a vessel appropriately known as a hydria. There was some variation in the ratio of water to wine, however, with early sources suggesting a mixture that ranged from one to one, to five to two.[49]

Despite warnings against overindulgence, inebriation was still so common in the ancient world that it engendered a mythic personification of its own. The dubious honour of symbolizing drunkenness was bestowed at some point in the fifth century BC on Silenus, one of the male followers of Dionysus.[50] Various legends are associated with his name, some of them attesting to his wisdom and his gift for prophecy. One claimed that he had been the older tutor of Dionysus (*Orphic Hymns*) while another (Herodotus) placed him in the court of King Midas. Yet his sagacity is typically overlooked in favour of his physical dissipation, while his portrayal as a shaggy-haired, paunchy old man made him unique in the pantheon of well-toned gods of Greek mythology. His temperament, on the other hand, was good-natured. A charming fourth-century BC sculpted vase (illus. 21) shows him seated next to an amphora holding a bunch of grapes in one hand and offering the viewer a cup of wine with the other. Silenus is not visibly drunk in this work although he surely is in a larger bronze in the Naples Archaeological Museum, a Roman copy of a Greek original from the third century BC. Any trace of sobriety, not to mention self-respect, has vanished from this pathetic creature who continues to argue a point after he has toppled over backwards.

Silenus' weakness for wine proved to be harmless both to himself and to his fellow revellers, but overindulgence came at a price for other Greek partygoers. The classic case was that of the centaurs, mythic descendents of Ixion and Nephele whose heads and upper torsos were human but whose lower bodies and legs were equine. Of all the followers of Dionysus, these bestial creatures were especially prone to drunken misdeeds that ended tragically. In two of the most famous incidents, a centaur named Nessus made the mistake of trying to rape Heracles' wife, Deianeira, and was killed by the offended deity on the spot. On another occasion, a group of centaurs overindulged at the wedding of the Lapith king Pirithous and one of them, Eurytion, attempted to abduct the bride, Hippodamia. The brawl that ensued all but led to the centaurs' demise, leaving in its wake a clear lesson on the dangers of intemperance. Numerous ancient authors describe this tragic event, but Homer, in Book XXI of the *Odyssey*, was the most direct in addressing its underlying cause.

> Remember Eurytion the centaur! It was the wine that got at his wits, in King Pirithous' house, when he was visiting the Lapithae. Fuddled with drink, what did he do but run amuck in the palace? His hosts . . . threw him out of doors, but not before they sliced off his ears and nose with a knife. Away went the maddened brute, with his woes heavy on his silly soul; and so the feud started between the centaurs and men. But he was the first to suffer, and he brought his troubles on himself by getting drunk.[51]

The tale of the lapiths and centaurs is famously prominent in the history of art, appearing on the François Vase and achieving canonical status on the metopes of the Parthenon. The most expansive

22 *Drunken Silenus on a Lion Skin*, 270–250 BC, bronze.

treatment of the subject is found at the Temple of Zeus in Olympia (*c.* 460 BC) where the entire west pediment is devoted to the epic encounter. The implacable figure of Apollo stands at the centre of this tumultuous composition, with lapiths and centaurs locked in mortal combat all about him. Nowhere is the conflict between the rational and irrational exemplified more directly than in this clash of Apollonian and Dionysian forces. Greek statuary of the classical period typically illustrated exemplary behaviour through positive role models – victorious athletes or valiant warriors – but the Olympia group carried a different message as it reminded viewers, particularly youthful viewers, of the perils of overindulging in alcohol.

Wine as Medicine

Just as wine brought spiritual benefits in Greek religious rites, so it attended needs of the body in Greek medicine.[52] The oldest witness to ancient healing practices was Homer in whose *Iliad* (datable to the eighth–seventh centuries BC) no fewer than 147 wounds are meted out with just a 22 per cent survival rate.[53] For the first time in history, one hears of the wounded being carried off the battlefield and being tended in barracks or on nearby ships. Medical care was spotty at best, but there were some notable exceptions. In Book XI, Homer has the 'lovely-haired Hekamede' tend to the needs of Machaon and Eurypylos, who had each been shot with arrows in Troy. The potion she prepared for their wounds was made from Pramneian wine, grated goat's cheese and barley meal.[54] Once they drank this concoction, the two 'were rid of their thirst's parching and began to take pleasure in conversation again'. Could there be any truth to this? In the *Republic,* Plato offered his contrary opinion, confessing he found it 'an odd drink for someone of [Eurypylos'] condition'.[55]

Among the surprises of modern medicine – as we shall see in chapter Seven – is proof that 'the antiseptic power of wine is no myth' as long as it is applied externally.[56] In Homer it is taken internally, but Hippocrates, writing several centuries later, recommended that 'surface lesions should generally not be moistened, except with wine'.[57] Treating wounds with wine seems to have been fairly universal in the ancient world for the same methods are described centuries later in the New Testament parable of the Good Samaritan (Luke 10:34).

Wine remedies were not always so beneficial, however. In the eighth century BC Hesiod recommended it be drunk 'in the wearying summer season' at the time 'women are most wanton and men most depressed'.[58] What he seems to have had in mind was a holistic view of human health that depended on the body being in balance with natural elements like the seasons. In succeeding centuries, this supposition evolved into humoral theory, the pseudo-scientific belief that health and disease were essentially dependent upon the four bodily humours, blood, phlegm, yellow bile and black bile.[59] Given the Greek disposition to believe in universal laws and formulations, it was perhaps only natural that they thought in such terms when it came to matters of health and disease.

Hippocrates, the most celebrated physician of the ancient world, wrote the classic text on the theory of the four humours some time around 400 BC. This was not his soundest piece of work and neither does it make for easy reading. Modern translators bemoan its disjointed prose, obscure references and 'seemingly intentional difficulties'.[60] Its arguments are supported by the author's other essays, 'The Nature of Man', 'Regimen in Health' and 'Fleshes'. The essence of the theory was that the humours were unstable, being easily affected by external factors that could alter basic human physiology. Thus, he writes, 'the humors vary in strength according to season and district; summer, for instance, produces bile; spring, blood, and so on in each case'.[61] The bodily changes that were thought to result were understood as binary oppositions between hot and cold, and wet and dry.[62] Gender also had a role to play, for as Hippocrates explains in his essay, 'On the Diseases of Women', women are by nature hotter than men.[63] The key to good health, in his view, was to keep everything in balance by harmonizing one's essential humour – whatever that might be – with the conditions prevailing in the outside world.

When maladies occurred through a 'distemper' – or disharmony – of the blend, a change could be effected by bleeding out the bad humours, starving the growth of new ones or purging those that remained. Hippocrates thought wine to be particularly effective as a purgative and a diuretic, and he recommends it for a number of humoral imbalances. Where water was 'cooling and moist', wine, by contrast, was generally 'hot and dry', although not all wines affected the body in the same way. Thus,

> dark and harsh wines are more dry, and pass well neither by stool, urine, or spittle. They dry by reason of their heat, consuming the moisture out of the body. Soft, dark wines are moister and weaker; they cause flatulence because they produce moisture. Harsh white wines heat without drying, and pass better by urine than by stool. New wines pass by stool better than other wines because they are nearer the must (unfermented grapes), and more nourishing; of wines the same age, those without bouquet pass better by stool than those without . . . thin wines pass better by urine. White wines and sweet wines pass better by urine than by stool; they cool, attenuate, and moisten the body, but make the blood weak, increasing in the body what is opposed to the blood.[64]

49

In practice, Hippocrates prescribed different wines for different illnesses, incorporating it into the regimen for almost all chronic and acute diseases, including consumption, fevers, fistulas, jaundice and uterine pain. Only for certain illnesses of the brain did he advise against its use. Wine was not the only gastronomic weapon in his pharmacological arsenal either, for in other chapters he discusses the humoral efficacy of eating cheese, eggs, honey, meat and fish along with countless fruits and vegetables.

After Hippocrates, a long chain of Greek physicians that included Athenaeus, Theophrastus, Mnesitheus, Erasistratus and Cleophantus upheld the therapeutic benefits of wine in treating illnesses and injuries of every kind. As their diagnoses and prescriptions became more exacting, the audiences for their writings grew wider. Pliny singled out Cleophantus in his *Natural History* as the one who 'brought into notice the treatment of disease by wine' just as some of his Roman contemporaries were beginning to explore the subject for themselves.[65] As we shall see in the next chapter, Celsus and then Galen went on to expand the discourse with significant contributions of their own.

three

Roman Wine

Greek wines of the classical period offered relatively few choices when it came to varietals, vintages or appreciable regional characteristics. Contemporary texts describe them as light or dark, strong or weak, sweet or dry, but seldom go into further detail. Eventually, connoisseurship grew more sophisticated in both Greece and Italy, and by the first century AD the Roman natural historian and philosopher Pliny the Elder (23–79 AD) wrote that 'there are altogether about eighty notable kinds of liquor that can properly be called "wine", and two-thirds of this number belong to Italy, which stands far in front of all the countries of the world on that account'.[1] Pliny's awareness of the role geography played in the cultivation of vineyards is apparent in his observation that 'grapes drink up the juice of the soil'.[2] His survey is encyclopaedic, with notations on the distinctive colour and character of wine from towns as small as Ariccia, Bevagna, Durazzo, Modena and Todi. A contemporary of Pliny, Lucius Junus Moderatus Columella, gave an even more comprehensive account of Roman viticulture in the twelve books of his *De Re Rustica*. Although his estimates of the profitability of vine production in the competitive agrarian economy remain open to question, his text leaves little doubt as to the growth of the wine industry as a whole.[3] Shop signs (illus. 23), winemakers' tombstones and other archaeological evidence clearly attest to the ubiquity of wine in the daily life of ancient Rome.[4]

Greek influence on Roman culture was so pervasive that the term Greco-Roman is often used to avoid the confusion that clouds the origin of many works produced in the later classical period. The first inroads on Italian soil occurred in the eighth century BC in the colonies of Magna Grecia, now the regions of Apulia, Calabria

and Sicily. The painted ceramics of Apulia, like the early Doric temples in Paestum, Metapontum or Agrigento, bear witness to the successful export of Greek ideals to the Italian peninsula over the course of the following centuries. Even today, a Greek-derived dialect is still spoken in a few isolated hamlets of Calabria. It did not take long for the culture of Magna Grecia to be absorbed by native Italic and Latin settlements to the north, particularly in the central Italian region of Etruria. Etruscan tombs have yielded a wealth of evidence –

23 Wine merchant's sign in Pompeii, 1st century.

much of it illegally excavated – that bears witness to the lively trade with Greece and its colonies as well as indigenous creations inspired by Greek models. This market may have been provincial, but the quality of luxury goods passing through it was sometimes extraordinary, as is exemplified by the splendid Euphronius krater (recently repatriated to Italy by the Metropolitan Museum of Art, New York). Etruscan civilization was instrumental, in turn, in shaping Rome's own cultural outlook. Given the succession of Etruscan kings who ruled the city before the founding of the Republic in 509 BC, further hybridization of Greek cultural prototypes was all but inevitable.

Romans were choosy, however, when it came to selecting cultural prototypes. The athletic contests so cherished by Greeks held little appeal for the Romans, while a taste for gladiatorial combat and luxurious public bathing led to major architectural innovations. Temple architecture followed a steadier course through the ancient world, as did sculpture, literature, theatre and, for the most part, viticulture and the consumption of wine.

Roman Banquets

The rituals of the Greek symposium were not among the cultural exports that took root on Italian soil, however. Romans preferred to drink and eat at the same time, and the *convivium*, or banquet, was for them the place to indulge, or overindulge, in food and wine. The emphasis on convivial meals led to significant changes in the furnishing of dining chambers themselves, the most popular being the

tightly arranged *triclinium* with its three couches – each holding up to three diners in comfort – placed around a central table.[5] This configuration clearly encouraged greater interaction among the guests who, unlike the homosocial participants of the Greek symposia, would have included women, men and even children.[6] The age and gender diversity of those attending Roman banquets is evident from a variety of literary and artistic sources. Representations of meals being consumed both by the living and the deceased portray figures of both sexes and all ages.[7]

Roman banquets also spanned class differences. Cato the Elder, we are told, gave 'frequent and plentiful dinners' at his Sabine villa, 'asking in the country neighbors, for he considered the table to be the very best promoter of friendship'.[8] Juvenal, though a social climber himself, satirized the degree of 'inclusiveness' he found in second-century Roman society. At a dinner that included the consul Lateranus, he laments the presence of 'assassins, sailors, thieves, runaway slaves, cutthroats, coffin-makers, and a priest'.[9]

It was wine, needless to say, that fuelled the festivities. Romans had more than three hundred names for their wine vessels and utensils, from the large *amphorae* in which the beverage was stored to the *colum*, or sieve, in which it was filtered (and sometimes flavoured with herbs), to the numerous types of cups and beakers in which it was consumed.[10] Although typically diluted with water, the alcohol content remained high. Pliny even describes a favourite wine (Falernian) that would ignite when a flame was put to it.[11] It is not surprising, therefore, to find Cicero recounting a typical Roman dinner party as an occasion marked by 'people coming and going, some wobbling from too much wine, some still unsteady from yesterday's drinking. The floor was filthy, muddy with spilt wine, covered with drooping garlands and fish bones'.[12]

Did Romans drink more wine than diners do today? As the wine scholar André Tchernia has noted, the only primary textual source to survive is an inscription of AD 153 decreeing the wine allocation to residents of a medical college on the Via Appia.[13] Each senior fellow was provided with nine *sextarii* of wine a day, the equivalent of 470 US gallons (1,780 litres) a year. While their junior colleagues received a daily ration of just two *sextarii*, both allotments exceeded the wine consumption of modern Italians which has now fallen to just 13.5 US gallons (51 litres) a year.[14] Yet real figures for the population as

a whole can only be estimates, with the disparity in consumption ranging from 27.4 gallons (104 litres) a year to as much as 48.2 (182 litres).[15] By the second century AD, the city's overall annual consumption – including men, women and adolescents – has been estimated to be sufficient to fill the Pantheon twice over.[16]

As in ancient Greece, Roman table talk followed its own protocols. Although Varro recommended that worrisome and complex conversations be avoided at the table, Catullus and Martial praised *vinum* as the catalyst of freer or more licentious speech.[17] At the most puerile level this could include sexual puns based on the suggestive shapes of fruit and vegetables, or even crude obscenities. More meaningfully, wine acquired a reputation for inducing revelations of a highly personal nature. Pliny offers a catalogue of such disclosures: 'lustful eyes bid a price for a married woman, and their heavy glances betray it to her husband; the secrets of the heart are published abroad; some reveal the provision of their wills; others say things of fatal import, and fail to keep to themselves words that will come back to them through a slit in their throat'.[18] A famous passage in Petronius's *Satyricon* transcribes the litany of insults exchanged by inebriated guests at a lavish banquet given by Trimalchio where among the injudicious barbs are ones mocking the pretensions of the host himself.[19] Aeschylus's aphorism 'wine the mirror of the mind', or Pliny's more famous *in vino veritas* seem to have captured the unfettered spirit of the Roman *convivium* perfectly.[20]

Pliny, like most ancient authors, deplored the behavior of those who overindulged, going so far as to name a few of the most notorious offenders: Novellius Torquatus of Milan, he claims, 'tossed off two and a quarter gallons at a single draught'; Lucius Piso 'caroused two days and two nights without a break'; and Mark Antony 'wrote a book on the subject of his own drunken habits'.[21] Drinking heavily on an empty stomach was particularly common, Pliny claims, during the reign of Tiberius.

Wine and Death

For some, the pleasures of wine led to ruminations of a darker and more probing nature. Propertius, for example, warned in the late first century BC that 'wine ruins beauty, wine spoils youth', while one of Persius's *Satires* describes a young wine drinker whose dissipation

ends with the funeral for his perfumed corpse.[22] Such gloomy meditations did not go unanswered, however. Horace, for one, popularized
the term *carpe diem* to suggest how wine might induce a more positive approach to debility and death. His advice was simple:

> Be smart, drink your wine.
> Scale back your long hopes to a short period.
> Even as we speak, envious time
> is running away from us.
> Seize the day, trusting little in the future.[23]

The philosophy of *carpe diem*, along with the related topos of
memento mori, had in fact been noted centuries earlier by Herodotus
in his discussion of Egyptian dining practices.[24] Numerous images of
memento mori run through the literature of Stoic Latin authors like
Martial and Seneca while at the same time finding visual expression in
the dining chambers of Roman epicures. Surprising as it may seem, ancient triclinia were frequently haunted with skeletons that embellished
drinking vessels, were depicted on walls, or were even handed out as
party favours. Petronius's *Satyricon* describes the last phenomenon,

24 Goblet with skeletons,
late 1st century BC–1st
century AD, silver.

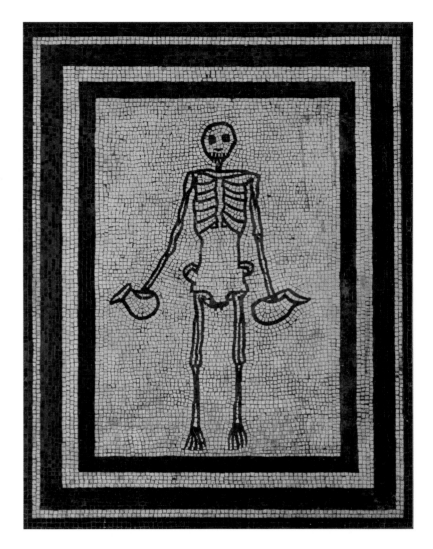

25 *Skeleton,* mosaic from Pompeii, 1st century.

again at a dinner hosted by Trimalchio. After the meal was under-way, 'a slave brought in a silver skeleton, so constructed that its limbs swiveled in every direction'.[25] A few such objects, known as *larvae convivialis*, still exist, while silver goblets from the same Vesuvian region as Trimalchio's mythic villa are iconographically related.[26] In one spectacular example from Boscoreale (illus. 24), a procession of skeletons ring the cup, merrily imbibing wine.[27] Two Roman mosaics from Pompeii offer variations on the theme, one from a tabletop in a summer triclinium that depicts a skull balanced on a wheel of fortune, and the other a floor mosaic of a skeleton with a jug of wine in each hand who stares back pointedly at the viewer. The *carpe diem*

message of each would have been especially poignant that day in August, AD 79, as the first rumblings of Vesuvius were heard in the distance.

The Roman memento mori should not be confused with later Judeo-Christian emblems of *vanitas*, whose purpose was to warn viewers not to forsake their spiritual lives in pursuit of worldly luxuries. Just the opposite was true in ancient Rome where the hedonistic philosophy was perhaps nowhere more evident than in the many funeral epigrams that speak of '*balnea vina venus*' (baths, wine and sex). Of all life's pleasures, wine-drinking was the one most frequently recommended in exhortatory inscriptions.[28] A remarkable example of this sanguine approach to life and death is found on a tomb from the second century AD that was discovered in the Vatican necropolis in 1626 as the foundations were being dug for Bernini's baldacchino.[29] The monument – known as a *kline* – shows a bearded man reclining on a couch, holding a drinking cup in one hand and adjusting a wreath on his head with the other. For those hoping to find the tomb of St Peter, stumbling upon this must have been a major disappointment. An epigram carved on the now-lost base of the effigy identified the deceased as Flavius Agricola and divulged his epicurean views on life:

26 Tomb monument of Flavius Agricola, 2nd century, marble.

Friends who read this, I advise you, mix up the wine and drink far away, wrap your brow with flowers, and do not spurn the pleasures of Venery [sexual intercourse] with beautiful girls; all the rest after death is nothing.[30]

Shocked by the discovery of the pagan monument, Pope Urban VIII had the base destroyed and threatened whoever divulged the inscription with 'the most rigorous excommunication and the most horrible threats'. The statue itself was then quietly spirited away to the garden of a papal nephew, eventually ending up far away from Flavius Agricola's native Tivoli in the Indianapolis Museum of Art.

Roman Religion

Devotions of all kinds were practiced in ancient Rome. By the third century AD, these included cults dedicated to the gods of Greek mythology, to Egyptian and Persian divinities like Isis and Mithras, to deified emperors like Augustus and Hadrian and to Jesus Christ. The Greek myths were among the earliest to flavour the polytheistic stew, having arrived in the south of Italy more than a millennium earlier, and from there spreading to Etruria and Rome. All the Olympian gods and goddesses, along with some other Greek deities, crossed the Adriatic with their identities more or less intact and entered the Roman pantheon of deities. Each, with the exception of Apollo, was renamed in Latin. Several were associated with wine: Jupiter (Zeus) presided over the spring *vinalia* when the first wine was opened, Saturn (Chronos) with the libertine rites of the December *Saturnalia*, and Venus (Aphrodite) with ritual libations of her own.[31] Bacchus, of course, was the reincarnation of Dionysus. Although it is unknown exactly when and where the Bacchic cult originated on Italian soil, it flourished in Rome perhaps even more vigorously than it had in Greece.[32] Driven by the need for mystical experience, devotees tested the tolerance of the Roman authorities to the point that in 186 BC the senate issued a decree suppressing Bacchic rites altogether. Such a prosecution – unprecedented in Rome as far as we know – suggests that the cult posed a major threat to the social and political order.

Livy's *History of Rome* provides a rich if perhaps fanciful account of the cult's activities. Claiming in Book XXXIX that 'the damaging effects of this evil spread from Etruria to Rome like the plague', he reports:

> Initiation into these secret and nocturnal rites was at first imparted only to a few, but then spread widely among both men and women. To *religio* were added the pleasures of wine and feasting . . . When wine had inflamed them, at night males mingled with females, young with old, and when all sense of modesty had vanished, every type of indecency began to occur: promiscuous sex between freeborn men and women; false witness, forged seals, wills, and evidence; poisonings and domestic killings . . . Much was ventured by trickery, more by violence, everything concealed since the voices of those crying for help could not be heard above the wails and the beat of drums and clash of cymbals.[33]

Even after the senatorial decree of 186 BC, the bad behaviour evidently continued, for Pliny's *Natural History*, written nearly two centuries later, gives practically the same account of the evils of drink. Many of the pleasures and transgressions associated with wine are vividly depicted in Roman art, although the picture that comes down to us is somewhat less complete than the one from Greece. Because Romans eschewed ceramic vessels with highly descriptive graphic imagery in favour of ones made of glass or precious metal, the narrative decoration tends to be more cursory and the surviving examples more limited. Fortunately, the Roman penchant for mosaics and wall painting made up for some of what was lost with the disappearance of the pottery painter's art.

Figurative imagery on Roman wine vessels is, nevertheless, revealing. A first-century glass beaker (illus. 27) depicts Bacchus, in the company of Pan and other dancing revellers, pouring wine in the mouth of a small panther while a contemporary silver cup (illus. 28) is decorated with a scene of Bacchic sacrifice before an altar. Although neither vessel is especially innovative in recasting the myth of Dionysus or the practices of his cult, the deity's personal appearance differs markedly from most Greek models in showing him in a state of semi-nudity. Furthermore, if Bacchus retains his early Greek character on the cup – gruff and full-bearded – on the beaker he appears younger, lithe and clean-shaven. The contrast

27 *Dionysian Revel*, cup, 1st century, glass.

28 *Bacchic Sacrifice*, cup, 1st century, silver.

OPPOSITE:
29 *Bacchus*, Roman copy of a Hellenistic original, marble.

30 *Bacchus, a Panther, and a Herm*, 1st–2nd century, fragment of a fresco.

between the two contemporaneous likenesses illustrates the remarkable change in persona that the deity underwent in the late classical world.

As we know from the previous chapter, the image of Dionysus in early Greek verse was of a ruggedly masculine and sometimes violent figure, but over time that reputation gave way to a more benevolent one in which his mythical persona was more commonly interpreted as the bearer of wine and good cheer in the spirit that Homer, Hesiod and the *Greek Scholia* had originally envisioned. Although fully garbed in most Greek representations of the god, the benign unclothed Dionysus was already known from vases dating from as early as 400 BC.

It is in this manner that Dionysus usually appears in Roman art, the archetype presumably introduced in monumental sculpture like one now in the Museo Nazionale Romano (illus. 29), or by textual sources like Callistratus's third-century AD ekphrasis of a lost – or possibly imaginary – bronze by Praxiteles. Callistratus describes the work as:

> a young man, so delicate that the bronze was transformed into flesh, with a body so supple and relaxed . . . it had the bloom of youth, it was full of daintiness, it melted with desire, as indeed Euripides represented him when he fashioned his image in the *Bacchae*.[34]

This was the image that spread through the empire most commonly in the form of drinking vessels like the glass beaker referred to earlier and in the decorations of private houses. In all of these depictions, conventional attributes of the deity appeared, like a wine cup or pitcher, *thyrsus* (staff), panther or satyr. Significantly, Bacchus is only rarely shown intoxicated in Roman art, and then never in free-standing statuary. Before Michelangelo envisioned his drunken god in the late fifteenth century (illus. 52), that was a role reserved for his older friend, Silenus.

For Ovid, Bacchus was the quintessentially metamorphic divinity, both for his own transformations and those that he brings about.[35] He plays a significant role in the *Metamorphosis*, where at the beginning of Book IV he and his followers are described:

The priest had ordered Bacchic celebration,
With serving-women, freed of toil, and ladies
As well as servants, dressed alike in skins
Of animals; all should unbind the ribbons,
Let the hair stream, wear garlands, carry wands
Vine-wreathed. The god, his minister proclaimed,
Would otherwise be fearful in his anger.
So all obey, young wives and graver matrons,
Forget their sewing and weaving, the daily duties,
Burn incense, call the god by all his titles,
The Loud One, the Deliverer from Sorrow,
Son of Thunder, The Twice-Born, The Indian,
The offspring of Two Mothers, God of the Wine-Press,
The Night-hallooed, and all the other names
Known in the towns of Greece. He is young, this god,
A boy forever, fairest in Heaven,
Virginal, when he comes before the people
With the horns laid off his forehead. Even Ganges
In far-off India bows down before him,
The slayer of the sacrilegious Pentheus,
Destroyer, too, of impious Lycurgus
Whose battle-axe, one time, was raised against him.
He turned the Tuscan sailors into Dolphins.
The lynxes draw his car, with bright reigns harnessed,
Satyrs, Bacchantes, follow, and Silenus,
The wobbling old drunkard, totters after,
Either on foot, with a stick to help him hobble,
As shaky on three legs as two, or bouncing
Out of the saddle on his wretched burro.
Wherever Bacchus goes, the cries of women
Hail him, and young men's joyful shouts, and drum
And timbrels sound, and cymbals clash, and flutes
Pipe shrill.[36]

Ovid's characterization of Bacchus as 'young, this god, a boy forever', represented a further transfiguration of the manly deity celebrated in Greek mythology. Over time, the persona of Bacchus merged with that of Liber Pater, another Roman god of fertility and wine, and that in turn led to additional mythic overlays. Macrobius,

31 *Dionysus and Ariadne*, sarcophagus, *c.* 190–200, marble.

one of the last pagan authors of ancient Rome, explained the aging of this composite figure as a matter of seasonal change. In Book I of his *Saturnalia,* Macrobius reports that

> sometimes [he is represented] as a child and sometimes as a young man; again as a man with a beard and also as an old man . . . These differences in age have reference to the sun, for at the winter solstice the sun would seem a little child . . . Afterwards, as the days go on and lengthen, the sun in the spring equinox acquires strength in a way comparable to growth in adolescence . . . Subsequently, he is represented in full maturity, with a beard, at the summer solstice . . . After that, the days shorten, as though the approach of his old age – hence the fourth of the figures by which the god is portrayed.[37]

By the time the *Saturnalia* appeared in the mid-fifth century AD, the tides of religion and art were running strongly in the direction of Christ. Only much later, during the Renaissance and Baroque periods, would the wine god again be shown in his infancy.

Depictions of Bacchus in Roman art tended to be limited to just a few of the episodes catalogued by Ovid. One of the most popular of these focused on a single event in his personal life, his rescue of Ariadne, daughter of the Cretan King Minos, from the island of Naxos where she had been abandoned by Theseus. Classical literary sources differ on a few of the details, but most agree that they married soon afterwards. Ancient representations of the lovestruck couple appear most commonly on sarcophagi, containers for burying the dead. One example dating to the late second century AD (illus. 31) depicts the very moment that Bacchus discovers Ariadne sleeping beside the sea.[38] Clearly besotted by wine and love, he stands a little unsteadily, his arm thrown around the shoulder of a young satyr for support while two of his companions strip away her garments to reveal her beauty and sensuality to the god and viewer alike. A full entourage of nymphs, satyrs, Silenus, a centaur and a panther complete the crowded scene.

The funereal context of such imagery suggests that Romans, like Greeks, viewed Bacchus as an agent of deliverance from earthly concerns, and devotion to his cult as a means of securing happiness in the afterlife. According to this way of thinking, Ariadne's slumber symbolized death, and her awakening the promise of resurrection in the afterlife. Wine, of course, remained critical to the passage from one level of existence to the other. The conjoining of *eros* and *thanatos* under the influence of alcohol must have offended at least one early viewer of the sarcophagus, however, since the head of Bacchus was defaced in the manner that often befell unpopular rulers and political figures in the ancient world. Even on a tomb, the excesses that Livy catalogued centuries earlier presumably remained targets of disapproval and censure.

Bacchic processions were a regular feature on Roman sarcophagi. Among the most popular were those depicting the deity's triumphant return from India accompanied by allegorical figures such as the seasons, whose presence implies the promise of renewal and raises Bacchic imagery to a level of greater cosmological significance.[39] In addition to the deity's agency in renewing life, the seasonal cycle introduces the notions of decay and rebirth that mark the annual passage of time. For the deceased entombed within – presumably a member of a Dionysiac cult – the sarcophagus offered the promise of a blissful afterlife modelled on the apotheosis of Bacchus and echoing the orderly patterns of the natural world. In some later examples, the message of renewal was made more personal by substituting a portrait of the deceased for the normative effigy of the god.[40]

Bacchic imagery could also be punitive, foretelling tragic consequences for those who stood in the way of the cult. A lesser theme in

Greek and Roman art, the tale of Lycurgus nonetheless served as a persistent reminder of what can happen to individuals who question the deity's magical powers. According to Homer's *Iliad*, Lycurgus denied Dionysus was a god and attacked him with an ox-goad, driving his terrified quarry into the sea (where he was quickly rescued by the kind-hearted nymph Thetis).[41] As punishment for his deed, Homer informs us that Lycurgus was struck blind, but later authors embroidered the myth with even more gruesome endings. The *Fabulae* of Hyginus, a Roman author who died in AD 17, envisions Lycurgus – with supreme irony – falling under the influence of wine himself.

> And in drunkenness trying to violate his mother, and then cutting down the vines because he said wine was a bad medicine that affected his mind. Having been driven mad (by Bacchus), he next killed his wife and son before being thrown to the panthers. He is said to have cut off his foot thinking it was a vine.[42]

Roman representations of Lycurgus tend to emphasize the misery of his punishment over the deed which led to his demise. The mosaic illustrated here (illus. 32) focuses on the moment when Lycurgus clubs his son to death while Ambrosia, another of his victims, is transformed into a grapevine, ensnarling him in her branches as a panther nips at his heels. Lycurgus was not the only mortal to pay the price of scorning Dionysus: Orpheus and Pentheus were both dismembered, and Proteus and the Minyades were driven mad for the same offence.

There is something almost comical, even cartoonish, about the Herculaneum mosaic. Indeed, not all depictions of Bacchus were motivated by metaphysical yearning of the kind represented on the sarcophagi. The decoration of private dining chambers like the one from which Lycurgus was presumably excavated are generally more attuned to the philosophy of *carpe diem* than to matters of spiritual redemption. Among the light-hearted subjects represented in these secular settings is the drinking contest between Bacchus and Hercules. Two mosaics from Roman houses in Antioch render the scene with exceptional realism. The first (illus. 33), dating from the late first or early second century AD, casts Bacchus as a pale, effeminate presence (not dissimilar from Ariadne in the sarcophagus discussed earlier),

reclining on a couch with a *thyrsus* in one hand and an overturned cup signifying victory in the other. Before him, the ruddy-skinned Hercules has fallen to his knees while a female flute-player attempts to spur him on. Both Hercules and his supplicant seem unaware that the contest is already over, despite the signals given by Ampelos and Silenus, the attendants of Bacchus. Here, the viewer of the mosaic knows the contest's outcome before the loser himself.

Although Hercules was a notorious tippler – at one point pausing between labours to sample a particularly fine vintage, or in

32 *Lykurgos, Ambrosia and Dionysus*, mosaic from Herculaneum, 1st century.

68

33 *Drinking Contest of Herakles and Dionysus*, mosaic, late 1st or early 2nd century.

Euripides's *Alcestis* drunkenly pursuing a servant girl – his drinking bout with Bacchus is unknown in mythological literature. The subject appears for the first time in images like this, but may reflect the reality of actual 'drinking matches' that were described by Pliny in his contemporaneous chapter on wine.[43] Pliny makes no secret of his disapproval of the prizes and debauchery that inevitably followed, but he was sober when he wrote his commentary and many early viewers of the mosaic presumably were not. Although some art historians wish to interpret the humiliation of Hercules as an illustration of behaviour to be avoided, it seems more likely that the message was understood by those who sat eating and drinking before it as encouraging and witty, rather than admonitory.[44]

Roman Medicine

Roman medicine got off to a slow start, in Pliny's opinion not so much for a lack of belief in its therapeutic benefits as suspicions about the ethics of the practitioners.[45] When the plague struck in 293 BC, the solution was to dispatch a ship to the shrine of Asklepios in Epidauros and bring back the Greek god of medicine in the form of a snake. According to Livy, the snake settled on an island in the Tiber and the plague abated.[46] This was nearly a century after the death of Hippocrates. Only in 219 BC was a practising physician by the name of Archagathus brought over from the Peloponnesus, but the reception he received in Rome was mixed. Again, according to Pliny, 'They say that he was a wound specialist [*vulnerarius*] and that his arrival was at first wonderfully popular, but from his savage use of the knife and cautery he was soon nicknamed the executioner [*carnifex*] and his profession, with all physicians, became objects of loathing'.[47] Martial, for his part, sustained the attack with epigrams like: 'Dialus was once a surgeon, now he is an undertaker', and 'You are a gladiator now, you were formerly an eye doctor. You did as a doctor what you do as a gladiator'.[48] By the time of Pliny and Martial (the second half of the first century AD), other Greek expatriate physicians had managed to venture forth, but not everyone agreed on the efficacy of wine therapy. Pliny dodges the issue with the comment 'there is no topic more difficult to handle [than wine] . . . medical opinion is very divided'.[49]

Asclepiades (124–40 BC) was the most prominent of the wine-prescribing physicians who emigrated to Rome. He was Cicero's personal doctor and the one generally credited with raising the standards of Greek medicine on the Italian peninsula. Some of his prescriptions for good health sound surprisingly modern: dietary restrictions, outdoor exercise and regular bathing (he is said to have invented the shower bath) being among them.[50] But wine was central to his medicinal treatments, and in an essay 'Concerning the Dosage of Wine', he discusses the therapeutic properties of various kinds of wine, both Greek and Roman. He prescribed wine to patients with fever and plied the insane with it in order that in drunkenness they might sleep. Alternatively, in cases of lethargy, wine was recommended to excite and awaken the senses. Over time, his reputation earned him the sobriquet *physikos oinodotes*, or giver of wine.

Other Greek and eventually Roman physicians followed in Asclepiades' footsteps. Aurelius Cornelius Celsus (*c.* 25 BC–AD 50) was the first native-born author of a medical treatise to promote the health benefits of wine. His encyclopedic *De Re Medicina* consists of eight books on ailments he believed treatable by diet, surgery or *medicamenta*, that is, pharmaceutical means.[51] Although based on earlier Greek texts by Hippocrates and Asclepiades, Celsus extended their arguments to include more discerning comments on the therapeutic values of different vintages and wines of different strengths. Thus he contrasted the laxative effects of sweet and salted wine and *mulsum* (wine to which honey or other aromatic substances were added) with the constipating capacity of undiluted wine, harsh or resinated, and *mulsum* that was served warm. Some wines he recommended for invalids (*vinum passum*), those in need of an astringent (*mustum defrutum*), and those who liked to drink in the middle of the day (*vinum siliatum*). Other ailments treatable by wine therapy were those of the eye, ear, teeth and digestive tract. To give but one example, he recommends flushing ear maggots with a decoction of horehound and wine, a treatment equally effective, he adds, for nasal and genital ulcerations.

The pharmacological utility of wine was further investigated by Dioscorides, a Greek physician who by legend was attached to Roman legions during the reign of Nero. His multi-volume *De Materia Medica* from *c.* 65 AD contains an entire book on 'Wine and Minerals' that extends the discussion of his predecessors on the subject of both pure and medicated wines.[52] Dioscorides's contributions were soon eclipsed, however, by those of Galen (*c.* 130–201 AD), another immigrant physician who, though born in Asia Minor, settled in Rome. For the last thirty years of his life, Galen served in the court of Marcus Aurelius and a succession of emperors. Over the span of a long career – and he lived to be seventy – Galen wrote so extensively that the sole modern edition of his work comprises twenty-two volumes and an estimated two and a half million words.

Galen for the most part popularized and refined Greek theories of medicine that had been around since the time of Hippocrates. Most importantly, he advanced the treatment of wounds through years of experience tending gladiatorial combats first in his native Pergamon and then in Rome. As one might expect, he favoured wine over all other antiseptics in the application of dressings: 'I cured the most seriously injured', he writes, 'by covering the wounds with a cloth soaked in astringent wine kept moist day and night by a superimposed sponge'. In cases of severe stabbing with evisceration, he bathed the viscera in wine before replacing them in the abdominal cavity. But wine was not the only substance he applied to wounds, for elsewhere he recommends dressing them with a mixture of flour cooked in oil, or with dove's dung (on which he has an entire chapter), or even writing ink.[53] Nevertheless, it was said that none of the gladiators died from infected wounds.

Galen's recommendations concerning the remedial effects of wine taken internally were not well founded, however. Like everyone in his day, he believed in the theory of the four humours and the efficacy of wine in maintaining the balance of humoral fluids. Thus he recommends that wine be given freely to 'the choleric, the sad, or the dreamer, but not to the irascible until after his passion has subsided'. Likewise, he suggests keeping wine from 'those patients who are chilled and are plethoric'.

Galen went down another wrong road in his belief in a class of pharmaceuticals known as theriacs. Theriacs were first used as antidotes for poisonous animal bites (the Greek word *theriake* is derived from *therion*, 'a wild or venomous animal'), later for poisons in general, and eventually as all-purpose drugs.[54] While they typically were prepared from dozens of different substances – mainly plant-based but with additives of viper flesh and assorted minerals – wine, pure, strong and unadulterated, was the binder that held the formula together. After a lengthy period of preparation and twelve years of maturation, the potion was finally ready for use. Marcus Aurelius was said to be among its biggest adherents, and as the remedy grew in popularity, its association with Galen led to the renaming of theriacs as galenics. In the words of one medical historian, the phenomenon 'mushroomed into one of history's best examples of the power of wishful thinking'.[55] Notwithstanding its many failings, Galen's system of healing was nevertheless so comprehensive, dogmatic and seemingly plausible that it dominated the practice of European medicine for the next fifteen hundred years. Only in the eighteenth century, during the Enlightenment, were his most specious ideas finally laid to rest.[56]

four

Wine in the Middle Ages

Christianity was but one of many religions that flourished in the West during the later classical period. By the time of Christ's crucifixion around AD 30, cultic practices were rampant in imperial Rome. Officially, Romans subscribed to a variety of different beliefs: in individuals thought to be responsible for the cosmic order such as Aesculapius for health, Fortuna for fortune, Juno for childbirth, Bacchus for wine; in ancestor worship of the *paterfamilias;* and finally, in devotions to certain posthumously deified emperors like Augustus and Claudius. With so much competition, Bacchic images and cults barely survived the early Middle Ages, and then only in places far from the centres of the Christian faith. The latest depictions of the pagan deity were made in Egypt, Iran or Syria, and date from no later than the sixth or seventh centuries.[1]

Unofficially, countless 'oriental mystery cults' also found supporters in Italy and the Western Empire. The nomenclature presumes an eastern origin for devotions to deities like Isis (Egypt), Cybele and Attis (Asia Minor) and Mithras (Persia), but the term is problematic since common structures can also be traced to Hellenistic Greece.[2] Christianity followed a similar itinerary, according to legend having been brought from the Holy Land to Rome by Saints Peter and Paul. The conversion of Romans to the Christian faith was fairly rapid. By the middle of the third century the construction of pagan temples had come to a halt, and it has been estimated that by the following century more than half the inhabitants of the Roman world had adopted the new faith.[3]

The primary sources for early Christianity are hardly ideal, for apart from the Acts of the Apostles, there is nothing that constitutes a contemporary record. The historical evidence, such as it is, consists of the four Gospels, letters from various apostles to different communities of believers, and later a number of polemical, apologetical and expository writings.[4] Typologically, some of this material sustains Old Testament metaphors, such as when Christ is called 'the true vine' (John 15:1, 5) or when his wrath is likened to 'a great winepress' (Revelations 14:19), a passage nearly identical to how the God of Israel is described in Isaiah (63:3).

Wine is central to Christ's first recorded miracle, his transformation of water into wine at a wedding party in Cana. Scripture is unusually descriptive about this, with John (2:1–11) informing us that once the miracle had occurred, the steward praised the bridegroom with the words 'Everyone serves the good wine first, and then the inferior wine after the guests have become drunk, but you have kept the good wine until now.' His comment is revealing in two respects: first, that Christ approved of drinking – perhaps even to excess – and second, that drinkers in Galilee had discerning tastes. More importantly, John goes on to add, Jesus transformed the water into wine, 'the first of his signs . . . and so revealed his glory; and his disciples believed in him.'

That the shortage involved wine, rather than, say, bread or meat, underlines the beverage's importance in the Judeo-Christian cosmography. At the same time, some Christian texts reveal an uneasiness with its cultural roots. The uncanonical Gospel of Thomas, for example, seeks to distinguish between the new and old religions with a string of metaphors voiced by Jesus:

> It is impossible for a man to mount two horses or to stretch two bows. And it is impossible for a servant to serve two masters; otherwise he will honor the one and treat the other contemptuously. No man drinks old wine and immediately desires to drink new wine. And new wine is not put in old wineskins, lest they burst; nor is old wine put into a new wineskin, lest it spoil it.[5]

This conceit – which Thomas extends with the even more famous analogy of an old patch sewn onto a new garment – was repeated in the three Synoptic Gospels of Matthew, Mark and Luke, an indication of its widespread acceptance.

The most momentous occasion in which wine figures in the New Testament is, of course, the Last Supper. According to the Synoptic gospels, the event took place at Passover, with Matthew (26:20) noting that the meal took place in the evening, and Mark (14:15) and Luke (22:12) adding that it was 'held in a large room, upstairs, fully furnished'. All four of the evangelists rightly emphasize the significance of Christ's institution of the Eucharist as well as his announcement of Judas's betrayal. In the words of Matthew:

> While they were eating, Jesus took a piece of bread, and after blessing it he broke it, gave it to the disciples, and said, 'Take and eat, this is my body.' Then he took a cup, and after giving thanks he gave it to them saying, 'Drink from it, all of you; for this is my blood of the covenant, which is poured out for many for the forgiveness of sins. I tell you, I will never again drink of the fruit of the vine until the day when I drink it new with you in my father's kingdom.

Although the words 'communion' and 'eucharist' do not appear in the New Testament, belief in the sacramental transubstantiation of bread and wine into the body and blood of Christ became fundamental to early Christian notions of salvation.[6] Echoing as it did both Jewish benedictions over shared food as well as certain rituals of the Greek symposium and the Roman banquet, the eucharistic rite guaranteed the survival of late antique wine culture for millennia to come.[7]

Early Christian Imagery

Although Christian iconography would eventually become the mainstay of Western art history, the use of painting and sculpture for devotional purposes did not have a promising beginning. Biblical injunctions against idols run though both the Old and New Testaments. One of the Ten Commandments declaims that 'Thou shall not make for yourself an idol' (Exodus 20:4), while Deuteronomy (7:5) includes the making of idols among the 'abhorrent' practices of the nations the Hebrews are to supplant in the land of Israel. The proscription survives in the Christian Bible as well, particularly with St Paul who, in the Acts of the Apostles (17:16), is 'deeply distressed' to see Athens 'full of idols', and again, in Corinthians (1,8:7–10), which deplores idolatry as a serious distraction from the 'one Lord, Jesus Christ'. Idolatry, however, goes unmentioned in the four Gospels, its

34 *Christ as Good Shepherd*, fresco in the catacombs of S. Priscilla, Rome, 1st–3rd century.

absence suggesting that the issue had all but disappeared by the time the evangelists were writing.

For nearly two centuries, Christianity steered clear of figurative art altogether, but by the end of the second or beginning of the third century, painted images began to appear in Christian contexts.[8] Until the conversion of Constantine around 312, these were limited to fairly schematic representations on the walls of catacombs that depicted Christian monograms, Christian symbols such as doves, sheep and fish, or, more promisingly, iconic renderings of biblical subjects drawn from both the Old and New Testaments. A painting like *Christ the Good Shepherd* from the catacombs of Santa Priscilla typifies the syncretic nature of such images, the figure's classic *contrapposto* pose echoing that of countless Greco-Roman prototypes. Although other mythological deities were also represented in this fashion, a comparison between this figure and *Bacchus with a Panther and a Herm* illustrated in the previous chapter (illus. 30) is particularly striking.

Images like these became more widespread after Constantine's conversion. Then, more than ever, the new faith took to *imagining* Christ, with the results affecting not only the history of art, but the history of Christianity itself. At the same time, the iconographic repertory expanded to include a broader range of scriptural themes based on the life of Christ and the saints, martyrs and apostles. The making of pagan idols did not cease, however, and 'a war of images' ensued between the old and the new. Nevertheless, by the end of the century, representations of ancient deities had begun to decline, with the last recorded raising of a statue of Jupiter occurring in 394.[9]

The traditional view of Early Christian iconography has been that once Christians had an emperor of their own faith and were free to begin building and decorating public places of worship, they looked to imperial imagery for visual models.[10] Since no genuine portraits of Christ existed, it is generally agreed that later depictions of his likeness were fashioned from Roman prototypes, but any certainty as to the precise nature of those prototypes remains open to question. Thomas Mathews, for one, has proposed that Christian artists rejected what he calls the 'Emperor Mystique' and turned to pagan sources of inspiration instead.

A sarcophagus representing the *Entry of Christ into Jerusalem* from the second quarter of the fourth century (illus. 35) supports

Mathews's point. None of the elements of this work – the beardless figure of Christ, his costume or those who attend his parade – suggest an imperial pedigree (illus. 31). Rather, both the composition and characterization of individual figures recall Bacchic sarcophagi from second-century Rome. If the resemblance noted above between the paintings of the *Good Shepherd* and the *Bacchus* was only generic, the similarity of these two works would seem more deliberate. Although there was considerable diversity in Early Christian representations of Christ, an indication of his 'utterly mysterious, indefinable, changeable, and polymorphous nature', the youthful, curly-haired and beardless type depicted here (and in illus. 36) was fairly common.[11] One might also ask if the reliance on pagan imagery was intended to be meaningful, or was simply an imitation of style.

It has been suggested that some aspects of Christian devotion derived from Dionysiac cult practices and that Dionysus himself was a prefiguration of Christ. The latter argument rests on a handful of legends culled from Homer, Euripides, Pliny and other ancient sources.[12] The principle points of overlap include the belief that, like Christ, Dionysus was born of a god and a mortal woman, and thus enjoyed a 'virgin birth'; appeared in human guise; travelled widely and performed miracles; made wine essential to his ritual; turned water into wine; consumed raw flesh (anticipating the Eucharistic communion); and was a saviour who was resurrected from the dead.

Wine was critical in both Dionysian and Christian rituals for its agency in attaining eternal life. Although this may simply reflect

OPPOSITE: 36 *Christ Teaching*, c. 350, marble.

35 *Entry of Christ into Jerusalem*, sarcophagus, c. 325–50, marble.

a common cultural heritage, the surviving visual evidence suggests that when it came to imagining Christ's physical appearance, some level of emulation was clearly at work. The beardless, curly-haired Christ so common in early representations does not reflect prevailing fashions for men, either for apostles or emperors.[13] Moreover, the fleshy – dare one say – effeminate features of *Christ Entering Jerusalem* and other fourth-century representations like the slightly later *Seated Christ* are wholly consistent with Greco-Roman portrayals of the pagan deities Apollo and Dionysus. Apollo was always depicted in the bloom of adolescence, his hair often abundant and ready to be shorn in token sacrifice at the time he came of age. More remarkably, Apollo was sometimes depicted in an androgynous manner, as when in his role of patron of the arts, he leads the muses in song and dance, and plays his lyre dressed in the long chiton of a woman.[14]

By the time Dionysus arrived on Italian shores, he had shed his uncivil image to become the androgynous personality later described in Euripides' *Bacchae* as 'soft, even effeminate . . . with girlish curls'.[15] When later in the play Dionysus induces his rival, Pentheus, to don women's clothing, it signals his acceptance of a transgendered identity as a means of mastering adversity. For Pentheus the effort was in vain, but androgyny provided a useful means for Dionysus to disrupt normative social categories and extend his mythic reach.[16] Since there were no biblical texts that suggest any comparable degree of sexual ambiguity on the part of Christ, the feminization that found its way into his early images – sometimes even including swelling breasts – can only have been suggested by visual sources. Other Hellenistic saviour deities like Apollo and Orpheus may have offered attractive models, but for believers in the 'true vine' of Christianity, Dionysus had special resonance.

Needless to say, parallels between the two religions should not be drawn too closely.[17] In Dionysian ritual, wine was imbibed in large quantities in order to achieve otherworldly union with the god, whereas for Christians, it was taken in small quantities as a symbolic memorial of Christ's death and resurrection. Furthermore, wine alone fuelled Dionysian ritual while Christian communion combined it with bread. Finally, there was nothing in the ancient religion to compare with the belief that Christ's blood was sacrificed to atone for human sin, and that the Eucharist was the instrument of salvation.

37 *Grape harvest*, detail, mosaic in S. Costanza, Rome, 4th century.

Nevertheless, two examples of vine imagery associated with Constantine's daughter, Constantina, underscore the recycling of Dionysian iconography in the art of the Christian era. The first, a mosaic ceiling in the ambulatory of her mausoleum, S. Costanza, in Rome, is so closely linked to Bacchic wine culture that Piranesi actually misidentified the building as the 'Tempo di Bacco' in his 1756 engraving. No doubt Piranesi took his cue not from the architecture but from the mosaic, which represents a sprawling grape arbour. The scene is devoid of any overtly Christian symbols and, like many Roman wall decorations, features putti at work performing simple chores. Throughout the composition, these industrious figures gather fruit from vines while at the sides they transport it to a winepress where it is crushed. If the press itself resembles a Roman temple, the spirited dance of the putti recalls the ecstatic frenzy of Dionysian maenads. Finally, in the centre of the mosaic is a classicizing portrait that can only represent Constantina herself. A companion mosaic with identical iconography commemorates her husband, Hannibalianus, who predeceased her.

The second monument linking Constantina to the grape harvest is her porphyry sarcophagus, presumably carved around the time of her death in 354. Now in the Vatican Museum (a copy remains in her mausoleum), this splendid tomb is also decorated with depictions of cherubic putti at work in the vineyards. Those on the front pick grapes, while others at the side crush them in a large vat, the juice flowing into storage jars below. The association of grapes with Christian salvation and the afterlife is further reinforced by the presence of lambs and peacocks – symbols of Christ and his resurrection – just beneath the vine garlands that encircle the figures.

Even in biblical narratives, vine imagery continued to add complementary layers of meaning. The first sarcophagus to be so decorated was that of Junius Bassus, a Roman prefect who was baptized a Christian on his deathbed in 359, five years after Constantina's own death. The front of his marble tomb, now in the Treasury of St Peter's, is embellished with ten scenes from the Old and New Testaments. The decoration of the sides abandons the architectonic organization of the

38 Giovanni Battista Piranesi, etching of porphyry *Sarcophagus of Constantina*, c. 354.

39 *The Antioch Chalice,* first half of 6th century, silver and silver-gilt.

front to illustrate the harvesting of grapes and the gathering of wheat, clear allusions to the Eucharist.

Vine imagery remained popular throughout the Middle Ages, appearing as a decorative border on tombs, in manuscript illuminations, on crucifixes, even on columns and capitals. In the liturgical context, it was especially commonplace on chalices. One famous example from the sixth century, the Antioch Chalice, represents Christ acclaimed by the apostles. The lamb at his side and the eagle beneath his feet obviously allude to the resurrection, but the proliferation of oversize grapevines along with the basket of grapes on which the bird perches reinforce the spiritual content of the chalice itself.

Unlike the Eucharistic bread – whose centrality to medieval notions of the 'mystical body' and 'spiritual flesh' of Christ remained unchallenged – the sacramental necessity of wine proved to be more problematic. The problem originates with scriptural accounts of what was served and said at the Last Supper. The three Synoptic Gospels specify the 'unleavened bread' of Passover, but only refer to 'the cup' of Christ's symbolic blood without mentioning its contents. Similarly, the Gospel of St Luke and the Acts of the Apostles designate other meals of significance for the Christian community simply as a 'breaking of bread' alone.[18] The second-century *Apologies* of Justin Martyr are often cited in support of the belief that such biblical cups may, in fact, have contained water and not wine.[19] The evidence is a little ambiguous, however, for Justin's description of a baptismal banquet actually recounts the presence of 'a cup of water and of wine mixed with water'.[20] While some Middle Eastern Christian communities in Palestine and Syria are known to have disavowed the ritual use of wine, it is unclear whether this was the result of theological pressures or was simply due to its unavailability. Cyprian, a Carthaginian bishop of the third century, sought to quell the matter by suggesting in one of his *Epistles* that a wineless Eucharist was practiced only by 'ignorant peoples' and was contrary to the institution of Jesus.[21] But the matter did not end there, and a certain amount of debate on the subject lingered throughout the Middle Ages.

Medieval Wine Production and Consumption

Economically and geographically, major shifts occurred in European wine production after the fall of the Roman Empire in the late fifth century.[22] In part, this was the result of the neglect or destruction of farms and vineyards by barbarian invaders who preferred barley or grain liquors to wine.[23] Numerous accounts in Gregory of Tours' *History of the Franks* chronicle the pillage and destruction that took place in the sixth century at the hands of those who did not share the taste of those whose lands they occupied.[24] Yet the greatest damage inflicted by the invaders may not have been the destruction of vineyards and farms, but the collapse of the economic and social structure of the Roman Empire, at least in the west. The division of Italy, Gaul and Iberia into a number of small warring kingdoms effectively undermined long-distance wine trade while the decline in urban population, particularly in Rome, dramatically curtailed the demand for such trade. The outbreaks of plague and epidemic diseases like smallpox further reduced population levels and lowered the overall demand for wine.

Finally, the use of airtight amphoras for storage and shipping – so essential to the fine vintages described by Pliny and other Roman authors – gradually gave way to less portable wineskins and wooden barrels. With all these factors in play, it is not surprising that wine production and consumption took on a more local character, almost exclusively concerned with the needs of the immediate market. It is often suggested that wine-making only survived in this period because of its symbolic importance in the Christian liturgy. Hugh Johnson explains the phenomenon as follows:

> The Church had been the repository of the skills of civilization in the Dark Ages. As expansionist monasteries cleared hillsides and walled round fields of cuttings, as dying vine-growers bequeathed it their land, the Church came to be identified with wine – not only as the blood of Christ but as luxury and comfort in this world.[25]

The theory is attractive, but it has not gone unchallenged. One argument suggests a different scenario:

> The church had little, if anything, to do with the transmission of viticulture from the ancient into the Christian worlds. Wine-growing was brought over the Dark Ages by private enterprise, and the traditions of viticulture were continued through the memories of lay *vignerons* rather than through the manuscripts of monastic libraries.[26]

Since the surviving evidence tends to be limited to the monastic archives – no written records are preserved from the secular sector – we will never know just what the overall wine industry looked like at the time.

The history of medieval wine-making begins with early bishops like Martin of Tours, Gregory of Langres and Felix of Nantes, who established and maintained vineyards in France. Centuries passed without much note being taken of either the process or the product, but by the early ninth century a leader emerged who is universally credited with reviving European viticulture. This, of course, was Charlemagne, the Holy Roman Emperor said to have been the light that ended the Dark Ages. The personal drinking habits of

Charlemagne – temperate in all things – were recorded in the *Vita Karoli Magni*, a contemporary biography written by his servant and friend, Einhard: 'Charles was moderate when it came to both food and drink, but he was even more moderate in the case of drink, since he deeply detested [seeing] anyone inebriated, especially himself or his men . . . He was so restrained in his consumption of wine and other drinks, that he seldom drank more than three times during a meal.'[27]

The same source, nevertheless, recounts a 'miracle' associated with the emperor that involved the transformation of one liquid – in this case beer – into wine. The event, which occurred in the royal residence at Sinzig, so unnerved Einhard with its resemblance to the Eucharistic transubstantiation that it kept him awake at night. Thoughts of Christ's 'Miracle at Cana' might also have entered his mind, but in searching for an explanation for what had taken place, he could surmise only that 'the divine and heavenly power through which these and other miracles occur never does anything without reason.'[28]

Under Charlemagne's rule, reforms took place in every area of the economy. Numerous directives were issued calling for improvements in agriculture and farming, with several in the *Capitulare de Villis* addressed to the making, storing, transporting and selling of wine. These mandated that

> The stewards take charge of the vineyards and see that they are properly worked . . . [and that] the wine-presses be kept in good order and no one dare crush the grapes with their feet, that everything is clean and decent . . . [that] the wine be put in good barrels bound with iron, that containers should not be made of leather . . . that particular care be taken that no loss is incurred in shipping it to the army or to the palace . . . and that each steward make an annual statement of the income.[29]

Winemaking, then, was part of the political and cultural *renovatio* initiated by Charlemagne. While viticulture merely survived in Southern Europe as part of a subsistence economy, it prospered north of the Seine and the Moselle, around towns and palaces such as Aix-la-Chapelle (Aachen), Rheims, and Köln (Cologne). The concurrent expansion of monasticism – however essential it may have

40 *Monk Drinking,*
manuscript illumina-
tion, 13th century.

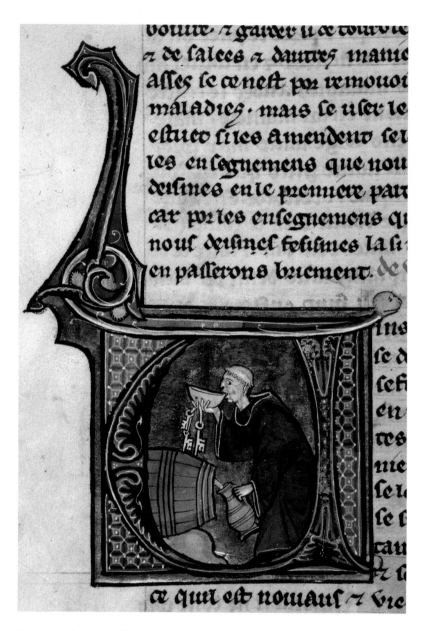

been in the overall enterprise – provided both continuity and the
means of valuable record-keeping. From accounts of Saint-Germaine-
des-Près in Paris, we learn that the abbey owned between 300 and
400 hectares of vines, about half of which were cultivated by the local
peasantry in exchange for a percentage of the wine produced. Each
year the abbey had approximately 6,400 hectolitres of wine at its
disposal, for use in Mass, for consumption by the monks, and for

sale.[30] One of the Rules of St Benedict – since the sixth century the *urtext* of monastic life – prescribed the ideal characteristics of the person responsible for dispensing it:

> Let there be chosen from the brotherhood as Cellar Master of the monastery a wise man, of settled habits, temperate and frugal, not conceited, irritable, resentful, sluggish, or wasteful, but fearing God, who may be as father to the whole brotherhood.[31]

Charlemagne had Benedict's rule copied and distributed to monks throughout western Europe. Another Benedictine Rule specified how much wine was to be furnished at each meal – less than half a pint – but abuses obviously occurred. A charming manuscript illumination from the thirteenth century (illus. 40) depicts a red-faced Benedictine cellar master at work in the monastery *cave*, filling a wine jug with one hand while drinking from a large bowl with the other. Surely this was not what St Benedict had in mind when he formulated the job requirements mentioned above. The tiny illumination is apparently the earliest known satire of an over-indulgent clergyman, a theme that will recur with some frequency in the art of the nineteenth century.

Medieval Medicine

Ancient wine remedies were not forgotten during the Middle Ages, and compilations of Greco-Roman sources are known from as early as the fourth and seventh centuries. The most complete of these is the tenth-century *Geoponica*, or *Agricultural Pursuits*, an anonymous collection of twenty books assembled in Istanbul for the Byzantine emperor Constantine VII.[32] Individual chapters of Book VIII discuss the healing properties or preparation of nearly three dozen medicated wines for ailments ranging from indigestion to snakebite. While it is true that medieval medical science made few advances of its own, monastic communities played a significant role in preserving those ancient manuscripts that came into their possession. In due course, studious monks translated into Latin the Greek texts of Hippocrates, Dioscorides, Galen and others, although not always with perfect accuracy. These texts had a major impact on medieval thinking, and new and even more specialized treatises extolling the therapeutic effects of wine appeared in both Italy and Spain. Galenic recipes underlie the eleventh-century *Regimen Sanitatis Salernitanum*, the health code of the prestigious Benedictine School of Salerno, which prescribed wine more frequently than any other therapeutic agent.[33] The ailments, not surprisingly, remained tied to humoral imbalances:

> The best wine engenders the best humors
> If wine is dark, it renders your body indolent;
> Wine should be clear, aged, subtle, ripe,
> Well diluted, zesty, and taken in moderation.

The remedy for over-indulgence, on the other hand, was anything but abstinence:

> If you develop a hangover from drinking at night,
> Drink again in the morning;
> It will be your best medicine.[34]

A Spanish text of the late thirteenth or early fourteenth century, the *Liber de Vinis* attributed to Arnauld of Villanova, catalogued some forty-nine different medicinal wines and, like a physician's desk manual, prescribed their use in the treatment of nearly every kind of disease. The primary practical benefit of wine – in addition to its antiseptic effect – was its ability to dissolve and disguise the taste of the substances with which it was mixed.[35] For that, if for no other reason, Arnauld's pharmacopoeia endured for centuries and, thanks to the printing press, eventually went through at least twenty-one editions in many languages.[36] Arnauld wrote other treatises as well, and one, *The Preservation of Youth and the Retardation of Age*, heralded wine as essential to a long life.

Medieval monasteries were more than places for monks to study and worship, for they provided services for the general public that included the accommodation of pilgrims, benefice for the poor, and perhaps most importantly, hospitals and pharmacies for the sick. In Florence alone, forty-one hospitals were founded before the Black Death of 1348, all of them based in religious communities.[37] Many of these, like S. Maria della Scala, S. Miniato al Monte and S. Trinità, still exist today. The same was true in other locations. The *Regola*, or

Rules, of the still-functioning hospital of S. Spirito in Rome, founded by Pope Innocent III in the twelfth century, envisioned 'the feeding and giving hospitality and clothes to the poor, looking after and housing the sick, pregnant women and abandoned children, and helping prisoners.'[38] Wine was clearly part of the normal hospital diet since it constituted twenty per cent of the food budget – more than six percent of the total budget – in the fourteenth-century account books of Santa Maria Nuova in Florence.[39]

A second contribution of the monastic community was the introduction of distilled spirits, also known as cordials (from the Latin *cor,* meaning heart).[40] These were byproducts of alchemical searches for the elixir of immortality, and they came about as the process of 'burning' wine was introduced – perhaps from Arabia – during the thirteenth century. The distilled product was called *Aqua Vitae,* the water of life, and it was extravagantly extolled as a universal panacea. In Italy, Thaddeus of Florence, founder of the medical school in Bologna, unreservedly recommended its health benefits in his treatise *On the Virtues of the Water of Life, which is also called Fiery Water.* Modern brandy is the direct descendent of *Aqua Vitae* and, like grappa and other distilled liqueurs, may still be purchased in the apothecary shops of old European monasteries. Benedictine and *vin santo*, in name alone, underscore the origins of many popular cordials.

Later Medieval Imagery

Few illustrations of the role wine played in medieval secular life have come down to us, but the existence of a lively drinking culture is, recorded in several Goliardic poems from the twelfth century.[41] In 'The Contest of Wine and Water', the anonymous poet speaks to the virtues of each in twenty-eight alternating stanzas. In one exchange, water belittles wine:

> Vile and shameless in thy going,
> Into cracks thou still art flowing,
> That in foul holes thou mayst lie;
> O'er the earth thou ought'st to wander,
> On the earth thy liquor squander,
> And at length in anguish die.

To which wine replies:

> How canst thou adorn a table?
> No one sings or tells a fable
> In thy presence dull and drear;
> But the guest who erst was jolly,
> Laughing, joking, bent on folly,
> Silent sits when thou art near.

Later in the poem wine makes another argument against water that can hardly be refuted, an accusation that speaks to an awareness of the perils of sewage-contaminated wells:

> Thou of things the scum and rotten
> Sewer, where ordures best forgotten
> And unmentioned still descend!
> Filth and garbage, stench and poison.
> Thou dost bear in fetid foison!
> Here I stop lest words offend.

Another poem, 'Bacchic Frenzy', is a rollicking drinking song that unambiguously captures the spirit of long-forgotten ancient rites. It begins with the apostrophe:

> Topers in and out of Season!
> 'Tis not thirst but better reason
> Bids you tope on steadily!
> Pass the wine-cup, let it be
> Filled and filled for bout on bout
> Never Sleep!
> Racy jest and song flash out!
> Spirits leap!

In the visual arts, sacred narrative proliferated in the later Middle Ages as religious devotions increasingly turned to visual aids as a means of captivating audiences. Once the Iconoclastic Controversy subsided in the eighth century, the Gregorian notion that 'images are the books of the illiterate' became even more widespread. But since the primary sources for artistic invention – the Old and

New Testaments – were typically spare when it came to describing narrative settings, artists – and painters in particular – were forced to rely on their imaginations when it came to elaborating the backgrounds and requisite furnishings for most biblical scenes.

Giotto di Bondone (*c.* 1267–1337) was the first painter to make naturalistic observation central to his strategy of story-telling. His 38 frescoes in the Scrovegni Chapel in Padua from around 1305 are milestones in the history of art for their realistic depiction of scenes from the lives of the Virgin and Christ. Where earlier medieval representations portrayed religious narratives in otherwordly terms, Giotto brought them down to earth as closely observed human dramas that

41 Giotto di Bondone, *Wedding at Cana*, fresco in the Scrovegni Chapel, Padua, 1304–6.

frequently unfold in domestic settings. Wine figures in two of his Paduan frescoes, most prominently in the *Wedding at Cana*, the tale of Christ's transformation of water into wine. Giotto stages the scene in a courtyard open to the blue sky, a clear rejection of the contemporary Byzantine convention of using a gold background to suggest the heavens above. Gathered around the table with Christ (the first figure on the left), the Virgin Mary and another disciple are seven mere mortals who are distinguishable by the absence of halos. While the two closest to Christ witness the miracle, the three to the right are members of the household staff who are responsible for the wine. Six large jugs with gadrooned decoration stand on a low table in the foreground tended by two of the men as the third raises a glass to his lips. The taster is easily identified as a cook both from the cap he wears on his head and the considerable size of his belly. Although he does not appear tipsy, as cooks often do in later representations, his conspicuous presence – and conspicuous girth – signals how such figures had become part of the popular culture of the day.[42] Contemporary viewers of the Scrovegni Chapel would have taken this as part of the artist's overall commitment to realism.

The most common subject involving wine in the Middle Ages was, of course, the Last Supper, a theme whose sacramental importance would, over time, be subverted by artists more challenged by the dramatic possibilities afforded by Judas's betrayal. The earliest known depiction of the Last Supper – a mosaic in Ravenna – dates from the sixth century, but in this iconic representation, the table is set with no more than a platter of fish and six loaves of bread.[43] Centuries would pass before such abstract compositions expanded into realistic narratives and, when they did, the food and drink laid before Christ and the apostles became a more conspicuous part of the picture. Duccio di Buoninsegna, a contemporary of Giotto, was among the first to engage in this kind of elaboration, and his *Last Supper* from the *Maestà* altarpiece (1308–11) depicts an ample feast being consumed by an animated group of diners (illus. 42). The main course is neither a symbolic fish nor the traditional Passover lamb, but a suckling pig, a curious choice given that Mosaic law deemed the pig to be an unclean animal. Several glasses of red wine are in evidence. An intricately painted ceramic *boccale,* or wine pitcher, occupies a conspicuous position in the foreground, directly before Christ. The detailing of the pitcher leaves little doubt that the object was painted directly from life. Later, during the

Renaissance, some artists would appear to be more preoccupied with depicting the material furnishings of the Last Supper than with explicating the narrative itself.

Like the miraculous Wedding at Cana and the Last Supper, the Old Testament account of the Drunkenness of Noah was also a popular theme in late medieval art. The post-diluvial tale is described in Genesis 9:20-23:

Noah, a man of the soil, was the first to plant a vineyard. He drank some of the wine and became drunk, and he lay uncovered in

42 Duccio di Buoninsegna, *The Last Supper*, from the *Maestà* altarpiece, *c.* 1308–11, tempera on panel.

43 The *Drunkenness of Noah*, manuscript illumination from the Holkham Bible, *c.* 1320–30.

Apres q̈ noe out uines plaunte · Hulcrescent grapes · a graunt pleinte · e tes venist · deles vendenger · Adunk noe · les sut culier · e en hoctes · a lou bel porter · e en graunz cuues · les alla fuller · e feseyt uin lou · si euleuoyst · dount meintenāt ivere estoyst · e chef dormiz · tut decouert · se membre apparutth · tut apert Cham son deusisne ensaunt · son pere trouua · illi dormant · Il sen moca · ne le vouisit couerir · por ceo estoyt · son fiuz le piz · ves alla · ses freres quere por lur pere houite fere · sem le esue · le alla couerir · Mal de son pere · ne vouisist oyr · Iaphet le ieuene se returna · e nevouisist regarter · endreit la · Ben tot apres Noe ueliac · e de uyl · estoyt tut mati · por sō fiuz · q deluy moka · E tot il dist Cham uen tei · ehea · ton fiuz canaan · seit maudit · pour le tunes en despit

his tent. And Ham, the father of Canaan, saw the nakedness of his father, and told his two brothers outside. Then Shem and Japheth took a garment, and walked backward and covered the nakedness of their father; their faces were turned away, and they did not see their father's nakedness.

The story highlights the shame of Noah's overindulgence and subsequent immodesty as well as the disrespect paid him by the youngest of his three sons.[44] While this might hardly seem an exemplary subject for Christian devotion, efforts to reconcile the Old and New Testaments by identifying typological 'prefigurations' of Christ in the Hebrew bible had been common from the early days of the faith. Noah was viewed by patristic writers as a key figure in the cosmogony since his deliverance from the Flood anticipated salvation through baptism, and his ark the building of the church.

An early fourteenth-century manuscript illumination from the Holkham Bible (illus. 43) condenses Noah's experience with wine into two registers, the upper one showing grapes being brought from the harvest for pressing, and the lower one the senseless Noah slumped against two wine casks with an empty cup in his hand. All three of his sons stand in the foreground while behind them Noah appears a second time, censuring Ham for his behaviour.

The manuscript's lower scene is like a medieval morality play: the weakness of the father's flesh leads first to self-degradation, and then to the sin of one of his sons; the good behaviour of two of the sons underscores the bad behaviour of the third; nowhere in the legend is there remorse or forgiveness; once Noah regains his senses (Genesis 9:24–7) he punishes Ham by cursing his son Canaan and enslaving him to Shem and Japheth who then, in turn, receive his blessing. Good finally triumphs over evil, but Noah is surprisingly vindictive in rebuking the wrongdoer. Yet his own drunkenness – the moral failure that precipitated the whole sequence of events – is beyond reproach in the biblical account. Where drinking to excess is heartily condemned in other books of the Old Testament, especially Proverbs (4:17, 20:1, 21:17 and 23:20–21), Noah goes unpunished.

What lesson, then, did Noah's drunkenness hold for Christians? Since he was considered a prototype of Christ, one would expect his insobriety to be explained. Certain early church fathers like Clement of Alexandria were disapproving, calling it 'the spectacle of transgression of ignorance,' while others tended to downplay or excuse the event. Both Origen and Jerome wondered if Noah was unaware of his wine's potency, Ambrose emphasized the patriarch's 'joy and spiritual gladness', and Epiphanius attributed it to his advanced age.[45] Later, Thomas Aquinas tackled the issue in his *Summa Theologica* (1265–74) where, in Question 150, he addresses 'Whether Drunkenness is a Sin:'

> Drunkenness may be understood in two ways. First it may signify the defect itself of a man resulting from his drinking much wine, the consequence being that he loses his sense of reason. On this sense drunkenness denotes not a sin, but a penal defect resulting from a fault. Secondly, drunkenness may denote the act by which a man incurs this defect. This act may cause drunkenness in two ways. On one way, through the wine being too strong, without the drinker being cognizant of this; and in this way too, drunkenness may occur without sin, especially if it is not through his negligence, and thus we believe that Noah was made drunk as related in Genesis 9.[46]

Aquinas's logic makes sense, since as Origen had already pointed out, Noah as the world's first *vigneron* had no way of knowing the potency of the wine he had made (John Calvin later questioned this explanation on the grounds that the Bible does not say it was the first time he had tasted wine). Interestingly, Genesis ends the account of Noah's life with the report that the patriarch lived for three hundred and fifty years after the Flood, suggesting that his taste for the grape can hardly have been detrimental to his health.[47]

Two other Old Testament tales of wine's leading to misdeeds are those of Lot and his Daughters and Judith and Holofernes. In the case of Lot (Genesis 19:3–38), the story again begins with a disaster, the burning of Sodom and Gomorrah. The righteous Lot and his family were spared, but after his wife is turned into a pillar of salt for disobeying the order not to look back, his two daughters set out to seduce him in the mistaken belief that no one else was left on earth by whom they could have children. Wine was the agent that allowed the incestuous acts to occur. On successive nights, each woman plies him with so much that he lost control and later 'did not know when she lay down or when she rose'.

The consumption of wine in the tale of Judith and Holofernes (Judith 12:10–20) leads to a better outcome, at least from the Jewish perspective. As the Assyrian army was about to overrun the settlement of Bethulia, the widow Judith, who 'was beautiful in appearance and lovely to behold', took it upon herself to save the Israelites by vanquishing their leader. After gaining Holofernes's trust, she is invited into his tent and appears compliant as they dine together. But he was in for a surprise, for once he 'drank a great quantity of wine, much more than he had ever drunk in any one day since he was born', he fell asleep, and she beheaded him.

Neither the drunkenness of Lot or the seduction of Holofernes was as popular a subject in medieval art as the accompanying narratives of burning and beheading. Most likely because of the female eroticism involved, such tales of the disinhibitory effects of wine tended to be overlooked. Yet later, as we shall see, the less prudish societies of early modern Europe viewed these same stories – especially Lot and his Daughters – in a very different light.

Theologically more intriguing was the allegory of *Christ in the Winepress,* a theme again based on the topological pairing of passages in the Old and New Testaments. Thus in Isaiah (63:3) we read: 'I have trodden the wine press alone; and from the peoples no one was with me; I trod them in my anger, and trample them in my wrath', while in Revelation (19:15) it is: 'From his mouth comes a sharp sword with which to strike down the nations, and he will rule them with a rod of iron; he will tread the wine press of the fury of the wrath of God the Almighty.' The wrath and the trampling allude to the bloody harvest of Judgment Day, but in the minds of the early church fathers the prophetic words pertained more to the suffering saviour, who was crushed like a grape in a winepress, and whose sacrificial blood led to the promise of redemption.[48]

The first images of *Christ in the Winepress* date from the second half of the twelfth century, not long after the Benedictine theologian Rupert of Deutz (d. 1129) revived the notion that Christ had 'worked the wine-press in that he gave himself for us; he was pressed like a grape under the weight of the cross, the wine flowed from his body as his spirit was exhaled.'[49] Early renditions of the subject typically depict Christ standing in a simple wooden vat and crushing the grapes with his feet, the common practice of the time.[50]

44 *Christ in the Winepress*, 15th century, woodcut.

Subsequently, the theme became more common in woodcut impressions, made possible by the reinvention of the screw press, a mechanical device already known to the Romans.[51] The screw press soon became the principle means for crushing grapes as well as printing books and woodcuts, and most later renditions of *Christ and the Winepress* reflect the rediscovered technology (illus. 44).[52] Typically, such images show a bloodied Christ crushing grapes under the weight of a beam attached to a tall screw, as the juice flows directly into a chalice. The popularity of these crude and inexpensive works – nine different prints are known from the second half of the fifteenth century alone – suggests that belief in the symbolic unity of blood and wine trickled down to every level of society.[53] Significantly, these images were all derived from conventional depictions of Christ in the sympathetic roles of *Ecce Homo* or Man of Sorrows, never depicting him as the wrathful figure described in Isaiah and Revelations. The humanization of the saviour, as we shall see, was the interpretation Renaissance artists would go on to eagerly pursue.

five

Renaissance Wine

The consumption of wine significantly increased as the Middle Ages drew to a close. After 1400, as Fernand Braudel has noted, 'the whole of Europe drank wine, if only a part of Europe produced it'.[1] Viticulture and the wine trade flourished as the transition from feudalism to capitalism sparked every sector of the economy. While most wine consumed before 1400 was produced by an indentured peasantry, the emancipation of the Renaissance farmer led to expanded commercial production at the very time that advances in the banking and credit systems were making trade more profitable. In addition to a refreshed labour force and a stronger profit motive, the population increases of the sixteenth and seventeenth centuries spurred both economic growth and an appetite for luxury goods.[2]

Wine consumption increased among people of every social class. It has been estimated that the daily average was between a half and two litres per person in the fifteenth century, with production steadily rising through the 1600s.[3] Those at higher socio-economic levels also drank better wine. The qualitative improvement resulted from two factors: better access to wines from other regions, and the cultivation of more specialized grape varieties. While this had already been true in the ancient world – Pliny's *Natural History* displays a true appreciation of wines from various terroirs, including some that had been aged – wine connoisseurship barely survived the Middle Ages. Signs of its revival are first recorded in a thirteenth-century poem entitled *La Bataille des Vins* by Henri d'Andeli. In it, more than 70 different wines from across Europe were compared, and the judge was an English priest who classified each as either 'Celebrated' or 'Excommunicated'. Naturally, most of the wines sampled were French, although a sweet wine from Cyprus won the overall tasting.[4]

The recognition of regional distinctions became more pronounced over time, as we discover in the fourteenth-century *Ruralium Commodorum,* a classically inspired discourse by the Bolognese agronomist Piero de'Crescenzi.[5] Here nearly two dozen Italian vines are catalogued by region, and advice is given on ageing wines before they are drunk. Other Renaissance minds went on to expand on these principles while refining the descriptive vocabulary and introducing personal preferences into the discussion. Thus Lorenzo de' Medici's poem 'The Partridge Hunt' has hunters celebrating their catch with a 'cask of cooling wine' described rather humorously:

The Trebbiano wine was most suspicious,
But longing will make anything delicious.[6]

Among the many sixteenth-century treatises on wine, two from the 1550s stand out. One is an account by Sante Lancerio, *bottigliere* (bottle master) to Pope Paul III, of the many wines he and his Holiness had sampled.[7] The text comprises a catalogue of 57 different wines – all Italian but for a generic 'vino francese' and 'vino di Spagna' – which are classified by region and evaluated for their appeal to the palate. Here, for the first time, the qualities of colour, texture, taste and aroma are carefully considered along with any medicinal properties the wine was thought to possess. Words like *tondo* (round), *grasso* (rich), *delicato* (delicate), *possento* (powerful), *fumoso* (smoky) and *maturo* (mature) flavour the prose while, on occasion, food pairings are suggested. Lancerio concludes many entries by noting if the pope did or did not drink the wine *volentieri,* with pleasure. Not surprisingly, he pronounced the French wine 'unfit for gentlemen', and the Spanish 'never worth drinking'. The red wine of Montepulciano earned the greatest praise, Lancerio calling it 'most perfect . . . in bouquet, colour, and taste'. For him, the distinction of this Tuscan wine lay in its being *odorifero* (fragrant), *polputo* (full-bodied) and *non agrestino* (not too sharp). It was clearly the pope's favourite as well, and the only wine he pronounced *vino da Signori* (wine for lords). To this day, the papal endorsement remains a source of pride for local wine producers, who label their own bottles of Montepulciano *Vino Nobile.*

About the same time Lancerio was writing his discourse, the poet Giovanni Battista Scarlino published a tract in *terza rima* entitled *Nuova trattato della varietà, e qualità dei vini, che vengono in*

Roma. Here, the reader is treated to a list of all the wines available for purchase in Roman wine shops. Scarlino's verse is more than a sales list, however, for like Lancerio he includes qualitative recommendations and occasional suggestions for food pairings. The gustatory linkage of wine and cuisine was fairly commonplace in this period, as we see from the culinary perspective in works like Bartolomeo Scappi's magisterial *Opera dell'arte del cucinare*. Comparing the texts, we find that Scarlino and Scappi even preferred some of the same wines such as Chiarello, Guarnaccia, Malvasia and Moscatello.[8]

The French have always taken wine seriously. Viticulture on their lands has an ancient history that began with the Gauls and prospered under the Romans before coming under monastic control. Regional preferences are known from the time of Pope John XXII (1316–34) who, although from Cahors, had a special fondness for the wines of the Rhône Valley. It was he who christened wine from his residence at Châteauneuf, 'Vin du Pape', an appellation that later became Châteauneuf-du-Pape. According to Nostradamus, by the sixteenth century this was already being exported to Italy.[9] In the Bordeaux region, Château Haut-Brion – founded by Jean de Pontac in 1550 – was the first wine to be named for the estate where it was made.

Burgundy, and especially the Côte d'Or, enjoyed an exalted reputation of its own in the Renaissance. There, perhaps more than anywhere else, the better monastic vineyards fell into private hands, as for example did the estate of Vosne-Romanée, which had belonged to the Abbey of St-Vivant, or Clos de Bèze, which was sold by the Cathedral at Langres. Studies show that by 1600 there were also many more small independent producers in France than there had been three centuries previously.[10] Named grape varieties along with wines that could last proved to be especially profitable. Among whites, Montrachet was the first (in 1600) to be mentioned by name.

At the other end of the social spectrum, wine had a markedly different character. Produced in quantity from common vines with high yields, these were short-lived wines typically made with an eye towards wholesale markets in the larger cities. Along with beer, and later grain alcohol, cheap wine contributed to what Braudel has noted as 'an ever-increasing number of ordinary drinkers . . . [and] widespread urban drunkenness'.[11] In sixteenth-century Rome, for example, the wine trade comprised a robust sector of the city's economy, with as many as seven million litres entering the port at Ripa

Grande annually. On the retail level, several hundred wine shops served the needs of a population that numbered only about 40,000.[12] Substantial revenue was raised from the taxation on wine. In one year this yielded some 180,000 scudi to the papal treasury, which was then directed towards the cost of new construction at the university.[13]

The drinking habits of Romans were replicated throughout most of Europe. By the fifteenth century, per capita allocations of wine in France had already reached one to two litres a day, a quantity not seen since the high-living days of ancient Rome.[14] Legal restraints on public drunkenness were soon to follow, and from Elizabethan England to the Republic of Venice, sobriety laws were passed, usually to little or no effect.[15] With this in mind, one wonders if some atrocities committed in the name of religion and politics during the era might have resulted from the miscreants being intoxicated, as so many were reported to have been during the 1527 Sack of Rome.[16]

Wine in Renaissance Art

Renaissance art illustrates the richness and diversity of contemporary wine culture. Just as there were 'high' and 'low' wines, so there were 'high' and 'low' subjects in art, the more elevated ones drawn from the Bible and classical mythology, and most of the others from daily life. In the Catholic countries, the greatest continuity with the medieval era naturally occurred in wine-related narratives like the Last Supper, the Wedding at Cana and even the Drunkenness of Noah. At the outset of the Renaissance in the early 1400s, the Bible remained the basic textual source which continued both to satisfy spiritual needs and to inspire artists to embellish its spare descriptions with ideas of their own. The depiction of sacred narratives in secular settings was among the ideals of fifteenth-century humanism, and it was only towards the end of the century that mythological subject-matter became acceptable in art.

A *Last Supper* dated 1466 in the church of San Giorgio in San Polo di Piave would at first glance seem entirely conventional, so closely does its composition echo earlier treatments of the subject. But the artist, Zanino di Pietro, taking his cue from Duccio's *Last Supper* from some 150 years earlier (illus. 42), rendered the food and drink in this otherwise naively painted fresco with considerable accuracy.

45 Zanino di Pietro,
The Last Supper,
fresco in S. Giorgio,
San Polo di Piave, 1466.

Viewed from a high vantage point, platters of fish, some already cut in sections, and a number of whole and dismembered *gamberi* (crayfish) are strewn across the table along with six carafes of wine and a glass for each diner. Mosaic law, of course, forbids the eating of shellfish, but the village of San Polo di Piave lies in a water-threaded region northeast of Venice that is known for both its freshwater crayfish and its wine. Even today, the crustaceans from this area are praised for their 'succulence', while the local red Raboso is touted for its 'marked and distinctive personality', and whites like Tocai and Verduzzo for the 'snappy acidity that offsets their youthful fruitiness'.[17] Interestingly, five of the carafes on the table are filled with red wine, and one with white.

If the choice of beverages suggests the artist's commitment to secular realism, the inclusion of white and red on the same table reflects the vagueness of Christian doctrine on the matter of Eucharistic wine. Despite its derivation from the saviour's blood, communion wine was not always red. According to Joseph Jungmann's *Mass of the Roman Rite*:

> In the East, red wine was preferred, and occasionally this was also the case in the West since thus any accidental confusion with the water [with which it was mixed] was more surely avoided. But there was at no time any regulation that was universally obligatory. Since the sixteenth century, white wine has commonly been preferred because it leaves fewer traces in the linen.[18]

Like Zanino, most fifteenth-century artists who painted the Last Supper downplayed the institution of the Eucharist in order to give greater emphasis to the apostles' response to Christ's announcement of the betrayal. The change in emphasis, although envisioned by Giotto and Duccio a century earlier, is typical of the discomfort Renaissance artists experienced with mystical or supernatural legends in general. Leonardo's *Last Supper* is actually quite conventional in this respect despite the unique role the picture has always played in the popular imagination. Compositionally, it differs from most quattrocento depictions of the theme, chiefly in Judas being placed on the same side of the table as his companions. And just as Duccio and Zanino took special interest in the meal itself, so Leonardo rendered the Lord's Supper in considerable – if somewhat idiosyncratic – detail.

The cleaning and conservation of this poorly preserved fresco in the late 1990s led to several revelations, among which was the observation that the Passover feast set before Christ and his disciples includes a plate of grilled eel garnished with orange slices.[19] In light of this, and Vasari's observation that the tablecloth 'was so cunningly depicted that the linen itself could not look more realistic', one might look more closely at the wine Leonardo put on the table.[20]

46 Leonardo da Vinci, *The Last Supper*, fresco in S. Maria delle Grazie, Milan, 1495–8.

Each man is provided with his own glass, and the wine is a pale red. The light colour may result from its dilution with water – a glass carafe of which is also on the table – or from the fugitive nature of Leonardo's experimental pigment. Yet for a banquet so realistically described, it is odd that Leonardo failed to include a *boccale*, or wine pitcher, among the dishes, plates and saltcellars that comprise the service ware. Copies after famous paintings often remedy what their makers consider to be deficiencies in the original, and Leonardo's *Last Supper* was replicated on several occasions. The most widely reproduced copy – that of Marco d'Oddiono – eliminates food and drink from the table altogether, while another – by Cesare Magni – intensifies the colour of the wine and adds a second carafe of water. The missing wine pitcher, however, was eventually introduced in a pen and ink copy attributed to Raphael that was freely based on the original. Around 1515, Marcantonio Raimondi made a reproductive engraving of that drawing, and it was his print that initially permitted Leonardo's modified work to reach a larger audience.[21]

No *Last Supper* was more awash in wine than the one Paolo Veronese painted in 1573 for the Dominican refectory of S. Giovanni e Paolo in Venice (illus. 47). Taking a liberal view of the biblical text, the artist staged a banquet attended by no fewer than four dozen richly attired guests in a distinctly Venetian setting. Sansovino's newly built library stands in the background and all the stemmed goblets in the picture are products of Murano's famed glassworks. Wine containers of nearly every type are also in evidence: silver and glass pitchers, leather flasks and even a raffia-wrapped bottle of the kind still seen on some chiantis.

Veronese's painting was made at the very time that religious orthodoxy was on the rise in the period known as the Counter-Reformation or Catholic Reformation. Thus his Dominican patrons, dismayed by the number of extraneous elements in the picture, referred the matter to the Holy Office of the Inquisition. The Inquisitors went after Veronese with particular zeal, given the recent recommendations of the Council of Trent that mandated didactic exactitude in the fine arts above all other considerations. When asked whom he supposed to have been present at the Last Supper, the artist admitted that 'if in a [narrative] painting there is space left over, I fill it with figures from my imagination'.[22] The hearing concluded with Veronese being ordered to make certain 'corrections' in the composition, but rather than doing so

he simply renamed the work *Feast in the House of Levi*. The enormous canvas (which measures nearly 40 feet by 17, or 12 by 5 metres) hangs today in the secular halls of Venice's Accademia Museum.

The festive, pageant-like atmosphere of Veronese's painting mirrored the social aspirations and genteel tastes of the Venetian nobility, a society whose *joie de vivre* seemed – on the surface at least – little affected by the economic and political uncertainties that marked the second half of the sixteenth century in most of Europe. The sumptuousness of Venice's religious imagery was unlike that produced in Florence or Rome. Indeed, depictions of grandiloquent banquets like the Feast in the House of Levi or the Marriage at Cana are rare outside Venice, while sparer narratives like the Supper at Emmaus became increasingly popular elsewhere. Yet wine flows liberally even in some of the most parsimonious interpretations of the Emmaus story. The biblical account (Luke 24:28–32) turns on the chance encounter, after Christ's resurrection, when two of his disciples initially fail to recognize him at the table they share in a country inn. Although the only nourishment mentioned in Scripture is the bread with which the Lord gave the blessing, most artists who treated the theme envisioned a fuller repast.

A *Supper at Emmaus* by the Florentine mannerist Jacopo Pontormo (1494–1557) is especially noteworthy for its incorporation of realistic details in a sacred setting. Vasari tells us that the five

47 Paolo Veronese,
The Feast in the House of Levi, 1573,
oil on canvas.

48 Jacopo Pontormo,
Supper at Emmaus, 1525,
oil on canvas.

108

white-robed figures standing in the background were 'marvellous portrait likenesses' of Certosan lay brothers who lived in the same monastery outside Florence where the artist resided during the plague of the 1520s.[23] Other realistic elements include two cats hiding under the table and a small dog and a fallen scrap of paper (bearing the date 1525) in the foreground. More puzzling is Pontormo's choice of the unnaturally high vantage point from which the scene is viewed, a perspective typically employed when an artist wished to emphasize the importance of what lies on a tabletop. Yet any expectation of an enticing meal is denied, for dinner consists of just two small loaves of bread.

With so abstemious a supper, it is surprising to see the apostle on the left – wholly distracted from the drama unfolding before him – caught in the act of filling his glass from a ceramic wine pitcher. A carafe of water is placed nearby, and two additional stemmed glasses are also in evidence. The biblical account says nothing about wine at this table, but allusions to the Eucharistic supper were not infrequent in depictions of the Supper at Emmaus. Pontormo may have had that in mind, or he may simply have been projecting his personal dining habits onto the narrative.

We know from a diary Pontormo kept later in life that his diet was erratic. One day he could eat 'fourteen ounces of bread, roast pork, an endive salad and cheese and dried figs', and on the next two, nothing more than fourteen or fifteen ounces (around 400 g) of bread.[24] Bread seems to have been as important a part of his fare as it is for Christ and the two apostles in the painting. The artist did not skimp on wine, however: the diary records frequent refillings of his cask from vineyards in Radda and Celenzano, as well as from a friend named Piero.

The Drunkenness of Noah was not as popular a subject in Renaissance art as in was in the Middle Ages, probably because the prophetic implications of Ham's condemnation that so fascinated the earlier age had lost much of their appeal. The patriarch's lapse in judgement was rescued from neglect in 1508 when Michelangelo depicted it as one of the nine scenes from Genesis that he depicted on the Sistine Chapel ceiling. His retelling of Genesis was somewhat idiosyncratic since he skipped the legends of Cain and Abel and reversed the sequence of the Flood and Noah's sacrifice. In concluding the cycle with Noah's drunkenness, Michelangelo expressed his own increasingly pessimistic attitudes on the prospects of human perfectibility.

49 Michelangelo Buonarroti, *The Drunkenness of Noah*, fresco in the Sistine Chapel, Rome, *c.* 1508–12.

Compositionally, his fresco is not dissimilar from the much earlier representation in the Holkham Bible: the recumbent Noah leans against a wine vat and faces in the direction of his three sons who stand to the right. Both images are double narratives, the earlier one including Ham's condemnation in the background, the latter Noah's role as winemaker to the side. Michelangelo, in contrast to the medieval illuminator, emphasized Ham's mockery (he is the finger-pointing boy in the centre), while avoiding any suggestion of his prophetic condemnation.

Michelangelo was particularly emphatic in highlighting the nudity of Noah as well as that of his sons (for which there was no scriptural justification). Grizzled and slightly flabby, the patriarch would seem at home in the circle of Bacchus, not in the role of the deity himself as Michelangelo envisioned him a decade earlier (illus. 52), but of Silenus, his drunken mentor. Noah's pose, on the other hand, was almost certainly modelled on that of the ancient River God that Pope Julius II had recently installed in the nearby Cortile del Belvedere. Significantly, Michelangelo depicted Adam in a very similar pose a few years later in the scene of his creation (the episodes from Genesis were painted in reverse chronological order).

Michelangelo's message in the *Drunkenness* was clearly a pessimistic one. Side-stepping the consequences of Ham's disrespect that intrigued earlier artists and theologians, he concentrated his attention on the weakness of Noah's flesh. For an artist known to have struggled with his own carnal appetites, Noah's weakness may have had a more personal meaning than is usually imagined. One can only wonder what Michelangelo's own attitudes were towards wine. While he never mentions it in his poetry or letters, the shape of the earthenware pitcher in the picture is identical to one that appears on an illustrated shopping list he made some years later.[25]

Significantly, the medieval image of *Christ in the Winepress* – the most unequivocal of religious subjects having to do with wine – did not disappear during the Renaissance. If anything, the theme gained relevance in the second half of the sixteenth century as a reaffirmation of the decrees and canons of the thirteenth session of the Council of Trent (1551), which took up the matter of the Eucharist. Responding to church reformers like Luther, Calvin and Zwingli who preferred to understand it as merely a 'token' or 'sign' of Christ,[26] the first two chapters of the session's decree reiterated both the 'real presence' of Christ in the Eucharist and the doctrine of transubstantiation.[27] It was thus in the context of a Europe divided over the meaning of communion that engravings like Hieronymus Wierix's *Christ in the Mystical Winepress* were made in support of the traditional Catholic position.

50 Hieronymus Wierix, *Christ in the Mystical Winepress*, before 1619, engraving.

Apart from engravers of illustrated religious tracts – like Wierix and a handful of others – artists tended to ignore Catholic Reformation dogma unless their creative interests happened to coincide with the didactic formulations of the Church. Such was certainly the case at the beginning of the seventeenth century with Caravaggio, an artist whose first-hand experience with violence prepared him to depict Early Christian martyrdoms in the realistic manner desired by his ecclesiastical patrons. More often, religious iconography followed the necessities of art, rather than the other way around.

Bacchus Returns to Italy

Bacchic imagery reappeared in poetry before it did in painting, with the earliest example coming in the verse of Chaucer's contemporary,

John Gower (*c.* 1330–1408). His poem *Confessio Amantis,* or *The Lover's Confession* (*c.* 1390), is not a celebration of Bacchus's wine, however, but a renouncement set within the structure of a Christian confession. In Book 6, which is devoted to the sin of Gluttony, the narrator is pardoned by the confessor after disclosing his affection for wine:

> And thus I rede thou assobre
> Thin herte in hope of such a grace,
> For drunkeschipe in every place,
> To whether side that it torne,
> Doth harm and makth a man to sporne
> And ofte falle in such a wise,
> Wher he per cas mai noght arise.[28]

Bacchus's rehabilitation took a little longer, emerging only in the fifteenth century in the work of Neo-Latin poets like Giovanni Pontano (1426–1503) and Jacopo Sannazaro (1458–1530). Pontano was a key figure in the enlightened Aragonese court of Alfonso 'the Magnanimous' in Naples, and among the earliest works he wrote for his patron was a long poem entitled *Parthenopeus* that contains a lengthy encomium to Bacchus and the restorative powers of wine. Written around 1450, this was among the first works of the Renaissance to praise the deity in a non-Christian context.

> Thanks to wine, sad cares are driven away from one's breast;
> This liquid lightens the heart of unwelcome sorrow,
> This god grants rest to the afflicted and hope to the destitute;
> Go page, and pour forth the Falernum with a generous
>   hand.
> Between draughts of wine (for Bacchus is the nurse of love),
>   I like
> To plant drunken kisses on the lips which are joined to mine
> And to stroke a soft thigh with my hand and to caress breasts
>   and to
> Engage in sweet battles in a tender lap.[29]

Sannazaro, writing nearly half a century later, modelled his image of Bacchus more closely on ancient prototypes, recalling the works of Tibullus, Propertius and Virgil in his own elegy to the god. His evocation is less erotic than Pontano's (or for that matter, Tibullus'), and more attuned to the pastoral tone of Propertius and Virgil. The final lines of the poem (Elegies 2.5) especially recall passages from the *Aeneid*:

> Holy father, drive away my gnawing cares: clear my clouded breast with aged wine. Bring quiet slumbers to my breast, and enlighten my weary eyes with your inspiration . . . And provide me with responsive Muses, and visit me graciously, your divinity peacefully disposed.[30]

Renaissance artists were slower to adopt pagan iconography despite the access they had to the many ancient statues and sarcophagi that survived the Middle Ages. The online 'Census of Antique Works of Art and Architecture Known in the Renaissance' lists over 100 documented statues and sarcophagi that represented the god of wine.[31] And it was doubtless some work of antiquity – probably a sarcophagus – that inspired Andrea Mantegna (1430/31–1506) to make his engravings of a *Bacchanal with Silenus* and *Bacchanal with a Wine Vat*. The two prints – which are believed to have been pendants – have been variously assigned from the mid-1460s to the early 1490s, but whatever their date, they remain among the earliest prints to be made in Italy. Mantegna worked primarily in Padua and Mantua rather than Florence or Rome, but was possessed with a passion for the classical

51 Andrea Mantegna, *Bacchanal with Silenus*, 2nd half of 15th century, etching.

past that surpassed that of any other artist of his age. He drew tire-
lessly after the antique, acquired what pieces he could for his own
collection, and recycled ancient motifs at every opportunity.

The *Bacchanal with Silenus* is set at the edge of a vineyard beside
a sedgy pool of water. Nine mostly naked men and one woman cavort
in rustic abandon in honour of Silenus, the drunken tutor of Bacchus.
In the center of this frieze-like procession, the paunchy god is held
aloft by a satyr and two fauns. His inebriation is evident from the
awkwardness with which he places a wreath of grapevines on his head
with one hand and unknowingly spills wine with the other. Behind
him, a drunken man is borne on the shoulders of another while at the
left an obese woman requires similar assistance as she exits the pool.
On the right, a pair of musicians serenade the motley assembly with
a syrinx and double tibia, or flute.

Mantegna's antiquarian interests permeate the print, which like
many of his works, emulates the style of classical relief sculpture in a
technique so crisp as to suggest a work carved in stone. As well as
being among the earliest Italian prints, Mantegna's *Bacchanal* was
also among the first works to incorporate classical subject matter.
Crucial to both developments was the invention of movable type and
the printing press in the middle of the fifteenth century. Not only did
classical texts become more available than they were when hand-
written parchment copies had been the only means of duplication,
but the related growth of the paper-making industry spurred the
development of the graphic arts of drawing and print-making.

For his subject-matter, Mantegna seems to have modelled his
Bacchanal with Silenus on Virgil, a fellow Mantuan and the town's most
illustrious ancient citizen. The relevant text is found in Book VI of the
Eclogues, a work from 37 BC that appeared in three printed editions –
all in Latin – between 1450 and 1476. In this passage, Silenus is aroused
from a drunken sleep by two satyrs and a nymph who induce him to
sing to the accompaniment of a pair of music-making fauns. The old
man sings of the mythic deeds of the Olympian gods until nightfall, as
his woodland companions drink along with him.

Mantegna never imitated the antique slavishly, and his engraving departs from Virgil in significant ways. Rather than idealizing the
pagan imagery – a risky venture at the time – he treated the participants as vulgar boors. His incapacitated Silenus is not the good-natured
toper known in ancient art but a humourless drunk. The woman at

the left, presumably 'Aegle, fairest of the Naiad-band', is treated even more harshly. Not only is she obese, but ugly and helpless as well. In effect, Mantegna transformed the lovely nymph into the personification of Gluttony and Sloth, two of the Seven Deadly Sins in the pantheon of Christian vices. Since other overweight women appear in his art among the vices expelled by Pallas – *Ignorantia* in the *Calumny of Apelles*, for example – one suspects he was familiar with ancient physiognomic theories that viewed a person's outward appearance as a key to their character.[32] With that in mind, one is tempted to read the print not so much as a tribute to classical mythology as a warning against the ungodly consequences that can attend the excess consumption of wine.

If Mantegna's *Bacchanal with Silenus* subverts its own mythic theme, Michelangelo's marble *Bacchus* single-mindedly challenges the classical ideal. The statue was begun in 1496 when the twenty-one-year-old artist had just moved from Florence to Rome. Inspired by the antiquities he encountered at every turn – the *Apollo Belvedere* had just been discovered – and pursued by a growing cadre of patrons and collectors, Michelangelo was evidently moved to create a work that might itself be taken for an antiquity. Ascanio Condivi and Giorgio Vasari – one a former student and the other a syco-phantic admirer – wrote biographies of the artist (published in 1553 and 1568 respectively) that took delight in recounting how the young genius had already 'counterfeited' an ancient statue while still in Florence.[33] From the beginning, an aura of uncertainty seems to have hung over the *Bacchus* as well.[34] Although commissioned by Cardinal Raffaele Riario, the statue is first recorded in the collection of Jacopo Galli, a Roman nobleman in whose sculpture garden the work was recorded in a drawing from the mid-1530s. From this sketch we learn that *Bacchus* was the only modern work among the owner's collection of antiquities, and, like them, was in a fragmentary state with one of its hands broken off and the penis mutilated. The circumstances of its transfer from Riario to Galli are unknown, as is any knowledge of how it came to be damaged. One sixteenth-century antiquarian, Jean-Jacques Boissard, suggested that Michelangelo had broken the sculpture himself so as to deceive viewers into thinking it was a genuine antiquity.[35] The game of deception – a favourite theme in Renaissance literature and theatre – reached its apogee in a 1556 guidebook to ancient sculpture in Rome that first titillated the

52 Michelangelo
Buonarroti,
Bacchus,
1496–7, marble.

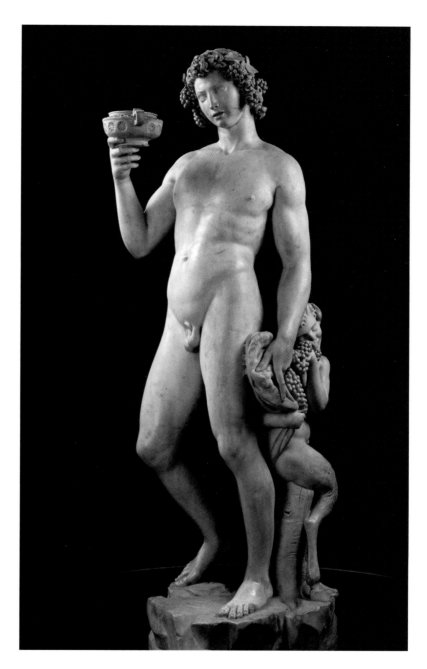

reader with a lengthy description of the marble before revealing that
it was, in truth, an *opera moderna*.[36]

Condivi's biography of Michelangelo describes the statue as
'corresponding in form and appearance in every particular to the
intention of the writers of antiquity', while Vasari, who was generally

unconcerned with iconography, found the figure 'a marvellous fusion of the youthful slenderness of the male and the fleshy roundness of the female'.[37] The two remarks are worth considering together since Vasari's recognition of the youth's androgyny actually confirms Condivi's assertion that the work was historically informed. Aeschylus and Euripides both describe the deity as 'womanly', and representations in later Greek and Roman art frequently depict him as a languid and effeminate figure. Nevertheless, as one art historian has noted, 'not only does the figure have a soft abdomen, but it also has slightly swelling breasts, both traditionally feminine features. In no known ancient image is the deity's feminine character so visually accentuated as in this statue'.[38] Beyond the youth's physical presence, Michelangelo also hints at his sexual nature by placing an animal pelt in his hand, a marginal yet suggestive attribute that turns the figure's nudity into an act of self-exposure.

Condivi further observed that *Bacchus* has 'the mirthful face and sidelong, lascivious eyes of those too much possessed by the love of wine'.[39] Michelangelo's figure does look tipsy as he lurches forward, but in this respect Condivi's assertion of the artist's dependence upon ancient textual sources did not apply. Drunkenness was not one of the traits typically ascribed to the deity in early texts, and some, like Athenaeus' *Deipnosophistae,* or *Learned Banqueters,* even claim 'the god of wine is really upright and does not totter when he is drunk'.[40] Significantly, no ancient statue shows Bacchus inebriated either, although the figure does sometimes lean on a satyr for support. Michelangelo's conception of the deity as inebriated is thus the work's most original feature.

Although the notion of a tipsy Bacchus did not directly derive from ancient sources, an alternative inspiration may have come from Renaissance texts.[41] It has been suggested that Michelangelo was influenced by the circle of Neoplatonists he met in Florence six years earlier when, at the age of fifteen, he joined the household of Lorenzo the Magnificent in the Medici Palace. There, among the poets and literati, he surely would have come into contact with Marsilio Ficino and Pico della Mirandola, the true apostles of the movement. Central to the tenets of Renaissance Neoplatonism was the philosophical compatibility of pagan culture and the Christian faith, as well as the belief that the senses could play a significant role in raising the soul from lower to higher realms of being. To this way of thinking, the drunkenness exemplified by Bacchus can lead to a state of grace, a proposition that Pico explains in his *Oration on the Dignity of Man*:

> Bacchus, the leader of the muses, in his own mysteries, that is, in the visible signs of nature, will show the invisible things of God to us as we philosophize, and will make us drunk with the abundance of the house of God.[42]

Ficino, in his *Commentary on Plato's Symposium*, gives the name 'divine madness' to this elevated state of the spirit, explaining:

> By divine madness, man is raised above the nature of man and passes over into God. The divine madness is a kind of illumination of the rational soul, through which God draws the soul slipping down to the lower world back to the higher.[43]

Bacchus plays a key role in the process of divinization for, as Ficino goes on to explain, the deity occupies an intermediary position in the four stages of divine ascension and assists in unifying the ascent to oneness. By the same logic, the animal skin that Bacchus has shed, and the little panisc, or satyr, on whom he turns his back, can only be symbols of the lower order the drunken youth leaves behind.

Was Michelangelo a Neoplatonist? Strenuous efforts have been made in the past – mainly based on readings of his poetry – to prove this the case, and some true believers continue the effort to this day. The leading text on Italian Renaissance art, in contrast, takes a dim view of such assertions, seeing Renaissance Neoplatonic writings as being so 'kaleidoscopic' in nature that any number of different meanings could be derived from the same classical legend.[44] Looking at Michelangelo's *Bacchus* in light of his other early works unfortunately does not resolve the issue.

By the turn of the sixteenth century, pagan mythologies became more acceptable in Italian art, particularly in Venice and the surrounding region. Bacchus was among the most popular deities, and his gift of wine and his rescue of Ariadne were seen as highlights of his complex and contradictory myth. It probably did not hurt that since the end of the Middle Ages the divinity of Bacchus had also come to be viewed as syncretic with that of Christ. Numerous editions of the so-called 'moralized' Ovid affirmed connections between pagan and Christian deities that first had appeared in ancient orphic literature.[45] Along with Bacchus/Christ, Juno was thus interpreted as a prototype of the Virgin, as was Diana, with her triple persona, considered an allegory of the Trinity.

Bacchus's rehabilitation in the Renaissance was most fully realized in the decorations Alfonso d'Este (1476–1534) envisioned in 1511 for his new picture gallery in the ducal palace in Ferrara.[46] Constructed of alabaster, the gallery was to have been filled with masterpieces by the leading painters of his day – Michelangelo and Raphael among them – but only after much delay, did the work proceed beyond its initial conception. Eventually, five canvases were completed, one by Giovanni Bellini, another by Dosso Dossi and three by the young Titian. The subjects all had Bacchic or festive themes: the *Feast of the Gods* by Bellini, a *Bacchanal of Men* by Dossi, and *Bacchus and Ariadne*, *Bacchanal of the Andrians*, and the *Worship of Venus*, by Titian. Unfortunately, all have since been dispersed, and the Dossi lost.

Pagan themes are never more sympathetically treated in Renaissance art than they are here. Each painting in the series was based on an ancient text like Ovid's *Fasti* or Philostratus's *Imagines*. The tamest and earliest of the pictures, Bellini's *Feast of the Gods*, begun in 1514, is taken from the description of a winter festival in the *Fasti*. As in the poem, Bellini (and later Titian who completed the work) depicts 'Pans and young sex-starved satyrs . . . nymphs with uncombed flowing hair . . . ruddy Priapus, his shameless member all too ready' and, of course, 'Bacchus with his ivy crown' pouring wine from a cask, and 'old Silenus on a braying ass'.[47] The image of Bacchus as a very young boy (he is the figure at the left dressed in blue) is not inconsistent with Ovid's claim in Book IV of the *Metamorphoses* that 'He is young, this god, A boy forever', or the passage in Macrobius's *Saturnalia* that likens the winter solstice to 'a tiny infant'.[48] Bellini was obviously intrigued by the notion of a child Bacchus, for in another canvas, also now in the National Gallery of Art, he depicted an even younger boy holding a wine pitcher sitting alone in a landscape.

Titian's *Meeting of Bacchus and Ariadne*, painted in 1522–3 (illus. 54), was inspired by another Ovidian passage, this one from Book I of the *Ars Amatoria*. Here Ovid tells how the fair-haired Ariadne, beset with grief from her abandonment by a previous lover on the island of Naxos, was rescued by Bacchus whose arrival on a

53 Giovanni Bellini and Titian, *Feast of the Gods*, 1514/1529, oil on canvas.

chariot drawn by tigers was heralded by 'the beating of cymbals and tambourines'. As usual, he was accompanied by an entourage of 'light-footed satyrs', 'wild-haired maenads' and 'Old Silenus [so intoxicated] he can hardly keep his seat on the ass'. Significantly, Titian's colourful and dramatic reenactment of the scene enriched the Ovidian text by including a man entwined with snakes in the foreground. Although the presence of this figure at a Bacchanal can only have been inspired by the lines of Catullus that described male bacchants as having 'girt themselves with writhing snakes',[49] the painter's visual conception was clearly based on the *Laocoön*, the celebrated Hellenistic statue that had recently been unearthed in Rome. Significantly, Titian's *Meeting of Bacchus and Ariadne* (illus. 54) was the first painting to recognize

this figure's potential for conveying powerful emotion, as well as its adaptability to different thematic circumstances.

The most intriguing of all the images conflating wine and love in the Alabaster Gallery was Titian's *Bacchanal of the Andrians*, also painted in 1522–3. This was mainly inspired by a passage in Philostratus's *Imagines*, the third-century account of a picture collection the author claims to have seen in a villa near Naples. First published (in Latin) just five years earlier, the *Imagines* was a classic ekphrasis, or rhetorical exercise in visual description. One of the pictures described by Philostratus was the 'Andrians', a subject otherwise unknown in ancient art.

54 Titian, *Meeting of Bacchus and Ariadne*, 1520–23, oil on canvas.

A stream of wine on the island of Andros, and the Andrians who have become drunken from the river, are the subject of this painting. For by the act of Dionysus, the earth of the Andrians is so charged with wine that it bursts forth and sends up for them a river . . . the men, crowned with ivy and briony, are singing to their wives and children, some dancing on either bank, some reclining. And very likely this also is the theme of their song . . .[50]

Titian's painting reverses the ekphrastic practice of turning pictures into words by translating the same text back into images. His Andrians are in a state of complete abandon, their inhibitions erased by the great quantities of wine they have consumed. The artist embellished his primary text in a variety of ways, most memorably by

55 Titian, *Bacchanal of the Andrians*, 1518–19, oil on canvas.

placing a voluptuous slumbering nymph in the right foreground. The nymph was unquestionably inspired by similar figures on Roman sarcophagi (illus. 31), but the shameless child who urinates at her feet was the artist's invention. Even more ingeniously, Titian introduced vocal music into the scene by placing a song sheet in the central foreground of the composition. One must crane one's neck to read it, but the music is recognizable as that of Flemish composer Adrian Willert who had just been appointed by Duke Alfonso as court musician in Ferrara. Translated, it reads: 'he who drinks and does not drink again, knows not what drinking is'.[51]

Given the intemperance and sensuality that permeates nearly every detail of the *Andrians*, it is hard to think of the picture as being anything but a tribute to the lost pleasures of paganism. Recondite arguments have attempted to interpret the series as signifying 'the harmonious relation between wine, love, and fertility, under the sign of temperance, symbolized by wine mixed with water', but this seems at odds with what one sees.[52] Since Bacchus began his existence as an elusive and unstable figure in Greek and Roman mythology, it is perhaps only fitting that certainty continues to elude his modern interpreters.

The rehabilitation of Bacchus, like the alleged espousal of Neoplatonic philosophy, seems never to have extended beyond courtly circles to a wider public. While some earlier Florentine depictions of pagan deities may have been lost in the 'bonfires of the vanities' ignited in the late 1490s by Savonarola and his fanatical followers, such themes clearly lost favour after the Reformation. Catholicism's response to the threat of internal revolt was a flight to religious orthodoxy, a move that in truth was as much a counter-renascence as it was a Counter-Reformation.

By the middle of the sixteenth century, the humanist ideals that so firmly underlay fifteenth-century culture had lost most of their patronal support. Although Titian would be the last major artist to paint a Bacchanal before Annibale Carracci did so some seventy years later, the celebration of wine among artists and poets by no means disappeared during the intervening decades. The Roman Accademia dei Vignaiuoli, or Academy of Vintners, and the Accademia della Valle di Bregno in Milan did their best to keep the Bacchic spirit alive. Founded in the 1530s, the Roman 'academy' was a centre for burlesque poetry that frequently took the clergy as a target. Fuelled with wine, poets like Francesco Berni and Francesco Molza were especially adept at casting various fruits and vegetables as sexual metaphors in innocent-sounding verses like 'Ode to the Peach'.[53] Painters dominated the Milanese 'academy', which took its name from a picturesque region of southern Switzerland whose inscrutable dialect was adopted as the official language of their spoken communication. The choice of Bregno (or Blenio, as it was also called), was not just a matter of whimsy, for that was the region that traditionally supplied the *facchini*, or wine porters, of Milan. Fittingly, the organization's seal depicted Bacchus riding in a chariot drawn by tigers with the motto 'Bacco inspiratori', while its regular programming included mock-Dionysian drinking rituals.

Giovanni Paolo Lomazzo was the most famous artist to belong to the Accademia della Valle di Bregno, which at its height boasted more than a hundred members. In 1568 he was inaugurated as its second elected director or 'abbot', and it was in this role that he appears in a self-portrait now in the Brera Museum. Self-portraits were commonplace in the period, but Lomazzo's compact image carries an unusually complex iconography. Numerous interpretations have focused on the symbolism of his bizarre costume and attributes, but most agree that the allusions primarily centre on Bacchus as protector of the academy.[54]

56 Giovanni Paolo Lomazzo, *Self-portrait*, 1568, oil on canvas.

Italian Wine and Wit

Ceramic wine pitchers known as *boccali* were in ordinary use since the end of the Middle Ages, many of them painted with colourful abstract or figurative decoration. Duccio's *Last Supper* from the *Maestà* altarpiece depicts a particularly fine example from the early fourteenth century, and the survival of so many from the following centuries attests to their ubiquity in Renaissance domestic life at every level of society.[55] By the sixteenth century, a clever variant on this common piece of tableware emerged with the reinvention of the trick or puzzle jug. Playing jokes on the inebriated was, of course, a pastime that originated in ancient Greece to accompany post-prandial symposia. In chapter Two we heard of Greek ceramic vessels specially constructed to baffle or embarrass drinkers who most likely had already lost their bearings. While there is no record indicating that such objects were known in the Renaissance, the fact that similar vessels were produced in sixteenth-century maiolica workshops can hardly be a coincidence. Themes of deception, as we have already seen, were extremely popular in this period, and deceptive service ware was part of the phenomenon.[56]

The Museo del Vino in Torgiano has several puzzle vases on view, each taunting the drinker with the inscription *'bevi se puoi'* (drink if you can). Cipriano Piccolpasso, author of *I tre libri dell'arte del vasaio*, or *The Three Books of the Potter's Art* (1557), divulges the

57 *Puzzle Jug*, late 16th–early 17th century, maiolica.

secret of what he calls 'vessels without a mouth, and puzzle cups, which are things that have no rules' by including cut-away drawings of such a jug being assembled from inner and outer containers.[57] A fine example of a similar vessel has perforations encircling its neck that ensure that the contents can never be poured, leaving its user feeling both thwarted and thirsty.[58] In this instance, the trick involves hidden channels within the handles and rim that allow the wine to be sucked with a straw through one of the small spouts on the rim. One imagines the survival rate of such easily breakable table toys was fairly low given the high levels of intoxication and frustration that presumably attended their use.

Wine and Medicine

Along with everyday *boccali*, ceramic vessels known as *albarelli*, or apothecary jars, were also made in great quantities during the Renaissance. These were intended for the storage of dry or viscous materials like herbs, spices, candied fruits, honey, ointments and electuaries in pharmacies and homes across Europe. Since the known pharmacopoeia totalled more than a thousand potions at this time, some potters earned a living making nothing else.[59] Early apothecary jars might be decorated with armorial insignia, foliate motifs or even figural representations, but after the mid-fifteenth century the Latin (or pseudo-Latin) name of their contents was often inscribed across the vessel's front. From these we learn what concoctions were available, and from numerous herbals and pharmacopoeias what ailments they were thought to cure.

The cataloguing of herbal remedies began in the ancient world with the texts of Hippocrates, Galen and especially Dioscorides, whose *De universa medicina* examined the medicinal effects of more than 500 plants. More than a millennium later, Hildegard von Bingen summarized the traditions of the twelfth century in her famous *Physica*, or *Book of Simple Medicine*, which offered a compendium of 230 therapeutic plants.[60] For about half of these she recommends the patient immerse the herb in 'good' or 'pure' wine before drinking. The maladies treatable by wine-borne concoctions included arthritis (tithymal), bad breath (sage), bleeding intestines (chervil), broken bones (cornflower), coughing (lungwort), fever (psyllium, peony, madder, masterwort and figaria), heart trouble (galingale), indigestion (tansy), migraine (elecampane), poisoning (calendula), ringing in the ears (borage) and scabies (gladiolus). For Hildegard, wine was not an active agent but a 'mixer' whose purpose was to liquefy and render bitter-tasting substances palatable.

For its therapeutic benefits, pure wine, on the other hand, continued to be taken, with every prescriptive text since the time of Hippocrates touting its salutary effects, and new applications appearing regularly. After the new-world disease of syphilis reached Europe in 1494, for example, the suggested remedies included washing the penis in white wine or bathing in a solution of wine and herbs.[61]

When comprehensive pharmacopoeias were first assembled in the Renaissance, they usually repeated the traditional claims. The earliest of these, Valerius Cordus' *Pharmacorum . . . Dispensatorium* (1546), thus combined wine therapy along with other bits of folk medicine that called for ingredients that might include the ashes of scorpions and centipedes, dog excrement or wolf's liver.[62] The *Pharmacorum* was first published in Nuremberg and later reprinted in thirty-five editions and eight translations, eventually becoming the standard reference work in apothecary shops all across Europe.

The strangest of the wine-based formulations to emerge in this period were based not on organic specimens but on the minerals antimony and iron. These were the invention of Phillip von Hohenheim (1493–1541), the man who renamed himself Paracelsus out of a sense of rivalry with Aulus Cornelius Celsus, the Roman encyclopedist. Paracelsus was an alchemist, astrologer, physician and occultist, and among his many prescriptions were cures for wounds, ulcers and leprosy from decoctions of antimony (a poisonous metal) mixed with tartar, colcothar or bitter almonds dissolved in wine. For the treatment of anemia he recommended the consumption of iron filings that had been immersed in wine until they rusted.[63] Paracelsus attracted a loyal band of followers, but his unorthodox methods – no less than his personal arrogance – made him a target of vicious diatribes from the conventional medical community.[64]

Wine may have played a secondary role in Renaissance pharmacology, but its importance in the world of medicine did not end there. Italian hospitals were awash in wine, as the well-preserved account books of the *Ospedale* of Santa Maria Nuova in Florence makes clear. In 1510–11, for example, the institution's wine cellar was provisioned with 'wines of every kind [stored] separately: sweet, smooth, dry, white, and red – 5,000 or 6,000 casks a year'.[65] At the same time, a narrative account of the hospital's services informs us that 'While the sick are eating, three servants go round the ward serving excellent wine. Each person receives an appropriate amount of the particular wine – white, red, smooth, sweet, or dry – suited to his illness and his appetite.'[66]

The choice of wines was not intended to pamper the patients but (as the phrase 'suited to his illness' suggests) to match the particular ailment. The link was based on the presumed needs of the individual in accordance with humoral theory. As we know from earlier chapters, this was a pseudo-scientific notion introduced by Hippocrates in the fifth century BC whose basic tenets remained unchallenged in Western medicine for more than two millennia. In essence, the theory maintained that the human body was sustained by four essential fluids: yellow bile, black bile, phlegm and blood. These four humours were assumed to be unstable, and easily affected by outside factors such as the four elements and four seasons, as well as by gender. One's humoral condition was also associated with temperament, internal temperature and humidity. In practical terms, yellow bile was linked with the choleric temperament and with the hot and dry; black bile with the melancholic and the cold and dry; phlegm with the phlegmatic and the cold and moist; and blood with the sanguine and the hot and moist.

Throughout the ages, wine's role in maintaining good health was believed to stem from its ability to keep the humours in balance, especially when it came to temperature and humidity. Numerous sixteenth-century treatises extolling its salutary benefits were composed with just this in mind.[67] The earliest, Giovanni Battista Confalonieri's *De vini natura disputatio* (Basel and Venice, 1535), begins with a review of the different opinions held in his day on the nature of wine and its linkage to the humours.[68] Some, he admits, considered wine to be hot and moist, others dry and yet others cool. Wine is also said to affect people in different ways. Depending on the 'complexion' of the drinker, the same wine can heat those who are cold, dry those who are damp and cool the bilious. A watery wine, he says, will affect the phlegmatic person differently than a bilious one; a hot and volatile wine will make hotter constitutions drink quicker because it rises more easily to the brain than in colder bodies. In general, he recommends that cold and dry people drink hotter and moister (sweeter) wines while those who are cold and moist should imbibe ones that are austere and tannic. By this logic, passing out from drunkenness was explainable in humoral terms, for it resulted from wine's chilling the inner heat, just as water puts out the fire. Confalonieri was correct in at least one respect, however, for he speaks of the *terroir* of vineyards in a way that recognizes that the qualities of soil and water can affect the taste of the final product.

A sampling of other medical tracts from the period confirms Confalonieri's remarks regarding the bewilderingly different linkages that existed between the four humours and the five types of wine.[69] So, too, are wine's benefits applied to an ever-expanding range of symptoms. To name but a few, these include colouring the complexion, curing sleeplessness, raising the spirits, provoking urination, helping to expel gas, facilitating coitus, sparking the appetite, sharpening wit, opening obstructions and remedying hangovers. At the same time, few sixteenth-century texts are free from warnings about wine's harmful effects, which include forgetfulness, insensibility, reduced energy, contentiousness, laziness, dishonesty, anger and homicidal tendencies, as well as its link to diseases like dropsy, paralysis, gout, stupor, spasms, tremor and vertigo. Clearly, these treatises were to some extent shaped by the social and moral climates of their day, with a few seemingly more concerned with behavioural control than with making a contribution to the medical discourse.[70]

Wine in Northern European Popular Culture

Although Bacchus would eventually become a favourite subject of artists as different as Poussin and Rubens, his rehabilitation took longer in northern Europe than it did in Italy. Wine was not mythologized in Renaissance France, Germany and the Netherlands in the way it was in the south, yet its linkage to more serious sins made it a natural *topos* for the moralizing images and texts that were so important a part of the northern sensibility. In painting, the most popular exemplary subject relating to wine was the tale of the Prodigal Son (Luke 15:11–32), a parable illustrating God's grace towards those who rebel but repent. Having left the comforts of home, the nameless son 'traveled to a distant country, squandered his property in dissolute living', and descended to the level of a swineherd before finally returning to his father's welcome. The tale was unique in its potential for

58 Pieter Coecke van Aelst, *Prodigal Son*, c. 1530, oil on panel.

evoking different social and emotional environments, allowing artists drawn to the lower genres to depict his life in the barnyard, and those interested in human expression the family reunion. For the Flemish artist Pieter Coecke van Aelst (1502–50), for example, the opportunity to depict extravagant living proved irresistible. His *Prodigal Son* envisions the still respectable young man in the refined company of female musicians who ply him with cherries and a large glass of wine. The prominence of wine in the composition suggests its seminal role in his eventual decline, just as it does in images of the *Temptation of Saint Anthony*, where it is often the first of the many enticements Satan uses to torment the stoical hermit.

The adventures of the Prodigal Son quickly expanded beyond the biblical account. Paintings set in brothels became particularly popular, and as their numbers increased, their moral censure tended to become less clear or disappear altogether. Van Aelst's contemporary and countryman Jan van Hemessen (1502–50) painted such a scene, now playfully titled *Loose Company* (illus. 59), that replaces the young man with an elderly one. Contemporary viewers probably would have identified this figure with *Elckerlijk,* the Everyman of Dutch morality plays who undertakes an adventurous journey of his own. In Hemessen's version, the man is overcome by the attentions of two buxom young women while the madam of the establishment looks on. Although symbols of sexuality abound – a cat, a dog, a pitcher and a bowl of cherries – the true object of the wayfarer's desire seems not to be erotic gratification, but the glass of wine the courtesan holds temptingly in the air.

Northern painters of the sixteenth century typically cast the evils of drink in no uncertain terms, associating it with folly or, worse, Gluttony, which was one of the Seven Deadly Sins. In *The Praise of Folly* (1511), the Dutch humanist Erasmus of Rotterdam repeatedly refers to Bacchus – his personification of wine – as a 'witless dullard [who is] always merry, always in the first bloom of youth, always entertaining everyone with fun and games', but also one whose spell is short-lived. 'Bacchus is praised', he continues, for 'clearing the mind of troubles – but that only for a short time, since as soon as you have slept off your little wine-drinking spree, all your anxieties come rushing back to your mind like a team of wild horses'.[71] Erasmus' book, 'poised [as it was] between the urbanity of the Italian Renaissance and the earnestness of Northern Humanism', proved to be immensely popular throughout all of Europe.[72]

When it came to envisioning folly, no artist had a freer imagination than the Netherlandish painter Hieronymous Bosch (*c.* 1450–1516). The iconography of his pictures is so complex and personal that even the great Erwin Panofsky had to admit defeat, confessing in *Early Netherlandish Painting* that 'This too high for my wit, I prefer to omit.' Arcane, alchemical images, many too bizarre and otherworldly to describe, abound in his oeuvre, but those relating to alcohol are relatively easy to read.[73] Wine jugs and casks predictably appear in his depictions of the *Prodigal Son* and the *Temptation of St Anthony*, and most prominently in his *Allegory of Intemperance* (illus. 60), a fragment from one of the panels of his now-disassembled and partially lost triptych of the *Seven Deadly Sins*.[74]

The sin Bosch portrays is Gluttony, but it is overindulgence in wine, not food, that is the focus of his attention. Entering the scene at the left astride a floating barrel pushed by swimmers, a pot-bellied boor wearing a funnel on his head trumpets his arrival on shore. The marine imagery relates to the complementary theme – depicted in the adjoining composition – of the Ship of Fools, the central metaphor in Sebastian Brant's contemporary discourse (1494) on human imperfection. Guided by a jester, Intemperance sails towards a shoreline carelessly strewn with discarded clothing (probably that of the swimmers), his destination a tent at the water's edge. Inside, there are two figures locked in an embrace with a raised wineglass between them.

Gluttony at the time was generally viewed more in terms of its social consequences than its most conspicuous effect, bodily corpulence. The association with drinking originates in the writings of the early church fathers but was more fully developed in the later Middle Ages when one Christian manual likened the tavern to 'the Devil's church, where his disciples go to serve him', and another catalogued the consequences of alcohol as 'lechery, swearing, slandering, backbiting, scorning, despising, renouncing God, stealing, robbing, killing, and many other such sins'.[75] The couple tippling inside Bosch's tent can only allude to Lust, a vice Gregory the Great grouped with Gluttony among the carnal sins.

Wine most commonly appeared in Northern European art in genre scenes whose allegorical meanings – if they existed at all – tended to be less programmatic. Such images were usually associated with wedding feasts or religious or seasonal festivals. The works of Pieter Brueghel the Elder (*c.* 1525–69) come immediately to mind for their unique ability to capture the everyday life of peasants carousing in the countryside. But it was typically beer and not wine that accompanied the festivities he so colourfully depicted. At the time, beer enjoyed a significant price advantage, costing as little as one-sixth of the price of wine in some parts of northern Europe, a fact that surely prompted its consumption among the lower classes.[76]

Nevertheless, wine predominates in the 'low' woodcut prints in which alcohol was depicted. Since many of them are humorous or satirical, one wonders if parody of the peasant class rather than the promotion of moral rectitude was not the primary goal. A woodcut made in Nuremberg by Erhard Schoen in 1528 exemplifies the genre as a whole (illus. 61). Entitled *The Four Properties of Wine*, this print systematically catalogues the various effects of the grape on human

behaviour.[77] Four vignettes are organized around the central motif of a heavily laden vine, with each scene consisting of five to seven topers accompanied by an animal whose instincts complement their own. Reading clockwise from the upper left, the first image acknowledges the beneficial effects of wine when taken in moderation, the facilitation of courtship chief among them. The bestial attribute is a lamb who gazes in the direction of the one unaccompanied figure as if to remind him that wine alone is not a cure for meekness. In the second image, the presence of the broken vessels indicates that the drinking has now progressed beyond the limits of moderation. No women are present, and all five men are fighting. The attribute here is a growling dog, a natural sign of incivility. The third vignette seems mainly about foolishness, although the expression on one man's face implies the more serious sin of licentiousness. This time the animal is a monkey, who, dressed as a jester, engages another figure in a game that no doubt involves more drinking. Finally, in the fourth scene,

59 Jan van Hemessen, *Loose Company*, 1543, oil on panel.

60 Hieronymus Bosch, *Allegory of Intemperance*, *c.* 1495–1500, oil on panel.

drunkenness leads to the loss of all inhibition as humanity descends to the level of vomit-lapping swine.

Schoen, a native of Nuremburg, converted to Lutheranism just a few years before he made the woodcut in 1528. In a sermon of 1525 and letters from 1530 and 1546, Martin Luther (1483–1546) gave his opinion on both the dangers and the rewards of alcohol consumption. Although beer was the drink of choice in his native Nuremberg

61 Erhard Schoen,
*Four Properties of
Wine*, 1528, woodcut.

– a town that boasted some 49 breweries in 1579 – Luther concentrated exclusively on wine when speaking of alcohol.[78] Thus in the 1525 sermon he was tolerant of those who 'may have drank of the wine a little beyond what thirst required, and became merry', but warned that 'the excess customary in our times is a different thing, where men do not eat and drink but gorge themselves with food and drink, revel and carouse, and act as if it were a sign of skill or strength to consume too much . . . [and] the intention is not to be merry, but to be full and crazy. But these are swine, not men.'[79] The final vignette in Schoen's *Four Properties of Wine* is perfectly attuned to Luther's concluding remark.

The stereotypical German of the sixteenth century seems to have engaged in the very habits Luther and Schoen warned against. In his 1581 essay on drunkenness, Montaigne claims that 'the grossest nation of our day is alone in honouring it', that 'Germans enjoy drinking virtually any wine. Their aim is to gulp it rather than taste it', and that 'they drink out of bigger glasses towards the end of the meal . . . when they start their drinking contests'.[80] Travel accounts from the period matter-of-factly report that 'In Germany . . . if the tourist did not find a companion for himself, the host chose for him, and his bedfellow might be a gentleman, or he might be a carter; all that could safely be prophesied about him was that he would be drunk when he came to bed'.[81] Sixteenth-century medical treatises confirm this stereotype, sometimes attributing it to the country's harsh climate.[82]

Neither Luther nor even John Calvin proved to be the strictest of reformers when it came to alcohol, however. That distinction was shared among Ludwig Haetzer, Sebastian Franck and Martin Bucer, each of whom published a tract denouncing the evils of drink.[83] Haetzer's *On Evangelical Drinking* (1525) started the trend, but Franck's treatise, *Concerning the Horrible Vice of Drunkenness* (1528), was more wide-ranging and more widely read. For him, the abolition of alcohol was an essential part of the moral reform he sought to advance in the German-speaking lands. Excess consumption, in his opinion, led to 'a wild confused mind, dizzy head, bleary eyes, a stinking breath, bad stomach, shaking hands, gout, dropsy, weeping leg sores, [and] water on the brain'.[84] Alcohol, he goes on, diminishes a person's already impaired reason, and inexorably leads to the sins of blasphemy, idolatry, theft and murder. Significantly, in calling for prohibition, Haetzer singles out wine as the main culprit, and leaves no segment of society unspared:

> Oh misery! We are not alone drunk from wine, but drunk, drunk with the lying spirit, error and ignorance. One should punish the public vice, preachers with the word and ban, princes with the sword and law. For so long as no ban exists . . . I recognize no Gospel or Christian community to speak of.

Martin Bucer's *On the Kingdom of God* (1550) was written when the author was in exile in England, and unlike Haetzer and Franck – whose texts fell mainly on deaf German ears – his views are said to have had an effect on English Puritans as well as on Calvin himself.[85]

Luther, by contrast, was more open-minded on the subject. In a letter of 1530 addressed to his young friend Jerome Weller, the melancholic reformer discloses some surprisingly libertine attitudes, notably that 'Whenever the devil pesters you with [dreadful] thoughts, seek out the company of men, drink more, joke and jest, or engage in some other form of merriment. Sometimes it is necessary to drink a little more, play, jest, or even commit some sin in defiance and contempt of the devil in order not to give him the opportunity to make us scrupulous about trifles.' The drink Luther had in mind was not beer or spirits, but wine, for later in the same letter, after confessing his penchant for consuming 'a generous amount', he asks, 'What do you think is my reason for drinking wine undiluted . . . if it is not to torment and vex the devil who made up his mind to torment and vex me?'[86]

Luther's reasoning may seem disingenuous, but viewed historically, his remark is simply another in the long list of justifications for wine drinking made in the name of religion. Years later, he went beyond the beliefs expressed to Weller in an even more revealing epistolary disclosure. Writing to his wife from Mansfeld just eleven days before his death in February 1546:

> We are living well here. At every meal the councilor presents me with two quarts of Reinfal [a wine from Rivoglio in Istria], and it is very good. Sometimes I share it with my companions. The local wine is also good. The Naumburg beer is excellent, except that I believe it fills my chest with phlegm. The devil has spoiled the beer everywhere with pitch, and he spoils your wine at home with sulphur. But here the wine is pure, although it is, of course, affected by soil and climate.[87]

Luther's younger contemporary, John Calvin (1509–64), held stricter attitudes towards conviviality in general, yet his pronouncements on food and wine were also surprisingly tolerant. Eating and drinking, he believed, were gifts from God that were sources of both enjoyment and nourishment. 'If we ask to what end He created food', Calvin wrote, 'we will find He did not do this for the sake of necessity only, but also wanted to recommend to us some enjoyment and merriment . . . . For if this were not true, the prophet [Psalms 104:15] would not mention that wine gladdens the heart and oil makes his face shine.'[88] Elsewhere, he notes Christ's provision of an abundance of excellent wine at the Wedding at Cana, as additional proof of its goodness.

The issue for Calvin was therefore not the enjoyment of wine, but its link to intemperance. Several of his sermons warn against immoderation, one going so far as to criticize Herod's birthday party (Matthew 14:6–11) for being beset by 'luxury, pride, unrestrained mirth, and other extravagances'.[89] Another sermon he delivered in Geneva focused on the public drunkenness he saw everywhere around him:

> We see how the world is behaving nowadays in this place. How many of those heavy drunkards don't we see, of those gourmands who are like pigs at the trough, without any intelligence or reason? They fill their stomachs, but there is no question of lifting their heads to heaven to praise Him who feeds them and supports them so richly. They always have their whole snout deep in the fodder.[90]

Again, the porcine image is evoked, just as it was in Luther's 1525 sermon and Schoen's woodcut. Man's bestial side, sometimes exaggerated to the point of grotesqueness, or embellished with scatological details, captivated the imagination of sixteenth-century northern Europe like almost nothing else. Wine was viewed with particular suspicion for its association with the worst forms of depravity.

No image captures the dehumanizing effects of drink better than Hans Weiditz's woodcut *Winebag and Wheelbarrow* (illus. 62). Made around 1521, probably in his native Strasbourg, the print depicts a man whose stomach is so bloated with wine that it has turned into a winebag itself, a burden the drinker bears in a wheelbarrow. The figure may seem comical, but his unhappy expression suggests an awareness of the tragic circumstances that have befallen him. A leitmotif in Weiditz's grotesque imagery is a long-necked leather wine flask similar to that strapped to the man's behind.[91]

In literature, the imagery of Schoen and Weiditz would soon be eclipsed – and its moral message contravened – by the imaginative excesses of Rabelais's *Gargantua and Pantagruel*, a four-book romance published between 1532 and 1548. The Rabelaisian world was a celebration of the earthy and the scatological, of deformation and depravity, of the monstrous, the miniature and the bizarre. The story begins with the birth of the gigantic Gargantua, an event initially confused with his mother's copious bowel movement after she

reportedly consumed 'sixteen hogsheads and enough tripe to fill two barrels and six jugs'.[92] Hundreds of pages later, near the end of the tale, Pantagruel observes a shower of frozen words that looked 'like sweets of various colors' that spoke in 'barbarous tongues' as they melted away.[93]

Wine (never beer or distilled spirits) runs copiously through all four books and attends nearly every adventure and incident in the fast-flowing narrative. Indeed, it is central to the author's vision of the nonsensical world in which his fiction is set. The first line of the author's prologue addresses readers as 'Most illustrious drinkers', Gargantua's first spoken words are 'Give me a drink! A drink! A drink!', and the final volume concludes with the exhortation, 'let us drink'.[94] Rabelais was renowned as a fantasist and satirist, but as Mikhail Bakhtin has pointed out, many images in the novel were based on popular festive forms associated with Carnival and Lent.[95] Thus in one instance, as Rabelais himself acknowledges, the gigantic stone bowl from which Gargantua ate his gruel was modelled on the famous *scudella gigantis,* or 'giant's cup', in Bourges that once a year was filled with wine for the poor.[96]

At times, Rabelais expands or even interrupts his narrative with a meditation on the benefits of excessive consumption. At the beginning, we are told that when the infant Gargantua happened to be 'crotchety, fretful, irritable, or grumpy', a glass of wine restored him to good humour. Later, his son Pantagruel vanquished the evil King Anarch by funneling wine down his throat to put him to sleep before setting fire to his encampment. Discovering that Epistemon had been beheaded in the same encounter, Panurge cleaned the man's wounds with 'a good grade of white wine', treated him with an extract of dung, and stitched him back together. Soon Epistemon was on the mend although 'he was hoarse for over three weeks, and suffered from a dry cough, which nothing but drinking could cure'. In Book Three, the seasoned imbiber is praised for his ability 'to metaphysically philosophize in wine' and to 'deliberate, ponder, resolve, and conclude'. And finally, in Book Four, wine is credited with the magical property of curing any 'disturbance to stomach or head' brought on by seasickness.[97]

Rabelais, though also trained as a priest and a physician, clearly set out to mock the voices of reason and moderation that prevailed in his day. His advocacy of the irrational quickly led to the scrutiny of his writings in both the academic and the ecclesiastical communities. In due course, his books were censored by the Sorbonne and he was accused of apostasy by the Catholic church, attacked by John Calvin, and put at the top of the list of 'heretics of the first class' on the Vatican's 1564 *Index Librorum Prohibitorum*.[98]

Even today, Rabelais's writings remain subject to differing interpretations, with little agreement on the significance of all the wine. The introduction to the most recent critical edition of his work informs us that 'Wine in his writings is not normally a symbol of something else', while another modern text, *Wine and the Will: Rabelais's Bacchic Christianity*, posits the view that beneath all the vulgar ribaldry engendered by wine, there lies 'a multitude of Christian and classical symbols'.[99] Perhaps at this point in its history, wine had become so immersed in conflicting social and religious attitudes in Europe that univocal interpretations of its meaning in Rabelais's text are all but impossible.

six

The Seventeenth and Eighteenth Centuries

The recognition of regional distinctions among wines of the Renaissance continued to expand in succeeding periods. Lancerio's encomium to the wine of Tuscany and Scarlino's oenological poetics were followed most notably by Francesco Redi's long dithyramb, *Bacco in Toscana*, published in 1685. Redi, another Tuscan, is better known as a physician than a poet, and *Bacco* has been described as little more than 'a tiresome catalogue' of the wines of his region. When, at the end of his long hymn to the wine god, Redi names his favourite, it is Carmignano, a hearty red he likens to 'ambrosia and nectar of the gods'.[1] Not surprisingly, the regional chauvinism of Italian wine writing of this period was mirrored in its culinary literature, and only in the seventeenth century were the cuisines of Tuscany, Bologna and Naples first celebrated in texts of their own.[2]

In France, Château Haut-Brion – founded in 1550 – was the first wine to be named for the estate where it was made. Before long, Haut-Brion went on to acquire an international reputation, especially among the British. In what has been called 'the most momentous tasting note in the history of bordeaux', Samuel Pepys jotted in his diary for 10 April 1663 (just three weeks after vowing to abstain from wine altogether) that on a recent evening at a London tavern he 'drank a sort of French wine, called Ho Bryan, that hath a good and most particular taste that I ever met with.'[3]

For evenings spent at home, Pepys kept his own supply of wine in a cellar that in 1665 contained '[more than a barrel] of Claret, two quarter casks of Canary, and a smaller vessel of Sack, a vessel of Tent [tinto], another of Malaga, and another of white wine.'[4] The fact that an Englishman possessed wines from France, Spain and even the Canary Islands at this date was remarkable in itself, but Pepys's cellar inventory also speaks to the recent improvements in the preservation of wine. Some sprang from new techniques invented in Spain for cooking wines (*vini cocti*) in order to increase their sugar content and make them less susceptible to spoilage, but most came about with the introduction of more airtight containers and stoppers.

Glass vessels had already been used in Roman times for drinking and possibly serving wine, but only in the seventeenth century did anyone think to use them for storage. Coincidentally, a new type of bottle was developed in England with the shift from wood-fired to hotter coal-fired furnaces.[5] These were still hand-blown – moulded ones only came a century later – but they were heavier, darker coloured and less costly than their predecessors. Known as 'English bottles', they were shipped in quantity throughout Europe, with 36,000 of them made in a single year in Newcastle alone.[6]

Around the same time, cork stoppers began to replace those made of wood, leather or glass.[7] The full potential of cork was not realized until the mid-eighteenth century, however, when further innovations in bottle-making, binning and uncorking came about. The first innovation involved changing the shape of bottles from globular to cylindrical to make them easier to store on their sides. With that, in turn, came the realization that a wet cork was more airtight than a dry one, and a fully inserted cork better still. The invention of the corkscrew followed next, along with the standardization of bottle necks and corks. The cork itself came from Spain and Portugal, a spur to increased trade with the English. In a conspicuous example of wine politics, Portugal and England enacted a trade treaty in 1703 that assured English consumers access to a steady supply of port, and English wine merchants to all the corks they needed.[8]

Increased demands in one economic sector frequently spur derivative innovations in other sectors.[9] The Italian economic historian Giovanni Rebora refers to the phenomenon as 'dominant demand theory', and among the examples he gives in the Early Modern period are the rise of the textile and leather trades in places of increased culinary demand for sheep and goats on the one hand and for cattle on the other.[10] For the wine industry, the most significant by-products that derived from the use of airtight corked bottles were fortified beverages like port and sparkling wines.

Sparkling wines sparkle because of the carbon dioxide produced by the 'base wine' undergoing a second fermentation in a sealed bottle.[11] Until the precise requirements for adding sugar were formulated in the early nineteenth century, bottles could explode from an excessive build-up of gas. Champagne, the first sparkling wine, is said to have been the invention of Dom Pierre Pérignon (1639–1715), cellar master at the Benedictine Abbey of Hautvillier, located just north of Épernay. Pérignon apparently developed the bubbles by accident, but was so delighted with the result of his unplanned vintage that he exclaimed, 'I am drinking the stars.'[12] As the story goes, the wine was then introduced by two local landowners to the court of Versailles whereupon it immediately became a favourite of Louis XIV.[13] The appellation 'the wine of kings' did not come from Louis, however, but from its association with royal coronations at Reims Cathedral. Louis XIV not only enjoyed his wine, but drank it on the recommendation of his doctor, Antoine d'Aquin, who suggested he have it with every meal. Unfortunately for the burgeoning industry, when the king's health began to deteriorate towards the end of his life, his new physician, Guy-Crescent Fagon, recommended he drink burgundy instead.[14] It did not take long for word of the substitution to travel, and before long a lively dispute ensued between the two wine-growing regions. The taste for champagne held its own, however, expanding beyond the borders of France by 1668 and acquiring the reputation as a love potion in English Restoration comedy.[15]

By the seventeenth century, viticulture had also reached the New World. In America, the colonies of Virginia and Carolina first attempted to make wine from native grape varieties, but a lack of success led them to import European vinifera vines. The process continued to be marred by native pests, an unreliable climate and various vine diseases. It took the chance creation of a hybrid like the Alexander grape in Pennsylvania to spur the industry forward, and the dream of commercial production of a native American wine was only realized in 1806.[16]

Seventeenth-century Medicine

The advice d'Aquin and Fagon gave to Louis was based on what each believed to be the humoral bases of the king's ailments, which included gout, fevers and fistular tumours. The medical community did not always agree on the appropriate remedy for balancing humours, which they thought were susceptible to many variables. Even as the scientific methods of the seventeenth century led to some remarkable insights in anatomy and physiology – the circulation of the blood, the function of glands and the better understanding of the respiratory and nervous systems, for example – belief in the all-encompassing effects of the humours remained nearly universal. Thus the century began with the publication in 1600 of Cesare Crivellati's *Trattato dell'uso et modo di dare il vino nelle malattie acute* (*Treatise on the Use of Wine in Treating Illnesses and Maladies*) – a volume whose 26 chapters quote Hippocrates and Galen extensively while offering little if anything new beside the author's promotion of wines from his native Viterbo.[17] And the period ends with the publication of numerous pharmacopoeias that acclaim the benefits of wine in similar fashion.[18] The Scotsman William Buchan, in his *Domestic Medicine, or, A Treatise on the Prevention and Cure of Diseases by Regimen and Simple Medicines* (1769) wrote that 'The effects of wine are to raise the pulse, promote perspiration, warm the habit, and exhilarate the spirits.'[19] Buchan goes on to mark the salutary effects of different types of wine, both as primary agents and 'when employed as a *menstruum* for extracting the virtues of other medical substances'. After reviewing numerous confections, decoctions, draughts, emulsions, infusions, elixirs, and so forth, he concludes his text with the remark, 'Indeed, to say the truth, [wine] is worth all the rest put together.'

Wine in Religious Art

The Baroque style begins with the arrival of Caravaggio (1571–1610) in Rome in the 1590s. Born in the Lombard village from which he took his name, his creative genius had a profound impact on painters throughout Europe. His works were renowned – and reviled – for their unidealized realism and for his disdain for the stylizations of his mannerist predecessors. A comparison between his 1601 *Supper at Emmaus* and that of Pontormo from 75 years earlier (illus. 48) reveals his commitment to the direct observation of nature.

Unlike Pontormo's picture, Caravaggio's compact, close-up composition envisions the *Emmaus* scene as an occasion for hearty dining and human drama. And unlike Pontormo – a figure whose dyspepsia is evident from both his own diary and Vasari's biography – Caravaggio was a man of social ambitions and carnal appetites. Baked guinea

63 Caravaggio,
Supper at Emmaus,
1601, oil on canvas.

hen is the main course, and there is fruit for dessert, but bread and wine play special roles in the composition. Set to one side, their alignment with Christ's outstretched arm, raised in a manner suggesting a Eucharistic blessing, emphasizes their symbolic importance. Caravaggio's reputation for centring his work *tra il sacro e profano* – between the sacred and the profane – is never more evident than it is here. His depiction of the table furnishings and dining customs follow contemporary practice even to the point of placing the carafe of water next to the wine pitcher, in keeping with the age-old custom of mixing the two to cut the wine's alcohol content.[20] Leonardo and Pontormo had included water pitchers in their own sacred suppers, but Caravaggio went further by colouring the wine in the glass a pale shade of red, suggesting that it had already been diluted.

Supper scenes were not the only sacred subjects in which wine appears. *Christ the Redeemer* by the Dutch artist Henrik Goltzius (1558–1617) envisions the Saviour as a half-length figure who faces the

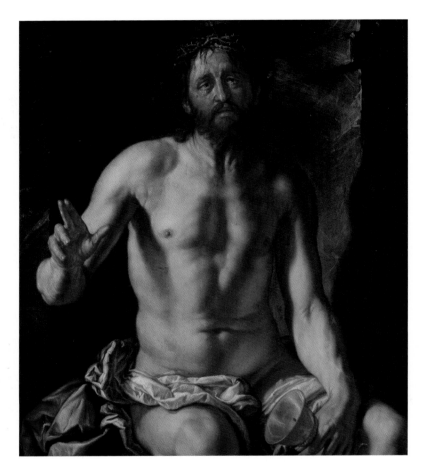

64 Hendrick Goltzius,
Christ the Redeemer, 1614,
oil on panel.

viewer as he emerges from a dark background into a dramatically illuminated foreground. Stylistically, the work is Italianate, but iconographically it recalls northern representations of *Christ in the Mystical Winepress* like Hieronymous Wierix's engraving of a few years earlier. But where Wierix fully elaborated the iconography, Goltzius limited it to the chalice alone. Although signs of the stigmata are barely visible on his body, no blood flows from the wounds and it is impossible to discern the contents of the cup. Yet the enervated expression on Christ's face and the nearly overturned chalice suggest he first filled the vessel with his blood before consuming it as wine. Moreover, the similarity of his pose to that of the typical medieval Man of Sorrows – a figure who bleeds directly into a cup – only affirms the primacy of wine as the instrument of redemption.

No biblical subject depicted the adverse effects of wine more graphically than the Old Testament account of Lot and his daughters

(Genesis 19:32–8). Although this incestuous tale occasionally appears in Medieval and Renaissance art, it became more popular in the more permissive atmosphere of the late sixteenth and seventeenth centuries. Like the (wineless) story of Susanna and the Elders (Susanna 1:15–27), Lot's drunken depravity was one of the few biblical subjects that justified the depiction of female nudity and male lust in a single image. Northern artists seem to have been especially fond of the story, although they typically emphasized the nudity over the lust. Peter Paul Rubens (1577–1640), an artist renowned for his renderings of voluptuous women and carnal appetites, was among the few to depict the obviously inebriated father embracing one of the daughters. The centrality of wine in the composition leaves little question as to what lay behind his behaviour.

Seventeenth-century northern European attitudes toward wine as the gateway to life's sensual temptations and subsequent fall from grace is reflected in the popularity of the story of St Anthony. In David

65 Peter Paul Rubens, *Lot and his Daughters*, c. 1611, oil on canvas.

Ryckaert's 1649 painting, wine is the primary temptation offered to the hermetic saint, with music being the only other earthly distraction on display. Like his better-known contemporary, David Teniers the Younger, Ryckaert populates the composition with an assortment of ghastly creatures reminiscent of the nightmarish fantasies of Hieronymous Bosch. The endurance of Boschian images of the evils of intemperance, along with wine's reputation as its most powerful agent, underlines the resilience of the trope in northern Europe. Only the pig sleeping at Anthony's feet – a symbol of victory over gluttony and lust – is based on reality, the rest being given over to the purely irrational.

66 David Ryckaert III, *Temptation of St Anthony*, 1649, oil on copper.

Bacchus and the Baroque

As the period of the Reformation and Counter-Reformation drew to a close, the religious uncertainties and orthodoxies that led to the demise of pagan imagery earlier in the century diminished to a point that mythological themes once again became acceptable. The phenomenon was evident in both northern and southern Europe, but the northern experience was especially remarkable given the absence of ancient prototypes; in the south, on the other hand, Bacchic imagery simply picked up where Michelangelo and Titian had left off.

The redirection of Northern art was largely due to the influence of Italian Mannerism on a handful of Netherlandish painters who journeyed south towards the end of the sixteenth century. Passing through France on the way to and from Italy, several of them also stopped in Fontainebleau, which was itself a centre of Italian ideals. There they would have seen the work of Francesco Primaticcio and Rosso Fiorentino, along with their French followers who espoused complex compositions populated with crowds of nude figures.

The Netherlandish movement took root in three cities: Antwerp in the Catholic south, and Haarlem and Utrecht in the largely Protestant north. Iconographically, artists in all three places tended to gravitate to profane rather than sacred imagery, and to mythological subjects over all others. Bacchic feasts and revelries were a favourite theme, as typified in the work of Joachim Wtewael (1566–1638). His 1612 *Wedding of Peleus and Thetis* (illus. 67) treats the marriage on Mount Pelion as a festive affair, with an abundance of wine on hand to raise the spirits of Bacchus and the many accompanying deities. Unfortunately the party ends badly, as Eris, an uninvited guest, contributes the golden apple that sets the stage first for the Judgment of Paris, and eventually for the Trojan War. Yet Wtewael, like most Dutch painters who took up the theme, only hints at the tragic consequences that can ensue from drinking too much wine. Significantly, the abundant food that lies at the centre of his composition remains untouched.

The Mannerist idiom espoused by Joachim Wtewael flourished in the north long after it had succumbed in Italy to the naturalism of Caravaggio and the classicism of Annibale Carracci (1560–1609). We have already seen how Caravaggio's *Supper at Emmaus* brought biblical narration down to earth, but even earlier in his career, during the 1590s, he had addressed Bacchic themes with some originality.

The so-called *Bacchino Malato*, or little sick Bacchus (illus. 68), was the first painting described by his early biographer, Giovanni Baglione. According to Baglione, the work was a self-portrait, disguised as 'a Bacchus with different bunches of grapes, painted with

great care though a bit dry in style'.[21] Opinions have differed about the young man's greenish pallor, some suggesting that the artist was recovering from malaria, and others finding his colouring emblematic of the poetic complexion or the natural look of satyrs. The lascivious quality of the work is clear, an indication that the picture alludes to the homoerotic activity that sometimes attended Greek symposia or, at the very least, the painter's familiarity with contemporary emblems of 'Lewdness'.[22] The presence of the peaches on the table adds to the erotic charge, posed as they are in the suggestive manner of human buttocks, a pun on the word *pesca*, defined in a contemporary Italian–English dictionary as both a peach and 'a young man's bum'.[23]

A few years later, Caravaggio returned to the Bacchic theme in a picture that leaves even less to the imagination (illus. 69). Here the

67 Joachim Wtewael, *The Wedding of Peleus and Thetis*, 1612, oil on copper.

68 Caravaggio,
Sick Bacchus,
c. 1593, oil on canvas.

deity faces the viewer and proffers a glass of wine while at the same
time unknotting the sash around his waist, his languid expression
clearly signalling his sexual intentions. The realism is exacting: the fruit
is blemished with insect predations, the fruit bowl is a contemporary
crespina, the carafe reflects the image of the artist standing before the
canvas, and the wineglass is a shallow Venetian tazza. Bacchus, moreover, has dirt under his fingernails and his hands (but not his arms)
are slightly sunburned. His androgynous physiognomy may appear
less realistic, but this may spring from the artist's fidelity to the texts
of ancient authors like Aeschylus, Euripides and Ovid who each describe the god as being effeminate or 'womanly'.[24]

Callistratus anticipated Caravaggio when, fifteen hundred years earlier, he wrote his ekphrasis of a supposedly lost work by Praxiteles: 'A young man . . . with a body so supple and relaxed . . . it had the bloom of youth, it was full of daintiness, it melted with desire'.[25] Caravaggio based his recreation of the mythically ambiguous Bacchus on more than just literary sources, however. The picture was painted

69 Caravaggio, *Bacchus*, *c.* 1596, oil on canvas.

around 1595–6 when the artist was residing in the palace of his first patron, Cardinal Francesco del Monte. Del Monte's Roman palace was filled with works of art, both ancient and modern, and among the antiquities listed in the inventory of his collections were a number with Dionysian themes, including five statues of Bacchus himself.[26] Unfortunately, there is no way of knowing what these looked like, but one can easily imagine Caravaggio being inspired by one. For Del Monte and his circle of friends, the opportunity to compare an ancient work with a modern one, and a sculpture with a painting, would have come at a time of unprecedented interest in such exercises.[27]

A year or two after Caravaggio painted his second *Bacchus*, Annibale Carracci began work in the Galleria Farnese in Rome. The most important commission of his career, this ambitious fresco cycle portrayed the *Loves of the Gods* in more than two dozen scenes depicting their often troubled relationships. The central image on the vault represents the *Triumph of Bacchus and Ariadne*, the tale of abandonment and rescue first told in Homer's *Odyssey* and subsequently repeated by Ovid, Hyginus and others.

Annibale stages the scene as a processional pageant, with the drunken Silenus preceding the blissful couple who ride in chariots drawn by tigers and goats. Despite its literary pedigree, the composition

70 Annibale Carracci, *Triumph of Bacchus and Ariadne*, fresco at the Palazzo Farnese, Rome, begun 1597.

seems more dependent on visual sources, like a Roman sarcophagus in Baltimore (illus. 31). But while this funerary sculpture separates Bacchus and Ariadne compositionally, Annibale combines the two, moving Ariadne to an adjoining chariot and replacing her at the corner with a voluptuous nymph. An exegesis by a seventeenth-century critic, Giovanni Pietro Bellori, explains her presence in the picture:

> In the foreground a half-nude woman lies on the ground . . . As though roused from sleep by the clamorous uproar she turns her head towards Silenus, who comes near and looks at her. This is vulgar and earthly Venus, with impure Love standing by her side, folding his arms and leaning on her shoulder . . . Her turning towards Silenus denotes the correspondence between drunkenness and lasciviousness . . . And so the nuptial dance continues, raging to the clamor of the Bacchantes, and in truth the painting is an incitement to dancing and music, and it expresses the fury and sweet madness that normally occupy spirits overcome by wine.[28]

One wonders how seriously this would have been taken by early viewers. For Bellori himself, Carracci's overall programme constituted a discourse on the struggle between divine and earthly love, 'showing that victory over irrational appetites elevates man to heaven'.[29] But given the apparent lack of thematic coherence in the cycle as a whole – not to mention the patently erotic nature of some of the subjects depicted – neither a unified nor a didactic meaning is readily found. One interpretation of the ceiling sees it as no more than 'a satire, spiced with a good-natured lewdness [painted] in the spirit of laughing derision, of bubbling merriment and mockery at the ridiculous aspects of the normally awesome pagan gods'.[30] Most recent readings, however, have all but abandoned the quest to explain the work in unequivocal terms.[31] Nevertheless, the centrality of Bacchus amid the many amorous dalliances – fulfilled or unrequited as they are – surely has a meaning of its own, one that would seem to underscore the importance of wine, and wine alone, in facilitating the progress of love.

Caravaggio and Annibale each had a profound influence on the art of their time, but when it came to Bacchic themes, the Caravaggesque idiom prevailed. A few followers like the young Guido Reni

71 Guido Reni, *Young Bacchus*, c. 1601–4, oil on canvas.

softened the edge of the master's imagery by transforming the deity into a wholesome boy. Recalling Ovid's claim in Book IV of the *Metamorphosis* that 'He is young, this god, a boy forever', or Giovanni Bellini's similar rendition in his *Feast of the Gods*, Reni removed any hint of sexual depravity from his interpretation. Indeed, his *Bacchus* looks like a child dressed in a Halloween costume. At the other extreme, Jusepe de Ribera (1591–1652), a Spaniard working in Naples, treated the theme of the *Drunken Silenus* (illus. 72) with a harsh naturalism. His 1626 painting in the Capodimonte Museum proved to be so popular that three editions of replicas were engraved before the middle of the century.[32]

Where traditional depictions of Silenus show him in motion astride a donkey or aided by satyrs, Ribera's picture envisions him

reclining on the ground before an enormous wine vat. He exposes his unlovely body to the viewer, attended by the boy Bacchus, an elderly satyr and several unidentified figures, one of whom refills his cup. The detailed description of his unshaven face and the sharp illumination of his body disclose Ribera's debt to Caravaggio, but the artist looked further back for the pose of the corpulent Silenus. Most likely, his inspiration came from the depiction of recumbent drinkers on Greek symposium vases, or in statues like the popular *Babuino*, then on public view near the artist's residence in Rome. Ribera's imagery, as one scholar has recently described it, was obviously layered with social and political meanings.[33] Sophisticated Neapolitans could affirm their personal erudition in recognizing the visual sources while experiencing a conflict between fear and fascination when it came to the underclass. Like Spanish readers of picaresque novels, the audience for Ribera's *Silenus* probably experienced a range of responses that included compassion, derision and disgust.

72 Jusepe de Ribera, *Drunken Silenus*, 1626, oil on canvas.

Peter Paul Rubens interpreted the Bacchic theme a little differently in several versions of the subject made early in his career. Typical of these is his *Drunken Silenus*, now in Munich, a picture in which a grossly overweight figure stumbles through a landscape surrounded by nymphs and satyrs. The atmosphere is both lusty and festive, and Rubens invested it with personal meaning by portraying himself as Silenus, his brother Philippe as a satyr, his wife Isabella Brant as a nymph and, at the lower right, his young son Albert.[34] Unlike Caravaggio's self-portrait as the *Bacchino Malato*, there is nothing unwholesome about this family gathering. Rubens was a man of principles and personal discipline, yet for him wine and its mythical

73 Peter Paul Rubens, *Drunken Silenus*, *c.* 1617–18, oil on panel.

personifications were less an evil to be avoided than a life-giving force that symbolized the fertility of nature itself.[35]

The seventeenth century continued to blur the distinctions first made in the Renaissance between the sacred and profane, the mythic and vernacular. If Rubens's *Drunken Silenus* merged the classical theme with the art of portraiture, other Baroque painters fashioned hybrid iconographies from ingredients drawn from mythology or the bible in combination with secular genres. Again, the practice was particularly popular among followers of Caravaggio. Bartolomeo Manfredi (1582–1622), the master's closest imitator in Rome, was the first to paint a *Bacchus and a Drinker* that conjoins a figure in modern dress with the historical Bacchus. A decade later, in 1628, the Spaniard Diego Velásquez expanded Manfredi's simple two-figure composition into a larger gathering in his *Los Borrachos*, or *Homage to Bacchus*.

The painting came at the point in Velázquez's career after he had left his native Seville to become court painter in Madrid. Most of his Sevillian works treated generic themes from everyday life, but in Madrid he was expected to concentrate on portraiture and classical mythology. *Los Borrachos* represents a transition between these worlds of fable and reality, enlivened at the same time with quotations from other works of art. Bacchus and the accompanying satyr have idealized physiques and are classically attired, while their companions are portrayed in a more individualized manner and are clad in modern garb. Together, the grouping represents the induction of ordinary drinkers into the world of classical mythology, a parody of both art and everyday life.[36]

What Velázquez represents in *Los Borrachos* is a Bacchic rite of initiation, not of the mystical and sometimes sado-masochistic kind described in Livy's *History*, but of the more playful variety ritually reenacted in contemporary academies of artists and poets. Two such academies – the Accademia dei Vignaiuoli and Accademia della Valle di Bregno – have been discussed earlier, but more is known about the practices of the seventeenth-century society of Dutch and Flemish painters in Rome known as the Schildersbent.[37] Founded around 1620 and disbanded by papal decree a century later, this group of artists also called themselves Bentvueghels (birds of a feather), and in its prime numbered over two hundred. The organization's professional tenets were twofold: in addition to refusing to pay taxes to the Accademia di San Luca, as was required of artists by law, the members favoured

74 Diego Velázquez, *Homage to Bacchus (Los Borrachos)*, 1628, oil on canvas.

genre scenes that, by Italian standards, were considered 'low' in both subject matter and style. Taking Caravaggesque naturalism to a point of no return, their work combined the fascination with everyday life with a contempt for the classical tradition as a whole.

Entry to the Schildersbent was accompanied by a set of arcane initiation rituals intended to undermine any social pretensions the enrollee might possess. Contemporary witnesses describe this so-called rite of 'baptism' in which the initiate, standing in a darkened room, first had to pass a test of courage that might involve gunpowder explosions or ghostly apparitions intended to frighten him out of his wits. Next the initiate had to kneel – in some cases naked – while one of the members intoned 'mysterious' words and poured wine over his head. The wine that dripped from his face was then collected in a goblet and given to the novice to drink. The entire affair was presided over by a *veldpaap*, or field pope, whose presence underlined the parodic nature of the ceremony as a whole.

With the initiation came the bestowal of a nickname that alluded to a personality trait of the *groentje*, or greenhorn. Most were harmless enough, but demeaning ones like 'Elephant' and 'Ferret', or 'Crab' and 'Goatsbeard', were not uncommon either. The popular name *Bamboccianti* was given to those Bentvueghels who worked in the manner of Pieter Van Laer (1592/95–1642), an artist whose physical deformity led to his being named *Bamboccio*, or 'Clumsy Puppet'.[38]

The Bentvueghels' initiation ceremony took the form of a banquet, paid for by the initiate, that could last an entire night and day. As one might imagine, the wine flowed freely at such events which typically ended with the participants stumbling out of the inn after daybreak to make their way across Rome to what they presumed was the tomb of Bacchus, but which was, in fact, the mausoleum of Santa Costanza. There they poured libations on the supposed grave and, as the party drew to a close, the initiates affixed their signatures and sobriquets to the walls of the ancient structure.

If the *Bamboccianti*, Ribera and the young Velázquez followed Caravaggio down the path of ever-grittier realism, a few seventeenth-century painters pursued the loftier goal of steeping themselves in classical literature. Of these, Nicolas Poussin (1594–1665) is the first who comes to mind, with more than half a dozen depictions of Bacchic themes among his mythological works. Poussin painted most of these early in his career as quiet meditations on the works of Bellini and Titian, but his final treatment of the subject, the *Birth of Bacchus* from 1657, signals the full maturity of his pictorial intelligence.[39] Poussin's friend, the art theorist and biographer Giovanni Pietro Bellori, provides an exegesis of what the picture represents: the infant Bacchus is presented by Mercury to the Nymph Dirce – daughter of the River Achelous – while his father Jupiter is depicted in the clouds above. Behind Dirce and Bacchus is a cave set into a rocky outcropping on which the piping Pan perches. In the left foreground, partially submerged in water, are a cluster of Naiads who look on attentively while two immobile figures close the composition at the right. This pair, Bellori continues,

> are not part of this fable, because the painter, following the description and sequence of Ovid's *Metamorphosis*, continued with another fable, that of Narcissus, who having died of self-love lies crowned with the flowers into which he was changed, and Echo sits nearby, miserably enamored, her harsh pallor indicating her tranformation into stone.[40]

75 Nicolas Poussin, *The Birth of Bacchus*, 1657, oil on canvas.

One may wonder why Poussin combined the *Birth of Bacchus* with the seemingly unrelated tale of the *Death of Narcissus*. The juxtaposition of the two myths makes more sense only after one realizes that Poussin looked beyond Ovid to Euripides's *Bacchae*, for that is the only text to name Dirce as the nurse of the infant Bacchus. Philostratus's *Imagines* – the source for Titian's *Andrians* – plays an important role in the iconography. In this, Poussin was attentive to two passages in particular, the first describing an image of Dionysus's mother, Semele, giving birth before a cave overgrown with ivy and grape vines with a spring of water nearby, and the second, a painting of Narcissus, again near a cave, with the pool that transfixes him being 'roofed over with . . . clusters of grapes . . . nor without some connection with the Bacchic rites of Dionysus'.[41] Poussin clearly recognized the connection Philostratus saw between the myths of Bacchus and Narcissus in their natural settings, and assumed the waters of Dirce, Semele, and Narcissus to be one and the same. In recollecting these ancient narratives and fashioning them into a single image, the artist created a work that has rightly (if prolixly) been called *The Fount of Dirce and the Cave of Pan*

163

and the Nymphs at Mount Cithaereron: The Birth and Consignment of Bacchus to Dirce, and the Death of Narcissus at Dirce's Fount.[42] The linking of the childhood of Bacchus with the death of Narcissus allowed Poussin to create a new cycle of birth and death based on the life-giving and life-ending properties of water, a theme that would occupy him throughout his career.[43]

The erudition of Poussin's picture demonstrates that the Dionysian myth remained capable of expansion even at this late date. His younger contemporary Pietro Testa (1612–1650) shared many of the same interests, condemning Caravaggesque painters as 'dirty and ridiculous apes of nature', while rejecting the illusionism of progressive artists like Giovanni Lanfranco.[44] Although Testa moved in the circles of Poussin, he had less success as a painter, and by his twenties turned his energies to printmaking. His large etching The Symposium, dated 1648, illustrates one of the final scenes in Plato's Symposium, the arrival of Alcibiades at a drinking party at the house of the poet Agathon.[45] Testa borrowed the figural arrangement of the recumbent participants from Poussin, but he embellished the setting with extraneous entertainers of the kind mentioned in Xenophon's Symposium. His interpretation of Plato's text, however, is entirely his own. It begins with explicit references to Pausanius's call early in the evening to limit the drinking after having indulged the night before – the attendants are shown clearing away wine and the symposiasts appear to be sober – but it focuses on the flamboyant entrance of Alcibiades who, 'very tipsy and shouting', immediately announces himself to be 'already drunk, utterly drunk'. The discussion he interrupts is one on the nature of love, but the only person who acknowledges his presence is Agathon, the host and his lover, while Socrates, seated next to him, ignores the intruder as he continues his discourse on truth and beauty. Alcibiades was known to be the object of Socrates' desire, and his exquisitely mannered pose embodies the very origin of the discourse. Testa was well acquainted with the dialogues and refers to them frequently in one of his notebooks.[46] His interpretation affirms the conventional Socratic view that beautiful appearances are virtuous only if they lead to a higher philosophical truth. Yet the artist did not stop there, for inscribed on a stone tablet on the wall behind Alcibiades and Agathon is the phrase: 'Vina, dapes onerant/animos Sapientia/nutrit' ('Wine weighs down banquets, Wisdom nourishes the soul'). Combined with the conspicuous absence of wine on the symposium table, the inscription undermines the assumption that these gatherings were primarily sites of overindulgence. Testa made temperance the issue instead, a sign perhaps of the sober and melancholic personality his early biographers describe.[47] Testa's apparent suicide at the age of 36 may even hint at a man deprived of the natural conviviality his print so resolutely censures.

Wine and Everyday Life

Images of ordinary people drinking wine appear in several contexts in this period. Louis Le Nain's *Peasant Family* (illus. 77), for example, is a simple portrayal of sober country folk consuming wine as part of their normal parsimonious diet. In this picture, painted in Paris in the 1640s, three generations of a family are gathered around a table before the hearth. Although a crock remains conspicuously on the floor, the only actual evidence of food is the loaf of bread clutched by the patriarch. The setting is so austere and the figures so restrained that the term classical comes naturally to mind. The artist clearly was sympathetic to his sitters whose spare existence must have been touched

76 Pietro Testa, *The Symposium*, 1648, engraving.

by the devastating Thirty Years War (1618–48). Because the meal they consume is limited to bread and wine, this dignified gathering is enriched with sacramental overtones one associates with depictions of the Last Supper. Artists frequently commingled the sacred and the profane at this time, and the prominence of the wine pitcher and glass held by the woman at the left, the bread at the centre of the composition and the solemnity of this wordless gathering clearly reverberate metaphorically.

Around the same time, an unidentified maiolica painter from the Tuscan town of Montelupo depicted a woman holding a wine pitcher and glass in her hands.[48] The message of this folkloric image could not be more different from the Le Nain, however. Swaying unsteadily in a vertiginous landscape, the woman is so drunk that she is unaware that her breasts have escaped from her bodice. The image thus puts the myths of both female sexuality and alcohol on trial. Women who drank to excess had long been viewed with suspicion, as Robert de Blois' thirteenth-century poem, *Le chastoiment des dames,* makes clear:

77 Louis Le Nain, *Peasant Family, c.* 1640s, oil on canvas.

78 *Drunken Woman*, plate, 20th-century replica of a 17th-century dish, maiolica.

And she who gluts more than her fill
Of food and wine soon finds a taste
For bold excess below the waist!
No worthy man will pay his court
To a lady of such lowly sort.[49]

Chaucer's *Wife of Bath's Prologue* affirms that lechers know from experience that a drinking woman has no defence against their advances, and San Bernardino of Siena warned that widows who overindulged 'would come to a bad end'. *Cuckold's Haven*, an English ballad from the same time as the maiolica plate, simply proclaimed that when a woman was drunk, ' all keys will fit her trunk'. Most of these sentiments were as misogynistic as they were disapproving, although a genuine concern is sometimes expressed for the shame that comes from unchaste behaviour. Thus we may read: 'Moderately take you thereof that no blame befalls you, for if you are often drunk, it reduces you to shame', or, 'A woman who drinks too much . . . whether widowed or married, often loses her good name.'

Nonetheless, alcohol's effect on female sexuality was not always viewed negatively. Indeed, wine was sometimes praised for its aphrodisiac properties, a notion derived from Terence's famous remark, 'Sine Baccho et Cerere fridget Venus' (Without wine and food, love freezes). Affirmations of eating and drinking as precursors of love are not uncommon in sixteenth and seventeenth-century texts, some openly cheering Bacchus for his capacity to 'seduce otherwise reluctant girls', or 'open every woman's door'.[50]

Genre painting flourished with particular vigour in Protestant lands, most notably in the northern Netherlands. Utrecht, the locus of Italianate mannerism a generation earlier, again took the lead in introducing the latest Italian fashions to audiences in the Low Countries. By the 1620s, the earthy realism of Caravaggio was particularly well-grounded. After decades of stylistic excess, many Dutch painters found the naturalistic immediacy of Caravaggio's early works irresistible, even if they all but ignored the artist's sometimes difficult iconography. The physical and psychological naturalism of these works was not just an artistic novelty, but a sign of the same open-eyed epistemology that characterized the age as a whole.[51]

Hendrick Terbrugghen's *Young Man with Wineglass by Candle-light*, dated 1623, exemplifies the Caravaggesque manner as it took root on Dutch soil. Like so many artists from Utrecht, Terbrugghen had been to Rome and he saw the work of the master at first hand. But his creation is clearly a hybrid for, unlike either *Bacchus* (illus. 68 and 69), there is nothing sordid or unhealthy about the fully clothed boy who cheerfully addresses the viewer with his glass of wine. The Utrecht School was partial to good-natured scenes, and one of the most popular settings was a brothel populated with attractive prostitutes and eager customers. In light of this new iconography, one only wonders if the moralizing fervour of earlier northern pictures has disappeared, or evolved into a different set of norms. Because the wine in Terbrugghen's picture is displayed so prominently, it is hard to imagine it carries no message of its own.

Seventeenth-century painters drawn to everyday subjects frequently justified their efforts by disguising them with a veil of allusion. The addition of a few pertinent details could transform a simple vase of flowers into an allegory of transience, a trio of topers into the *Three Ages of Man*, or a cycle of landscapes into the *Four Seasons*. The focus on wine in Terbrugghen's painting might thus be emblematic of *Taste*

79 Hendrick Terbrugghen, *Young Man with Wineglass by Candlelight*, 1623, oil on canvas.

as one of the *Five Senses*, a common theme in seventeenth-century art and literature. As of now, however, just a single pendant composition has been identified, and that seems to represent the sense of smell.[52]

Terbrugghen's allusion to the sense of taste may have simply been for the sake of expediency, an iconographic overlay that imbued an otherwise lowly work of genre with higher status. Yet like many works of Dutch Baroque art, the *Young Man with Wineglass/Allegory of Taste* can be read in more than one way: as an expression of Caravaggesque 'realism' and harbinger of pre-modern 'modernity', as a sign of the period's penchant for cataloguing sensory perceptions, and finally, as a still-resonant emblem of ethical values. The moral interpretation is supported by a text which, in this case, is a discourse on the five senses published in 1620. In it, the author sees all sensory perception as basic temptations of the devil, with taste's 'delightful fullness' a provocation to 'meditate on God's goodness', in order to 'quench my thirst of sin with a desire of an heavenly inheritance'.[53] In truth, even if Terbrugghen did intend his canvas to lead to moral improvement, his message could hardly have been couched in more ambiguous terms.

The paradigm of ambiguity with respect to alcohol was Jan Steen (1626–1679). The artist's *As the Old Sing, so Pipe the Young* captures a fleeting moment in a domestic interior as three generations of a family celebrate around a table. The focus is on two activities: the wine being poured into the glass of the already supine mother, and the father offering a tobacco pipe to his young son. Significantly, the mother's costume and most of the attributes – a foot warmer, a bird out of its cage, a plate of oysters and some luscious fruit – are those of a prostitute. Since the father is a self-portrait and the mother a likeness of his wife, the picture is autobiographical. Steen was himself a brewer and tavern keeper, and he could hardly have disapproved of alcohol; the centrality of the wine in the composition presumably indicates what in his mind was the truest marker of high times. What is the message in this lavish display of moral lassitude? The first clue comes from the inscription on the grandmother's song sheet: 'Song/ As it is sung, thus it is piped, that's been known a long time, as I sing, so (everyone) does the same from one to one hundred years old.' From this, we learn that the picture illustrates the Dutch proverb *As the Old Sing, so Pipe the Young*, a trope of the deterministic belief that poor child rearing produces ill-behaved adults.

While a nature/nurture debate was already underway at the time – Calvinists arguing for the former and Catholics for the latter – the fact that Steen was a Catholic hardly explains the picture's meaning. Multiple readings are possible: that the artist was engaging in free-spirited self-satire; that he was illustrating behaviour for the viewer to condemn; that he was offering fictive transgressions in place of the real thing; or finally, that he was making no moral judgement at all, with the admonitory inscription simply being disingenuous or hypocritical.

Disingenuousness is not hard to find in contemporary Dutch texts. As Simon Schama has observed, moralists like Jacob Cats devoted hundreds of pages chronicling the deeds of the lascivious; by the second half of the century an entire subgenre of pornographic literature sought to disguise itself behind implausible masks of respectability.[54]

80 Jan Steen, *Merry Company* ('As the Old Sing, so Pipe the Young'), 1663, oil on canvas.

One such title *Amsterdamsche Hoerdom (Amsterdam's Whoredom)* purported to be a lament by the city sheriff on the vices that flourished in the city. Sounding like a cry of despair over the fallen city, the narrator compiles a catalogue of Amsterdam's iniquities, complete with addresses, prices, customs, available liquors and advice on how to avoid being cheated or infected.[55]

As Schama went on to elaborate in *An Embarrassment of Riches*, members of Dutch society were deeply conflicted over their attraction to material goods and bodily pleasures, given their constitutionally parsimonious natures.[56] *As the Old Sing* might be understood in terms of this dichotomy, one which in Schama's words, constituted 'a permanent condition of cultural schizophrenia'. On balance, Steen's picture seems to mock the zeal of Calvinist reformers while pretending to expose his own dissolute behaviour. The result was comical, but not out of character in the context of his career as a whole.[57]

171

As Dutch society prospered and the market for art expanded, specialization within the genres increased. The new iconography included scenes of public and private life drawn from both ends of the socio-economic spectrum. Some artists like Adriaen Brower and Adriaen van Ostade specialized in the lower levels, highlighting the uncouth behaviour of those for whom taverns offered the only escape from the harshness of life. Recent studies have linked the increased consumption of intoxicants in this period to the psychological needs of the burgeoning lower class and, not surprisingly, the most popular beverage in pictures like David Teniers' *Tavern Scene* of 1680 is beer, not wine.[58] Unlike the silently dignified Le Nain peasants, Teniers' subjects are raucous boors who gamble, quarrel, smoke and are slovenly and shameless in scatological matters. Women are rarely present and disdain for the workaday world is indicated by the faint

81 David Teniers the Younger, *Tavern Scene*, 1680, oil on canvas.

daylight that enters the gloomy chamber. One can assume that the audience for such pictures was the urban middle class, whose own work ethic and tidy ways were inimical to the laziness and boorish behaviour on display. Early viewers must have wavered between amusement and repulsion, fear and fascination, as they confronted the successes and failures of their own open society.

At the other end of the spectrum, painters like Jan Vermeer (1632–75) and Gerard ter Borch (1617–81) made wine a symbol of Dutch social life at its most refined. Their milieu was naturally not the public tavern, but the well-furnished domestic interior populated with figures drawn from the leisure class. Always a master of understatement, one of Vermeer's favourite themes was a couple engaged in quiet but flirtatious conversation over a midday glass of wine, their mood intimating an illicit tryst or perhaps a more licentious transaction.[59] His *Officer and Laughing Girl* from around 1657 (illus. 82) is typical in this regard, the wineglass in the woman's hand hinting at her possible compliance with any advances her companion might make. Vermeer never made debauchery explicit – a contemporary treatise condemned such pictures – and he was usually content to leave the moralizing to the viewer's imagination.[60]

Ter Borch, by contrast, had little compunction about moving beyond innuendo to illustrate the improvident effects of wine on young women. His painting *The Gallant Officer* of 1662–3 (illus. 83) carries the moment forward to the point that the woman has now drained her glass, and the man offers her a handful of coins in an overbearing manner that contrasts with her own modest expression. The eroticism of this wordless encounter is underscored by the presence of numerous sexual symbols as well as a canopied bed in the background.

Wine and Death

In previous chapters, it has been noted that drinking wine in ancient Greece and Rome was sometimes accompanied not by the mirthful figure of Bacchus but by the baleful presence of death. Memento mori were surprisingly popular totems of early Epicureanism, their *carpe diem* message encouraging the consumption of food and wine in the face of the unknown. The concept vanished during the Middle Ages when the search for transcendental meaning outweighed such hedonistic pursuits, but came back into play during the Renaissance.

173

82 Jan Vermeer,
*Officer and Laughing
Girl*, c. 1657,
oil on canvas.

83 Gerard ter Borch, *The Gallant Officer*, 1662–3, oil on canvas.

And when it did, the meaning was not the same. The change occurred in the wake of the Reformation as more pessimistic attitudes towards life and the afterlife led to the renouncement of evanescent earthy pleasures in favour of long-term spiritual rewards.

Still-life painters, particularly in the Protestant lands of northern Europe, expanded the ancient iconographical repertory beyond skeletons and skulls to include hourglasses, extinguished candles and other symbols of transience and decay. By the seventeenth century, lavish displays of luxury goods that mirrored the materialism of the Dutch middle class but were reviled by Calvinists and Neo-Stoics were added to the mix.[61] Luxury, in Calvin's view, was an evil to be avoided: 'When men enjoy abundance', he wrote, 'they become

luxurious and abuse it by intemperance . . . eating and drinking be-yond their ordinary portion.'[62] Neo-Stoics, on the other hand, railed against material pleasures as one of the temptations that distract one from spiritual closeness to God.[63]

The underlying meaning of the anodyne term *still life* (*stilleven* in Dutch) is spelled out, more unflinchingly, as *nature morte* and *natura morte* in Romance languages. As if to strengthen the signifi-cance to northern audiences, the Latin term *vanitas* was coined in the sixteenth century to designate images and texts that explicitly alluded to the transience of life and its pleasures.[64] The iconography took on special meaning in the years after the Thirty Years' War (1618–48) when tragedy was still a fresh memory, and prosperity seemed fragile. The etymology of *vanitas* stood on a solid biblical foundation, with count-less Old Testament passages alluding to the brevity of human life. 'Vanity', in fact – the traditional translation of the Hebrew *hebel* –

84 Pieter Claesz.,
Still-life with Roemer,
1647, oil on panel.

176

occurs no fewer than thirty-eight times in the Book of Ecclesiastes alone, most memorably in its opening lines (1:1–4):

The words of the Teacher, the son of
David, king in Jerusalem.
Vanity of vanities, says the Teacher,
Vanity of vanities! All is vanity.
What do people gain from all the toil,
at which they toil under the sun?
A generation goes, and a generation comes,
But the earth remains forever.

Wine was frequently included among the worldly pleasures depicted in seventeenth-century still-life painting, and some artists like Pieter Claesz. (*c.* 1590–1661) made a speciality of probing its multifaceted nature. His forte was the so-called 'breakfast piece' (*ontbiktje*), a composition that dispenses with skulls and hourglasses to concentrate on tables laden with food and fine service ware. Although he occasionally depicted beakers of beer, his trademark was the *roemer*, a tall wine goblet with a large spherical bowl and thick cylindrical stem decorated with 'raspberry' prunts, or bosses.[65] The wine in question is always white and presumably came from the Rhineland.

While a pheasant, some oysters and a partially peeled lemon appear on the right of the composition, the left is dominated by the *roemer*, an overturned silver dish, and a popular Dutch roll known as a *brootje*. Could the combination of bread and wine allude to the Eucharist? There is usually more to Claesz.'s pictures than first meets the eye, and the frequency with which overturned *roemers* and tableware appear in his pictures suggests sudden, calamitous events, a fairly unequivocal allusion to human mortality. Significantly, a number of *roemers* survive that spell this out with etched inscriptions and images referring to the fragility of life.[66]

A painting by Judith Leyster (1609–1660) called *The Last Drop* (illus. 85) reduces the *vanitas* message to the temptations of drink alone. Two figures in an indefinite setting seem well on their way to inebriation as one drains the last drops of wine from a jug and the other displays his empty tankard to the viewer. To judge from their costumes, these are carnival revellers enjoying the festivities of Shrovetide.[67] But where the permissive atmosphere of most *Merry Companies* goes unchallenged, this pair is taunted by a leering skeleton who holds an hourglass in one hand and a skull and candle in the other. The scene recalls popular images of the Dance of Death, and the pose of the toper the figure of Gluttony, after Lust the second of the Seven Deadly Sins.[68] For Leyster and her contemporaries, memento mori clearly meant something quite different than it did for ancient viewers of the mosaic skeleton from Pompeii (illus. 24).

The message in Leyster's picture was echoed by countless moralizing verses of the period. One engraving from 1633, also embellished with a skeleton, carries the inscription:

> Oh ye, oh ye. Surprise! Surrender (you) beasts,
> Do you never make an end to your Bacchic feasts?
> Your merriment will be cut short
> Your joy will become confined to an eternity of
> Hellish crying.[69]

Several emblems in Jacob Cats's *Spiegel van den Ouden en Nieuwen Tyt* (*Mirror of the Old and New Times*, Amsterdam, 1632) make the same point. 'Time goes, Death comes' reads one, while another warns:

> Early to wine, early corrupted,
> Early a drunkard, early death.[70]

The message of Leyster's picture proved to be so affecting to one later owner that he had the skeleton painted out and a low table put in its place. Only when the canvas was cleaned in 1993 in preparation for an exhibition did the original composition and its morbid message reemerge.[71]

Wine in Seventeenth- and Eighteenth-century English Art and Literature

William Shakespeare (1564–1616), wrote frequently of wine, especially Spanish sherry, or sack, as it was known. Computerized concordances now allow us to catalogue them by type. In the 26 plays in which they are mentioned, sack appears 44 times, Rhenish wine four, and claret and malmsey once each.[72] James I's 1606 decree against insobriety 'in the

85 Judith Leyster, *The Last Drop*, c. 1639, oil on canvas.

streets, in the theatres, and in other public places of London' implies that playgoers imbibed along with those on stage.[73] Falstaff – a true Dionysian – delivers the lengthiest discourse on sack in *Henry IV, Part II*:

> A good sherry-sack hath a two-fold operation in it. It ascends me into the brain; dries me there all the foolish and dull and crudy vapours which environ it; makes it apprehensible, quick, forgetive, full of nimble fiery and delectable shapes; which deliver'd o'er to the voice, the tongue, which is the birth, becomes excellent wit.[74]

Shakespeare obviously had humoral theories in mind when he has Falstaff declare that

> The second property of your excellent sherrie is the warming of the blood; which before cold and settled, left the liver white and pale, which is the badge of pusillanimity and cowardice.

The soliloquy ends with the confession, 'If I had a thousand sons, the first principle I would teach them should be, to foreswear thin potations [light wines from the North] and to addict themselves to sack.'

Nevertheless, the effects of alcohol are not so positive in Shakespeare's dramas: in *Othello*, the villain Iago sings its praises as it leads to the downfall of Cassio who, in an earlier scene, recognizes its dangers when he says: 'O thou invisible spirit of wine, if thou hast no other name to be known by, let us call you devil!' Wine leads Claudius to lose sight of right and wrong, is the curse of Denmark in *Hamlet*, and the agent of the Duke of Clarence's death in *Richard III*. The most balanced voice is that of the Porter in *Macbeth* who lectures Macduff on wine's effects on sexual conduct:

> Lechery, sir, it provokes and unprovokes; it provokes the desire but it takes away the performance. Therefore much drink may be said to be an equivocator with lechery; it makes him and it mars him; it sets him on and it takes him off; it persuades him, and disheartens him; makes him stand to and not stand to.[75]

Perhaps most revealingly, in *Henry IV, Part II*, when Hal rejects Falstaff in his quest for social responsibility, it is made clear that the latter's dissipation had been a detriment to the character development of the future king. From all this one might ask if Shakespeare himself was a latent Puritan, but the evidence is far from clear and, as everyone knows, the man was a genius when it came to erasing traces of himself from his work.[76]

Since England was a country in which beer offered an inexpensive alternative to wine, it is surprising that it appears in Shakespeare only a third as often as wine. That the preference for one or the other was already an important marker of class is evident from the frontispiece of a 1617 tract on English drinking habits (illus. 86).[77] Entitled 'The Lawes of Drinking', a tavern (where wine was sold) is contrasted with an alehouse (where it was not). The tavern is set behind an elegant loggia with a classical landscape in the background while the alehouse is shown in nondescript surroundings. The furnishings of the two establishments, the attire of their habitués, and even the music – a Greek lyre in one, and a lowly bagpipe and jig dancer in the other – highlight the differences between gentry and common folk. Finally, the inscriptions that accompany the scenes suggest the existence of intellectual as well as social divisions between the classes. The tavern sign advertises 'Poets Impalled with Lawrell Coranets', an allusion to the nobility of the poetic calling, accompanied by the inscription *Nectar ut Ingenium,* a tribute to wine as an attribute of genius. By contrast, the alehouse is identified by a simple rose and the name 'Puddle-Wharf'.

The crude little images make two significant points, one linking wine with social class, and the other with poetic inspiration. The ties between the creation of literary texts and the culture of drink and conviviality are well-known.[78] In particular, the poetry of Robert Herrick (1591–1674) stands out for its celebration of the grape, as both a liberating agent and as a catalyst for good fellowship. One of his 'Hymnes to Bacchus' ends with the apostrophe:

> O Bacchus! Let us be
> From cares and troubles free;
> And thou shalt heare how we
> Will chant new Hymnes to thee.[79]

Or in another verse, 'How he would Drink his Wine', the poet derides those who followed the custom of mixing it with water:

86 'The Lawes of Drinking', frontispiece from Richard Brathwaite, *The Solemn Jovial Disputation*, 1617.

Fill me my wine in crystal; Thus and thus
I see't in's *puris naturalis*: unmix'd
I love to have it smirk and shine;
'Tis sin I know, 'tis sin to throttle wine.
What madman's he, that when it sparkes so,
Will cool his flames or quench his fires with snow?[80]

The masterpiece among Herrick's Bacchanalian verse is his 'Welcome to Sack', a poetic tour-de-force that substitutes wine for an absent mistress.[81] A life-long bachelor, the poet bestows upon his beloved sack all the rhetorical flights, extravagant compliments, and passionate fervour of an Elizabethan sonnet. Thus he begins 'A Lyrick to Mirth' with the lines:

> While the milder Fates consent,
> Let's enjoy our merriment:
> Drink and Dance, and pipe, and play;
> Kiss our dollies night and day;
> Crown'd with clusters of the vine;
> Let us sit, and quaffe our wine.[82]

Despite the presence of the 'dollies', the fellowship Herrick enjoyed would have been predominantly male, just as pictured in the print. The homosocial associations would remain steadfast in England, eventually taking on political significance of their own. Herrick's own sympathies were, in fact, hardly apolitical since he was among the Cavalier poets who supported Charles I during the civil wars and thus disavowed Puritan proscriptions against the pleasures of wine and other expressions of courtly gallantry.

Puritan attitudes are most poetically expressed in the verse of John Milton (1608–74). According to a contemporary biographer, the poet 'was extremely temperate in the use of wine or any strong liquors, at meals and at all other times; and when supper was over, about nine o'clock, he smoked his pipe, drank a glass of water, and went to bed'.[83] Sprinkled throughout his poetry are lines disparaging 'The barbarous dissonance/of Bacchus and his revellers', or 'Bacchus, that first from out of the purple grape/Crush'd the sweet poison of misused wine'.[84] Milton's final word on the matter appears in his 'Dramatic Poem', *Samson Agonistes* [1671], where the Semichorus of the Danites invokes the poet's own blindness as a metaphor for ruination:

> While their hearts were jocund and sublime,
> Drunk with idolatry, drunk with wine
> And fat regorged of bulls and goats,
> Chaunting their idol, and preferring
> Before our living Dread, who dwells

In Silo, his bright sanctuary,
Among them he a spirit of phrenzy sent,
Who hurt their minds,
And urged them on with mad desire
To call in haste for their destroyer.
They, only set on sport and play,
Unweetingly importuned
Their own destruction to come speedily upon them.
So fond are mortal men,
Fallen into wrath divine,
As their own ruin on themselves to invite,
Insensate self, or to sense reprobate,
And with blindness internal struck.[85]

Wine, poetry, and English politics continued to inspire one another throughout the early modern period. The authors of broadside ballads from the interregnum years (1649–60) politicized drinking by labelling radical leaders in terms of drink and drunkenness while raising their own spirits with verses that call for free expression:

Come Noble Hearts
To show your loyall parts,
Let's drink a lovely cup and banish care
Why should not we
Which are of spirits free
Dround grief with sack and cast off all dispare.[86]

After the monarchy was restored, balladeers cheered the king's return with other drinking songs, albeit ones that tended to endorse moderation as part of the reordering of society. More than ever, wine was the choice of loyalists while ale smacked of the anarchic. By the last quarter of the century, the political divide between the two widened to the point that Whigs and Tories – the two parties founded in 1679–81 – regularly attacked each other with the language of the ballad-based discourses. New Tory ballads even suggested that a benefit of wine-drinking was rendering the drinker incapable of political plotting. 'When the head's full of wine', according to one, 'there's no room left for thinking.' By the same logic, it was implied that Whiggish ale-drinking habits could lead to acts of treason:

We that good sack in plate
To make us blithe and jolly
Never plot against the state
To be punished for such folly
But the merry glass and pipe
Makes our senses quick and ripe
And expels melancholy.[87]

The beer–wine conflict eventually diminished towards the end of the century, only to be replaced by another locus of contention related to English drinking habits. This time, the issue had to do with the importation of the 'new' or 'luxury' French clarets, as wines from the Bordeaux region are known in England. These reds were of higher quality and deeper colour than their predecessors, and were estate-bottled. Samuel Pepys, one recalls, had already tasted Haut Brion in a London tavern in 1665, and Lafitte, Latour and Margaux were soon to follow across the channel.[88] With the arrival of the new wines, the preoccupation with class conflicts and political beliefs shifted to the expression of attitudes towards France itself.[89] Naturally, the new claret was more popular with Tories who favoured French trade, but a succession of embargoes and tariff increases levied under Whig governments quickly put this wine out of reach of all but the most wealthy and politically well-connected. Whigs eventually acquired a taste for claret themselves, but over time came to prefer port, a dividend of better relations with Portugal. When the British diplomat John Methuen negotiated a treaty with the Portuguese in 1703, an adequate supply of port and, perhaps more importantly, an adequate supply of bottle corks was virtually guaranteed.

For Englishmen who at the same time looked to the French court for models of conduct and etiquette, drinking luxury claret was also a sign of good taste.[90] Indeed, the English culture of 'politeness' made French wine an essential ingredient in the same cosmopolitan world of manners that prompted the Grand Tour to Italy, the adoption of continental styles of architecture and the decoration of country house with imported pictures. British painters occasionally recorded the pleasure the gentry took in their wine, as we see in *Mr Woodbridge and Captain Holland* (illus. 87), a portrait of 1730 from the circle of William Hogarth. Set in what appears to be the library of a law office, the two men appraise a wine as a servant enters the room to deliver a message. More than anything, it is the wine in this 'conversation piece' that connotes the breeding and good taste of the two gentlemen.

The second half of the eighteenth century witnessed the trickling down of social pretensions to the middle class, a phenomenon captured with classic English wit by Thomas Rowlandson in his satirical lithograph *The Brilliants*. The only requirement of this establishment was that 24 full toasts be given before the drinking began in earnest. Rowlandson's composition suggests that the behaviour of this convivial group hardly differed from that of the beer-swilling peasants and lowlife depicted in earlier Dutch and Flemish genre pictures, an indication that by his time, the sophistication associated with wine-drinking had plummeted.

A clue to the evolution of English wine culture during the period that separated the Hogarthian portrait and Rowlandson's print is indicated by the shape of the bottles depicted in each. The wine Woodbridge and Holland consume is stored in a globular flask while the Brilliants drink from cylindrical bottles. Greater ease in storage was, of course, the primary advantage of the newer shape, and although wine could not be commercially sold in them until 1860, increasing its shelf life through corking and horizontal binning did much to democratize the wine cellar in England and elsewhere.[91]

87 Circle of William Hogarth, *Mr Woodbridge and Captain Holland*, 1730, oil on canvas.

88 Thomas Rowlandson, *The Brilliants*, 1801, lithograph.

Benjamin Franklin (1706–1790) and Thomas Jefferson (1743–1826), statesmen, world travellers and bon vivants, are credited with introducing many Old World tastes to the New.[92] Jefferson's drinking habits are particularly easy to trace from the well-kept inventories of his wine cellars at Shadwell, Monticello and the White House. We know, for example, that in 1769, he had 83 bottles of rum, 54 of cider, 15 of Madeira and 4 of Lisbon wine. Over the years, and particularly after his time in Europe (1784–9), his preferences became more sophisticated. As United States president (1801–9), his cellar included Hermitage from the Rhône – then France's most expensive wine – Chambertin from Burgundy, Châteaux Margaux from Bordeaux, a Champagne from Ay, Montepulciano and Aleatico from Tuscany and Nebbiolo from the Piedmont.[93] Unfortunately, however, what would have been Jefferson's most lasting contribution to American wine culture came to nothing, and that was his attempt in 1774 to open a commercial winery on the slopes of Monticello in partnership with an Italian entrepreneur and physician, Philip Mazzei. Thirty years

187

earlier, Franklin's *Poor Richard's Almanac* had offered instructions on how to do so with 'grapes that grow wild in our woods', but a killing spring frost followed by the outbreak of war brought Jefferson's enterprise to a halt, and Mazzei's prediction that 'the best wine in the world will be made here', remained but a dream.[94] Only in 1806 was wine successfully produced in the United States, and then not in Virginia but Indiana.[95]

Jefferson's recorded thoughts on wine may be disappointingly terse, but Franklin's more than make up for the deficit. In *Poor Richard's Almanac*, we find the memorable lines:

> There cannot be good living where there is not good drinking. Wine makes daily living easier, less hurried, with fewer tensions and more tolerance. Take counsel in wine, but resolve afterwards in water.[96]

seven

Modern Wine

Along with increased production and consumption, the modern era witnessed sharper qualitative differences between wines made for mass consumption and those intended for export. This was especially true in France where more land came under cultivation, higher-yielding varietals were introduced, and improvements in transportation and marketing led to the creation of 'a vast wine-producing complex'.[1] At the higher end, systematic classifications of Bordeaux began to appear as early as 1815 – when some 323 separate *crus* from the Médoc region were listed – and the catalogue was refined in 1855 when the four-tiered division (now increased to five) was introduced at the *Exposition Universelle* in Paris.[2]

Exports to England, Germany, the Netherlands and, for a while, even the United States of America, grew dramatically. American imports, which began with a trickle in the era of Jefferson, increased until the 1860s when the outbreak of the Civil War, the emergence of California's own wine industry, the passage of protectionist tariffs and the influence of the temperance movement led to their demise.[3] Coincidentally, an Anglo-French treaty substantially reduced the duty on wine imports, prompting a surge of claret to enter the British Isles.[4]

Italian wines underwent a similar expansion in the wake of the country's unification in 1860–61. Two of the leading architects of the movement, Camillo Cavour and Baron Bettino Ricasoli, took particular interest in developing viticulture in their native regions of Piedmont and Tuscany, which were already important centres of Italian wine production. Ricasoli is widely credited with having created the popular wine we now know as Chianti, and his estate-bottled Brolio remains among the best of its kind. In terms of taste, Italian wines also became drier in the nineteenth century, a phenomenon that extended from one end of the peninsula to the other.

In America, the centres of wine production gradually drifted westward. From its unsuccessful beginnings in the southern colonies, vineyards in Indiana, Ohio and Missouri began producing an acceptable alternative to European wines during the first third of the nineteenth century. The California wine industry, which only took root in the Franciscan missions at the end of the 1800s, received a major impetus with the state's annexation in 1847 and the beginning of the gold rush a year later. From the southern missions, viticulture quickly spread northward, and before long encompassed Sonoma, Napa and Santa Clara counties, a territory with a combined yield approached something like 30 million US gallons (113.6 million litres) a year with than 300 *vinifera* varieties.[5] So successful was its progress that by mid-century American vine cuttings, roots and must were being exported to parts of Europe. While the French preferred the rootstocks, the English liked the concentrated must, to which they had only to add water to make wine. In 1891 a London agent wrote back to his San Gabriel Valley supplier: 'California wines are becoming quite the rage here and I hope in a few years time to make a very large business indeed in them.'[6]

Unfortunately, the world-wide wine boom suffered severe setbacks in the nineteenth century. Two major infestations struck the European continent, both originating from vines imported from North America. The first, which arrived in the 1840s, was a powdery mildew (*oidium*) that affected the flavour and yield of certain popular French varieties like chardonnay and cabernet sauvignon.[7] Of even greater concern, however, was the phylloxera epidemic that overran Europe in the 1860s.[8] Phylloxera is a small yellow aphid that kills vines by attacking their roots. In 1863 its effects were first noted in England and France, and despite intensive efforts to control its migration, the insect had reached vineyards in Spain and Italy by the late 1870s. Numerous scientific commissions were created and the French government at one point offered a reward of 300,000 francs for a cure, but for decades the pest went unchecked. By the end, more than 1,000 remedies had been suggested and evaluated, the most promising calling for flooding vineyards, injecting insecticides into the soil or grafting resistant rootstocks (again from America) onto vulnerable vines. Ironically, the latter proved to be the most effective

89 Roger Fenton, *The Wounded Zouave*, 1856, salt print photograph.

deterrent, but not before wine production in France had declined by some 75 per cent.

Just as the phylloxera epidemic was getting underway, Louis Pasteur (1822–1895), a scientist from the wine-producing district of Jura, began to devote his genius to the challenges of fermentation and micro-biological disease. Pasteur's efforts were commissioned by Napoleon III, and his discoveries presented in a 1866 book entitled *Etudes sur le vin, ses maladies, causes qui les provoquent. Procèdes nouveaux pour le conserver et pour le vieillir*. Here, Pasteur proved himself to be the father of modern oenology by discovering the underlying causes of grape fermentation and the role that micro-organisms played in the process. Most importantly, Pasteur discovered that fermentation was the result of yeast attacking sugar in the must, and bacteria were the cause of wine turning to vinegar. Oxygen's part in fermentation and degradation was central to his theories, as was his discovery that heating, which soon became known as 'pasteurization', was the most effective means of killing bacteria. His recommendation that the sealed containers of wine then be stored at cooler temperatures was his final piece of wisdom. For all these insights – which unfortunately did not include a way to eradicate phylloxera – Pasteur rightly became known as the man who turned the art of winemaking into a science. He did not neglect wine's physiological and spiritual benefits either, for in a much-quoted remark he once pronounced wine 'the most healthful and hygienic of beverages. That is why, of all the drinks known today, wine is the one human beings prefer to all others.'[9]

Contemporary evidence of the therapeutic consumption of wine is preserved in a remarkable photograph of 1855 made by Roger Fenton during the Crimean War (illus. 89). It shows a female 'canteen-seller' (or *cantinière*) offering a restorative glass to an injured Zouave, propped up in the arms of a fellow soldier.[10] The solace the French take in wine, however, was especially marked during the First World War. After both French and German studies concluded – remarkably enough – that its impact on performance was insignificant, the daily ration for French soldiers increased from a quarter litre in 1914 to half a litre in 1916, and to as much as a full litre in 1918, the year the conflict ended.[11] The impetus behind these acts of generosity was a surplus in Languedoc in 1914 that led local producers to contribute 200,000 hectolitres of wine to military hospitals to boost the morale of the wounded, and presumably hasten their recovery.[12]

Wine and Modern Medicine 1

Wine therapy by tradition was linked with humoral beliefs, but it continued to flourish even after its theoretical support grew fainter. Its discrediting began in the seventeenth century when the scientific methods of observation finally put the suppositions of Galen and Hippocrates to the test. William Harvey's *An Anatomical Essay Concerning the Movement of the Heart and the Blood in Animals* (1628) was the first treatise to question the canon. Harvey occasionally lapsed into humoral metaphors when describing the 'native heat, or innate warmth' of his subject, but his method was resolutely empirical as he laid aside books of science and theology to study vivisected frogs and chicks at first hand. The Flemish physician Joan Baptista van Helmont also dismissed traditional humoral theory in his *Ortus medicinae*, published posthumously in 1648. Despite his brilliance (he was the first to identify carbon dioxide and a number of other gases), Van Helmont, like Harvey, never let go of other specious beliefs in the areas of alchemy and Paracelsianism. In general, this is true of Western medicine for the next few centuries. Even as the gap widened between laboratory discoveries and superstitious beliefs, therapies based on scientific bacteriology and traditional practices like blood-letting continued to exist side by side. Therapeutic treatments have never been fully unified – 'alternative' medicine still flourishes more actively today than ever – and it is not surprising that wine therapy grew in popularity even after humoral theory was sacrificed on the altar of modern science.

Wine continued to be used medicinally for both its intrinsic benefits and as a solvent, or *menstruum*, in which other substances were dissolved. The advantages of *vina medicata*, as the latter was known, were still being heralded as late as the 1920s and '30s. *The United States Dispensatory* of 1926, for example, states the following:

> The reported advantages of wine as a pharmaceutical menstruum are that, in consequence of the alcohol it contains, it dissolves substances insoluble in water, and, to a certain extent, resists their tendency to spontaneous change, while at the same time it is less stimulating than strong or diluted alcohol.[13]

A review of the many pharmacopoeias published in the nineteenth century attests to the popularity of *vina medicata*. The *London Pharmacopoeia* of 1836, for example, includes wines of aloe, meadow saffron, ipecac and white hellebore, while among the 164 wines listed in the 1840 *Pharmacopée Universale* of Paris are ones mixed with gentian, mustard, rhubarb and squill.[14] The number of medicated wines steadily increase through the first half of the century, rising from a low of nine in the first *Pharmacopoeia* of the United States (1820) to a high of 175 in the Heidelberg version of 1835.[15] The beneficial effects of wine and wine-based medicines were perhaps best summarized in 1883 by Robert Edes, author of the *Therapeutic Handbook of the United States Pharmacopoeia*. *Vinum album* (white wine) is recommended, for example, to treat 'dyspeptic disorders, as a cardiac stimulant, and in cases of acute and typhoidal diseases'.[16]

Some publications of the late nineteenth century were less enthusiastic about wine therapy. Roberts Bartholomew's *Treatise on the Practice of Medicine*, also published in 1883, speaks of wine only in a censorious chapter on alcoholism.[17] The inevitable death knell for medicated wines sounded in 1902 when a pharmaceutical conference in Brussels advised against their use, not for their dubious efficacy, but 'because of the lack of uniformity in the commercial wines used in their preparation'.[18] By 1917 Remington's *Practice of Pharmacy* – then the standard pharmacopoeia of the United States – still listed one pure wine (sherry), and fifteen medicated ones among its approved remedies, but the die had been cast.[19] The demise was prompted, in part, by the imprecations of the temperance movement, whose charismatic figurehead, Carrie Nation, undertook the 'hachetations' of saloons and taverns during the early years of the century. Because one of the defences against prohibition was the belief that wine was medicinal, the zealots of reform set themselves to disproving claims made on its behalf. The fact that some 'pharmacies' were little more than unlicensed liquor stores made their job even easier.[20] In the end the reformers were successful, and by 1919 the 'Noble Experiment', or official era of Prohibition, was underway, with the ban on alcohol lasting until 1933. The toll Prohibition took on the burgeoning California wine industry was staggering; where there had been over 700 wineries before, only 140 survived to the end. Those that did were constrained to sacrifice the finest varietals and make altar wines and vinegars instead.[21]

In England – itself a cradle of temperance at the time – the 1932 edition of the national pharmacopoeia also dropped wines it had listed for centuries.[22] The pharmaceutical literature of Catholic countries like France, Italy and especially Germany continued to list *vina medicata* up through the 1950s and '60s.

Wine and Modern Art

Modernism hardly brought an end to artistic representations of wine. Traditional iconography may have held little appeal for avant-garde painters of the nineteenth century, but many of the subjects they favoured – café scenes and picnics in particular – included people imbibing wine. At the same time, academic masters like Thorvaldsen, Corot, Alma-Tadema, Bouguereau and Gérôme continued to be drawn to bacchanalia and other classical themes. One may not immediately associate Jean-Baptiste-Camille Corot (1796–1875) with classical mythology, but bacchantes and bacchic revelries frequently appear in his oeuvre, even in late pictures like the *Bacchanal at the Spring*. Typical

90 Jean-Baptiste-Camille Corot, *Bacchanal at the Spring*, 1872, oil on canvas.

of his woodland landscapes from the 1870s, the atmosphere is luminous and cool, with subtle tonal variations that unify sky and forest into a nature that is at once serene and quivering with life. The figures in the center of the composition may first seem like *staffage* – the designation for meaningless scale figures in French landscapes – but closer inspection discloses their mythic identities: the recumbent figure in the foreground is a river god, while the one to his left is the young Bacchus astride his panther. The mood is exquisite, and although Corot claimed to have retained nothing of value from his academic training, late pictures like this remain among his most provocative works.[23] Yet it was the lure of classicism and not the wine itself that seems to have held the most appeal for nineteenth-century academic painters and viewers. Compared to the true Dionysian spirit captured by Titian and Rubens, the mythic iconography of Corot seems but an overlay to formal ideals.

The truly progressive French artists of the nineteenth century drew their inspiration from the social and political realities of the world in which they lived. Since wine, along with other alcoholic beverages, was an increasingly important part of that reality, the subject fitted as naturally into the new pictorial repertory as it did the old. Most commonly, the focus was on the world of individual leisure, detached from the established rituals and behavioural norms that justified so much revelry in the past. The socio-economic context varied widely. At the lower end of the spectrum, a work like Honoré Daumier's *Le Chanson à Boire* (*The Drinking Song*) of 1860–63 captures the spirit of four ordinary men enjoying their wine at what we may assume is the end of the workday.[24] The conception recalls the tavern scenes of seventeenth-century Holland, but the restrained colouring and rough handling are trademarks of Daumier's unidealized

91 Honoré Daumier, *The Drinking Song*, *c.* 1860–63, pencil, watercolour, conté crayon and pen and ink on laid paper.

92 Edouard Manet,
*Déjeuner sur l'herbe
(Luncheon on the Grass)*,
1863, oil on canvas.

naturalism.[25] Significantly, the beverage is not the beer that English
and Dutch workmen would prefer, but wine, purchased in a country
where it was priced for every pocketbook. At the time Daumier fashioned his image, the explosive growth in French wine production had
nearly reached its height. Although the phylloxera epidemic would
soon bring wine-making to its knees, Daumier's drinkers appear bliss-
fully unaware of any deprivations as they drain their glasses and
break into song.

   Unlike Daumier, who tended to focus on the grittier aspects of
urban life, Edouard Manet was drawn to the leisure-time pursuits of
middle-class Parisians who fled the city for the beauty of the Bois de
Boulogne or nearby countryside. His *Déjeuner sur l'herbe,* or *Luncheon on the Grass,* of 1863 introduced the theme in a manner that was
at once respectful of Titian and Raphael and strikingly fresh in its

unidealized depiction of the figures and landscape. The large silver flask that lies on the ground next to the anomalous nude undoubtedly contains wine or another alcoholic beverage, clearly the source of her brazen lack of inhibition.

After Manet's work was exhibited at the first Salon des Refusés in 1863, other Impressionist painters took up the theme for themselves. Claude Monet was particularly attentive to the social realism of such gatherings as we see in his *Déjeuner*, begun in 1865. The figures in this fashionably informal picture include portraits of the artist's future wife and some of his friends. Although Monet never completed the enormous canvas he intended to paint, a preparatory oil sketch in Moscow preserves his original thoughts. In this, four bottles of wine – two overturned and two upright – reinforce the scene's naturalism, although like Manet, Monet does not show anyone consuming the beverage.

By contrast, Pierre-Auguste Renoir's *Luncheon of the Boating Party*, painted in 1881, views wine consumption as an integral part of everyday life. Again the party is personalized by the inclusion of

93 Claude Monet,
*Déjeuner sur l'herbe
(Luncheon on the Grass)*,
1865–6, oil on canvas.

the artist's friends and fiancée, now depicted on the waterfront terrace of a restaurant in Chatou. The atmosphere is charged with a boisterous spirit not found in the work of Manet or Monet. Because the viewpoint is high, the spectator is allowed a full view of the assorted glassware, wine bottles and small wooden keg that rest on the dramatically receding table. The disinhibitory effects of alcohol are everywhere in evidence, and a convivial sensuality permeates the air. Several partygoers have raised their glasses, the woman at the left – Aline Charigot, the painter's fiancé – has lifted her dog to the table and the man at the right sits backwards in his chair. The lushness of the image recalls the work of old masters like Titian and Rubens without the mythic underpinnings, or the festivity of Jan Steen without the moralization. Renoir, on the contrary, set out to capture the timeless pleasures of wine and friendship to be had on a sunny summer afternoon on the outskirts of Paris.

94 Pierre Auguste Renoir, *Luncheon of the Boating Party*, 1881, oil on canvas.

One consequence of the urban renewal of Paris carried out under Napoleon III (d. 1873) and Baron Haussmann (d. 1891) was the widespread displacement of residents from their old neighbourhoods and the influx of immigrants from other parts of France. As the demographics shifted, cafés and café-concerts proliferated as places where foreigners, new arrivals, and the dispossessed could meet, or sit in silence.[26] As a visitor from abroad noted in 1867, these establishments were central to the city's identity: '[Paris] gossips at the café; it intrigues at the café; it plots, it dreams, it suffers, it hopes'.[27] There is no shortage of works of art that document the phenomenon. Manet's *Bar at the Folies-Bergère* (1881–2) is perhaps the most famous for its seemingly candid glimpse into one of the city's glamorous music halls. The statuesque barmaid (modelled after a woman who worked there) faces the viewer/customer with the impassive gaze of someone awaiting an order to be placed. Despite the perplexing spatial distortions of the imagery reflected in the mirror behind her – the focus of considerable art historical debate – the picture is realistic in its depiction of the

95 Edouard Manet, *Bar at the Folies-Bergère*, 1881–2, oil on canvas.

96 Henri de Toulouse-Lautrec, *The Hangover (Suzanne Valadon)*, 1887–9, oil on canvas.

beverages for sale: champagne and beer are the mainstays, along with Crème de Menthe and Grenadine. No still wine is in evidence, but the presence of six bottles of Bollinger champagne and three of Bass ale presumably mirrored the preferences of the habitués of Parisian cabarets at the time. In the case of the champagne, it was increased production that made the desire affordable: champagne yields in France rose from 20 million bottles a year to 36 million between 1850 and 1883, with better marketing responsible for expanding the range of consumers beyond the moneyed elite.[28]

Paris's annual wine consumption rose from 86 million litres to 300 million litres in approximately the same period, an increase that exceeded the growth of the population as a whole.[29] Not surprisingly, the increased consumption led to increased dysfunction, and cafés became havens for those inclined to wash away their unfulfilled hopes and dreams with alcohol. Painters like Henri de Toulouse-Lautrec (1864–1901) were drawn to café life for this very reason. No stranger to life's disappointments, being a dwarf, crippled, and an alcoholic, Lautrec was a well-known figure in the bars and dance-halls of Paris. Suzanne Valadon, his model, student and friend, was a denizen of the same environment, and his portrait of her seated at a café table when both were in their early twenties is among his most moving works (illus. 96).[30] Like the painter, she knew about disappointment after her career as a circus performer ended with a fall from a trapeze at the age of fifteen. The picture, titled *The Hangover*, captures Suzanne in an enervated state as she stares vacantly into space, a single glass and a half-empty wine bottle on the table before her. Her lack of affect is hardly unique for its time, and likenesses like this are common in the café scenes of Manet, Degas and others. This is the face of urban modernity, detached from a world which on the surface appeared so vibrant and fresh.

Alcoholism had by this time become a serious problem through-out Europe, although the term itself was only coined in 1849 by a doctor from a country (Sweden) that produced no wine of its own.[31] The combination of alcoholism and café life preoccupied French social reformers more than any other vice, while public drunkenness became so troublesome that in 1873 the French government enacted a law against it. Other, stronger beverages joined wine on the table, with distilled spirits becoming especially popular after the phylloxera epidemic took its toll. High-yielding distilleries reduced the cost of brandy and other liquors while at the same time offering a higher alcoholic content. And then absinthe, a relative newcomer, appeared on the scene.[32] The 'green fairy', as it was called, was thought to be the worst inebriant of all, inducing

> a drunkenness that doesn't resemble any known drunkenness. It is not the heavy drunkenness of beer, the fierce drunkenness of brandy, the jovial drunkenness of wine. No, it makes you lose your footing right away . . . like all great dreamers you are only headed towards incoherence.[33]

To her credit, Suzanne Valadon chose to stick with wine. Significantly, there is no carafe of water on hand to dilute the beverage since that age-old habit had finally fallen into disuse earlier in the century. Thus even a glass of wine, when taken 'neat', had a higher alcoholic content than it did previously.

If the theme of the solitary or alienated drinker was fairly common in nineteenth-century art, the individual who drinks themselves unconscious was more unusual. The most poignant example of this comes not from France, but Norway, a country whose rates of

97 Edvard Munch,
The Day After, 1894–5,
oil on canvas.

alcoholism have always been among the highest in the world. Edvard Munch (1863–1944), another artist who battled alcohol in his personal life, treats the subject unsparingly in his painting *The Day After*. There can be little question that the slatternly woman flung across the bed has had too much to drink, for two empty bottles – one obviously containing wine – are prominently placed in the foreground. Both the alcohol and the prostrate female must have had a special meaning for the artist, for he composed and recomposed the image on several occasions.[34] There is no joy in this iconography, no sociability, no insights, no redemption. *The Day After* abandons the ageless myths linking wine with the elevated spirit to emphasize its contrary capacity for alienating the drinker to the point of oblivion.

Most artists of the twentieth century tended to take a brighter view of wine's transformative effects. The most successful of these were usually abstract artists capable of envisioning the frenzy of Bacchic rites more stirringly than their academic predecessors had done. André Derain's 1906 watercolour *Bacchic Dance* is among the most expressive works to take up the theme. Here, a single dancer gyrates between two companions who have fallen to the ground. The uninhibited figure recalls the frenzied maenads in Greek red-figure vase painting, but now the human energy is augmented by nature itself as the trunk and limbs of the nearby tree rephrase the swaying movements of the dancer. A palette of primary colours raises the emotional pitch even further, and it was this untamed spirit that led a Paris critic to label Derain, along with his friends Matisse and Vlaminck, *Fauves* (wild beasts).[35]

Other abstract painters of the twentieth century who exploited the expressive possibilities of Bacchic imagery include Lovis Corinth, Raoul Dufy, Max Ernst, Hans Hofmann, Gustav Klimt, André Masson, Jules Olitski and Georges Rouault.[36] But even in their most energetic compositions, the spiritual presence of wine is usually hard to find, and free movement and colour seem to be ends in themselves. Pablo Picasso was exceptional in this respect for he typically emphasized its importance in the many Bacchic scenes he rendered over the course of his career.[37] The most explicit link between wine and myth appears in his Vollard Suite of the 1930s which features the Minotaur in the company of beautiful women.[38] According to Virgil, Ovid and others, this monstrous bull-headed creature consumed an annual tribute of maidens in his labyrinth until Theseus, aided by Ariadne, entered the maze and killed him. One of the etchings shows the Minotaur and a lecherous male companion – presumably the artist himself – toasting one another with champagne as two voluptuous women sprawl at their sides. The uninhibited demeanour of the women suggests both intoxication and sexual availability, while the shape of the glasses – curvy coupes, rather than straight flutes – reinforces the sensuality of the scene.[39]

Religious art by no means disappeared in the twentieth century – the Vatican museum owns nearly 800 modern works – but few contemporary artists have found wine's agency in Christian redemption to be a compelling theme.[40] One exception, however, is Arnold Rainer (b. 1929), an Austrian abstractionist who has long been fascinated with the residual meaning of cruciform shapes and stains. His painting, *Wine Crucifix* (illus. 100), was commissioned in 1957 as an altarpiece for the Student Chapel of the Catholic University in Graz and

99 Pablo Picasso,
Vollard Suite 85:
Bacchic Scene with
Minotaur, 1933,
etching on copper.

100 Arnulf Rainer, *Wine Crucifix*, begun 1957, oil on canvas.

subsequently reworked by the artist prior to its acquisition by the Tate Gallery in 1983. In its original setting, the canvas hung, unframed, in a window that allowed light to flow through it. Like the transubstantiation itself, the effect would have been mystical, the oil pigments simultaneously suggesting both blood and wine. After reworking the picture, the artist claimed its 'quality and truth . . . only grew . . . darker and darker'.[41]

The twenty-first century has already seen a renewal of interest in more representational depictions of mythological and biblical narratives. Leonard Porter (b. 1963) has devoted his career to this, and his 2009 ink and watercolour *Ariadne Discovered by Dionysus* provides an eloquent example of how the classical language of ancient Greece can still be spoken and understood.[42] In Porter's words,

> I was thinking of that moment when Ariadne is just about to be awakened by Dionysus, existing on the cusp between one state and another, sleep/waking, sobriety/intoxication, mortal/divine, love/rejection. Dionysus raises his hand to halt the current song to prolong the moment, before allowing a new tune (and her new life) to begin.[43]

101 Leonard Porter, *Ariadne Discovered by Dionysus, Asleep on the Island of Naxos*, 2009, ink and watercolour on paper.

David Ligare (b. 1945), in turn, has depicted still-lifes of bread and wine in what he calls 'altar-like' and 'metaphysical' spaces that unequivocally evoke the sacrament of the Eucharist (illus. 102).[44] In addition to being 'fully aware of the Christian symbolism' involved, Ligare also emulates Roman still-life paintings and mosaics of food.[45] Ultimately, viewers have to determine the meaning of such arresting

102 David Ligare, *Still-life with Bread and Wine*, 2007, oil on canvas.

images for themselves, but whether they are moved primarily by the stylistic nostalgia or the iconographic message, they will see that the timeless story of wine and the Western imagination has come back to life just when it seemed to be at an end.

Wine and Modern Literature

Writers, for their part, have never stopped musing about wine, either directly or through metaphor. In fiction – a relative newcomer to the world of letters – wine plays a central role in several nineteenth-century plots, most prominently, perhaps, in Edgar Allan Poe's short story 'The Cask of Amontillado' (1846). A Gothic tale of revenge and terror, the narrator tells of luring a friend who has insulted him into his labyrinthine wine cellar in search of a barrel of special sherry.

To put the man at ease, he plies him with a Médoc suggestively named De Grâve. The unsuspecting victim thinks only of the treasure that awaits him as his host proceeds to wall him into the vaulted crypt that houses the fictional cask. The tale is memorable even if Poe mistakenly thought Amontillado was a rare Italian wine and not the common Spanish sherry that it is.

Wine plays a more metaphorical role in Robert Louis Stevenson's equally dark novel *The Strange Tale of Dr Jekyll and Mr Hyde* (1886). In the chapter 'The 'Incident of the Letter', Dr Jekyll is conversing with the lawyer investigating the mysterious Mr Hyde when a servant produces

> a bottle of a particularly old wine that had long dwelt in the foundations of his house. The fog still slept on the wing above the drowned city . . . But the room was gay with firelight. In the bottle the acids were long ago resolved; the impartial dye had softened with time, as the colour grows richer in stained windows; and the glow of hot autumn afternoons on hillside vineyards, was ready to be set free and to disperse the fogs of London.[46]

Using a vintage claret to evoke a patch of colour in the fog-bound city of London was a clever literary device, and Stevenson – unlike Poe – obviously knew his wine. After moving to California to marry Fanny Osborne in 1879, the tubercular author fled the fogs of San Francisco to spend his honeymoon in the Napa Valley. His journal for those days furnished the basis of *The Silverado Squatters* (1883), a volume in which the author admits 'I was interested in California wines . . . Indeed I am interested in all wines, and have been all my life . . .'. In the lines that follow, Stevenson goes on to reminisce,

> If wine is to draw its most poetic countenance, the sun of the white dinner cloth, a deity to be invoked by two or three, all fervent, hushing their talk, degusting tenderly, and storing reminiscences – for a bottle of good wine, like a good act, shines ever in the retrospect . . .[47]

And finally, it is here, in his most memorable remark, that the author offhandedly suggests that 'wine is bottled poetry'.

209

The links between wine and verse were so strong in the nine-teenth and twentieth centuries that computer indices cite hundreds of poems with apposite titles or references. They appear in virtually every language, and from talents as diverse as Emily Dickinson, Lord Byron, Charles Baudelaire, Tennessee Williams and Pablo Neruda. In some instances, the ideas and imagery follow tradition, recalling the classi-cal *carpe diem* philosophy of Theognis and Horace. Such was the tone Byron evoked in Canto Two of his epic poem *Don Juan* (1819–24):

> let us have wine and women, mirth and laughter,
> Sermons and soda-water the day after.[48]

Later in the same poem, Byron compares the legendary lover's fond-ness for wine with his attraction to women:

> Some people prefer wine – 'tis not amiss;
> I have tried both; so those who would a part take
> May choose between the headache and the heartache.[49]

The poet then admits the difficulty of deciding between the two:

> And if I had to give a casting voice,
> For both sides I could many reasons show,
> And then decide, without great wrong to either,
> It were much better to have both than neither.[50]

Among the most succinct lines on the subject – tinged with a touch of memento mori – are those William Butler Yeats penned in his 1910 poem, 'A Drinking Song':

> Wine comes in at the mouth
> And love comes in at the eye;
> That's all we shall know for truth
> Before we grow old and die.
> I lift my glass to my mouth,
> I look at you, and I sigh.[51]

In 1819, the same year the first Canto of *Don Juan* appeared, John Keats (1795–1821) touched on a different aspect of wine in his

'Ode to a Nightingale' (1819). Unlike his earlier poem, 'Women, Wine, and Snuff' (1816), in which the poet envisioned little beyond the pleasures of his 'beloved Trinity', the 'Ode' is not about the joy wine brings. Rather it casts wine as a metaphor for the idylls of summer amidst the sweetly melancholic nature of life itself, a world in which beauty inevitably fades. The second stanza reads:

> O for a draught of vintage! that hath been
> Cooled a long age in the deep-delved earth,
> Tasting of Flora and the country green,
> Dance, and Provençal song, and sunburn mirth!
> O for a beaker of the warm South,
> Full of the true, the blushful Hippocrene,
> With beaded bubbles winking at the brim,
> And purple stained mouth;
> That I might drink, and leave the world unseen,
> And with thee fade away into the forest dim.[52]

Even if the moment does not last, the 'beaded bubbles' of wine, like the poetry of the nightingale's song, are capable of bringing solace to the heart of the reader.[53]

Wine's capacity for broader significance reached a milestone in 1857 with the publication of Charles Baudelaire's *Les Fleurs du mal*, a collection of one hundred poems grouped in thematic clusters.[54] One of the clusters, *Le Vin*, is comprised of five poems that tell the story of wine's tragically mixed blessings. The first, 'The Soul of Wine', begins happily enough:

> One night the wine was singing in the bottles:
> 'Mankind', dear waif, I send to you, in spite
> Of prisoning glass and rosy wax that throttles,
> A song that's full of brotherhood and light.

'Like ambrosia from above', the poem continues, wine 'dives down the throat of some work-wearied slave', lighting the eyes of a 'delighted wife' and giving 'health and muscle . . . to that frail athlete of this life'. The second poem, 'The Wine of the Ragpickers', is more prosaic as it speaks of those 'mired in the labyrinth of some old slum', and 'ground down by toil, decrepitude, despair', who turn to wine

to lull their laziness and drown their rancour
For storm-tossed wrecks a temporary anchor . . .

But this is nothing compared with what happens in the third segment, 'The Murderer's Wine', when the narrator confesses, with no remorse, to having drowned his disapproving wife.

My wife is dead. I'm free. From hence
I'll drink my fill, and that's the truth!
Each time I came back with no pence,
Her screechings drilled me like a tooth.

The fourth poem, 'The Wine of the Solitary Man', details the inevitable degradation of the narrator as he descends into the world of gambling and prostitution. Yet just when things could hardly seem worse, the tale ends on the same felicitous note with which it began. The first stanza of this last poem, 'The Wine of Lovers', begins

Oh, what a splendour fills all space!
Without bit, spur, or rein to race,
Let's gallop on the steeds of wine
To heavens magic and divine!

Despite the unexpectedly upbeat ending, Baudelaire makes it clear in his prefatory notes 'To the Reader' that *Les Fleurs du mal* was intended as a morality play, a retelling of the 'folly and error, avarice and vice' that 'employ our souls and waste our bodies' force'. 'Boredom' with 'this drab canvas we accept as life' is what drives people to drink and drugs, a condition the reader is accused of sharing:

you know this dainty monster, too, it seems –
Hypocrite reader! – You! – My twin! – My brother!

The naturalism of Baudelaire's urban imagery found favour among authors like Victor Hugo, the Goncourt brothers and Emile Zola, but *Les Fleurs du mal* struck some French critics as tasteless and bewildering, with one complaining that everything in it 'which is not hideous is incomprehensible, everything one understands is putrid'.[55] The authorities were even less impressed, and charges were brought against the author that resulted in Baudelaire's being fined and prohibited from reprinting several of the poems.

Despite growing concern over the social consequences of alcoholism, poetic celebrations of wine continued to thrive in England and America. In some instances, the old tropes survived, as in Robert Browning's poem 'Aristophanes' Apology' (1875). Linking wine with the archaeology of literature itself, the ancient playwright muses:

> Our Art began when Bacchus . . .
> Found – not the least of many benefits –
> That wine unlocked the stiffest lip, and looses
> The tongue late dry and reticent of joke . . .[56]

Or in another classicizing poem, 'Apollo and the Fates', Browning linked wine with the god of sunshine who raises his glass to toast and taunt the gloomy Fates:

> proffer earth's product, not mine
> Taste, try, and approve Man's invention of – Wine!
> Quaff wine,—how the spirits rise nimble and eager . . .
> The juice, I uphold,
> Illuminates gloom without sunny connivance,
> Turns fear into hope and makes cowardice bold –
> Touching all that is leadlike in life turns it to gold![57]

One of the more surprising places to find wine imagery is in the poetry of Emily Dickinson, a seemingly abstemious individual who once described herself in a letter to a prospective mentor as having 'eyes like the sherry in the glass that the guest leaves'.[58] Dickinson referred to wine on a number of occasions in the oblique manner for which she is so famous. A concordance to her verse reveals seventeen citations for wine (and seven more for liquor) while tea, by comparison, appears just four times.[59] In one poem, 'Impossibility, like Wine', Dickinson uses the image as a simile for the wonder of unknown experience:

> Impossibility, like wine
> Exhilarates the Man
> Who tastes it; Possibility
> Is flavorless – Combine

A Chance's faintest Tincture
And in the former Dram
Enchantment makes ingredient
As certainly as Doom.[60]

Dickinson's search for transcendent meaning found a natural metaphor in wine's capacity for intoxification. The more metaphysical poems that address issues of love and immortality employ wine imagery to its greatest effect. Her masterpiece in this respect is probably 'I Bring an Unaccustomed Wine':

I bring an unaccustomed wine
To lips long parching
Next to mine.
And summon them to drink;

Crackling with fever, they Essay,
I turn my brimming eyes away,
And come next hour to look.

The hands still hug the tardy glass –
The lips I would have cooled, alas –
Are so superfluous Cold –

I would as soon attempt to warm
The bosoms where the frost has lain
Ages beneath the mould –

Some other thirsty there may be
To whom this would have pointed me
Had it remained to speak –

And so I always bear the cup
If, haply, mine may be the drop
Some pilgrim thirst to slake –

If, haply, any say to me
'Unto the little, unto me',
When I at last awake.[61]

Taken literally, the poem seems to speak of her passion for a would-be paramour or departed relative or friend, but on another level, the thirst could refer to the eternal life of the soul. Dickinson's religious beliefs were tinged with scepticism, but one cannot exclude the possibility that she intended the 'unaccustomed wine' to suggest a desire for salvation.[62]

In contrast to the mystery of Dickinson's poems, Pablo Neruda's 'Ode to Wine' leaves relatively little to the imagination. Neruda turned to the straightforward conventions of the ode during the 1950s, turning out three volumes of verse that addressed elemental themes like the artichoke, the bicycle, summer and sand. His 'Ode to Wine' (1954) begins with a tribute to the multivalent aspects of the beverage ('never has one goblet contained you') before turning into a meditation on a woman whose hip reminds him of 'the brimming curve of the wine goblet', breast a grape cluster, and nipples the grapes.[63] Neruda was married to Delia del Carril at the time, but the woman pictured in the poem was probably Matilde Urrutia, his long-time mistress.[64]

Twentieth-century luminaries like Sylvia Plath, Tennessee Williams and Richard Wilbur also evoked wine imagery. For Plath, the result was a dark little poem titled 'Maenad'; for Wilbur, 'A Wedding Toast', that plays on the biblical imagery of the wedding at Cana. Wine's capacity to stir the poetic imagination in new ways is especially evident in Tennessee Williams' poem 'The Wine Drinkers', from his collection *Androgyne, Mon Amour* (1977).[65] Williams, like Emily Dickinson, is believed to have inscribed his emotional autobiography in his poems, and *Androgyne* has been called 'the clearest road-map we have to [his] deepest feelings, especially in regard to his sexuality'.[66] With this in mind, one cannot help but read 'The Wine Drinkers' with the author's tastes for alcohol and barbiturates, not to mention homosexuality, in mind.

> The wine-drinkers sit on the porte cochère in the sun
> Their lack of success in love has made them torpid.
> They move their fans with a motion that stirs no feather,
> The glare of the sun has darkened their complexions.
>
> Let us commend them on their conversations.
> One says 'oh' and the other says 'indeed'.

The mention of 'bright and very delicate needles', comes next, and inevitably the question is asked:

> What do they dream of? Murder?
> They dream of lust and they long for violent action
> But none occurs.

Viewed from a historical perspective, Williams's poem – like Munch's painting – takes the destructive powers of wine to the point of no return. Neither joy nor insight attend 'The Wine Drinkers', but a message that proclaims the modern mythology of nothingness. Five years after the poem was published, Williams choked to death on a medicine-bottle cap in his hotel room. According to the police report, alcohol and drugs had been contributing factors.[67]

In recent times, wine has made major inroads into popular culture. Of the dozens of songs and films that have taken up the subject, the 2004 movie *Sideways* is perhaps the most memorable. Jack and Miles, two old college friends from Southern California, take a wine-tasting trip to the Central Coast region on the eve of Jack's wedding. The 'perfect week' they envision is comically disrupted by Miles's brooding over his recent divorce as well as Jack's attempts to seduce every woman he meets. Wine runs through the narrative as the pair, soon accompanied by two women, sample or discuss more than a dozen labels, both domestic and imported. In one restaurant scene Miles proclaims 'If anyone orders any merlot, I'm leaving. I am not drinking any fucking merlot', while in another, he discourses on pinot noir: 'It's a hard grape to grow – thin skinned, it ripens early, it's not a survivor. It requires constant care and attention, and can only really grow in these specific tucked away corners of the world.' What he says really applies to himself, and part of the genius of the film is the way wine preferences are used to express the personalities of the protagonists. Thus for Maya, the uncomplicated, good-natured woman to whom Miles delivers the lecture about pinot noir, wine is

> a living thing . . . I love how wine continues to evolve, how every time I open a bottle, it's going to taste different than if I had opened it on any other day. Because a bottle of wine is actually alive – it's constantly evolving and growing in complexity . . .

[before] it begins its steady, inevitable decline. And it tastes so fucking good.[68]

Not surprisingly, after *Sideways* was released – and named 'by far the year's best American movie' – by a widely read magazine, domestic sales of merlot and pinot noir were affected accordingly.[69]

Wine and Modern Medicine II

If wine's traditional ties with mythology and religion have weakened in modern times, they have grown stronger with medical science. Ancient wine remedies, one recalls, were applied topically for lesions and wounds, or taken internally for a bewildering assortment of ailments. Modern experiments and studies, especially ones from the last few decades, have proven both treatments to be essentially correct, even if for reasons other than those originally proposed. The most definitive results have come from experiments proving wine's effectiveness as a disinfectant or bactericide.

Among the surprises is proof that 'the antiseptic power of wine is no myth'.[70] The primary therapeutic ingredient is not the alcohol, the low pH or the added sulphites – all of which do have antibacterial properties – but the anthocyanins, a subgroup among the many polyphenols present in wine. Laboratory tests conducted in the 1970s have confirmed that immersion in wine destroyed five different strains of bacteria, all in the space of six hours. The wines in that experiment were Italian, French and Spanish, but in an even earlier test, a traditional Greek wine from Samos reportedly killed an entire culture of *E. coli* within three minutes.[71] A more recent study tested the resistance of *Staphylococcus aureus* – the most common wound infection – against Portuguese table wine, red wine vinegar, two different concentrations of ethanol (40% and 10%), with sterile tap water as a control.[72] The 40% ethanol eradicated the bacteria immediately, the vinegar within 20 minutes, while the wine destroyed virtually all the colony counts within two hours, and the 10% ethanol showed no effect over the same period of time. Because ethanol or vinegar is painful when applied to open wounds, the study concluded that 'wine, on the other hand, has sufficient antibacterial effect against *Staphylococcus aureus* to prevent it from causing infection, while also being acceptable to the patient'.[73] Homer, it thus turns out, was right when he described the success of Hekamede's treatment of the wounded Machaon and Eurypylos. So why, one may ask, is wine no longer used for this purpose? The answer is that its active ingredients are short-lived, being rapidly bound and inactivated by proteins.[74]

Even more remarkable are the recent discoveries that suggest 'moderate' internal consumption – one or two glasses a day – protects the body from a wide variety of ailments.[75] The rehabilitation of wine therapy – which had been dropped from most pharmacopoeia by the 1960s – began with a modest article published in 1979 in the British medical journal *The Lancet*.[76] In this, the authors redirected the scientific discourse away from its prevailing concern with alcoholism to one suggesting its role in lowering the risks of heart disease. A number of highly specialized studies followed, and the now-famous 1991 television documentary, 'The French Paradox', introduced the notion to a wider public.[77] The 'French Paradox' referred, of course, to the fact that French mortality rates from cardiovascular disease were lower than those in other industrialized countries despite a national diet rich in saturated fats. The suggestion that something in red wine accounted for the finding led to an explosive growth in wine sales, especially in the United States, where consumption rose by 40 per cent within a matter of weeks.

More laboratory studies and specialized publications quickly followed, most addressing the preventative rather than curative effects of 'moderate' wine consumption. In 1996 the *British Medical Journal* had reviewed 25 studies; by 2003 47 were cited in the journal *Cardiology Clinics*, and hardly a week now passes without a new contribution being made to the literature. Publications for the general reader have followed, with *The Red Wine Diet: Drink Wine Every Day and Live a Long Healthy Life* appearing in 2007, and a special section devoted to 'Wine and Health' in the *Wine Spectator* in 2009.[78] That issue of the *Wine Spectator* catalogued the maladies for which regular wine consumption has been recommended:

Ageing
Alzheimer's Disease and dementia
Cancer (breast, colon, esophageal, lung, and ovarian)
Cardiovascular disease
Cataracts
Colds and influenza

Diabetes
Fatty liver
Indigestion
Insomnia
Ischemic stroke
Macular degeneration
Rheumatoid arthritis

Strangely absent from this and most such lists is the fact that alcoholic beverages reduce anxiety and stress, which may itself lead to a healthier life. Unfortunately, there is little if any supporting data to back this hypothesis.[79] Rather, most studies focus on finding the active ingredients responsible for wine's beneficial effects. The average glass of wine, it should be said, consists of 80% water, with alcohol making up another 12 to 15%. What remains is a mix of acids, proteins, sugars and other organic compounds, and it is on these that researchers have concentrated their efforts. A class of chemical compounds known as polyphenols seem the most promising ingredients, and among them Resveratrol is the best known, a compound now synthesized and marketed as a nutritional supplement. But Resveratrol is not the only polyphenol in red wine. Quercetin and the procyanidins are also present, and these too have become the subject of laboratory studies. A second avenue of inquiry involves the higher levels of omega-3 fatty acids that accompany alcohol consumption. These acids – which cannot be manufactured by the body alone – have been found to lower the risk of heart disease as well. Finally, some of the most exciting current research has looked at how human genes known as sirtuins can be activated by polyphenols in a process that may slow down the ageing process.[80]

The rehabilitation of wine in the medical community has other, less clinical implications. Wine drinkers can now derive personal satisfaction on learning that something pleasurable may actually be good for you; that one need not feel guilty when enjoying it, and that the reproach of non-drinkers can be countenanced with a recitation of its health benefits.[81] The caveat, of course, remains *moderate* consumption, which typically is defined as a glass or two a day. Indeed, other sobering studies chart the harmful cardiovascular effects of drinking to excess.[82]

Wine's return to the annals of medicine has been complemented by claims made for it as a beauty product. The French have been the most active in this area, and since the 1990s a number of wine-based lotions and cremes have been introduced to the cosmetics market. The purported active ingredient in these – not surprisingly – are poly-phenols, and the most prominent of these products is Christian Dior's 'Capture'. Since 1999, a number of *vinothérapie* centers have sprung up in France and Italy, and a professional society founded to promote polyphenol-based beauty treatments.[83] With this, the culture of wine expanded once more, and in a fashion that even the ancient Greeks might have admired.

eight

Outside the Western Tradition

Our study has focused on the Western world, where the cultural history of wine has been the longest and most continuous. Although the origins of viticulture occurred elsewhere – probably in Asia Minor – wine cultures outside the West never left the imprint they did in Greece, Rome and later Christian lands. The archaeological record in ancient Egypt attests to the use of wine in both cult worship and medicine, but the proprietary gods Osiris, Hathor and Thoth did not survive the Roman conquest in 30 BC, and wine-making on a significant scale only returned to the country in modern times. Wine was certainly known in ancient India and China, and later in medieval Japan as well, yet the beverages in question were typically made from rice rather than grapes.[1] Since meditation rather than inebriation offered the preferred path to the divine, only through the efforts of European missionaries and colonists did *Vitis vinifera* return to these lands, albeit independent of the cultural traditions developed in the West. Wine consumption among the other major producers – Australia, New Zealand, South Africa and America – only began in colonial times and has left an even fainter cultural impression.

With this in mind, it is surprising to learn that grape wine was mythologized in early Islamic lands. Modern proscriptions against alcohol in these countries fail to suggest the role it played in the early Muslim imagination. The new religion left no visual record behind, but an abundance of texts – revelatory, legal, historical and exegetical, both Sunni and Shi'ite – suggest a surprising degree of ambivalence towards alcoholic beverages.[2] Indeed, Islam's early history is marked by striking incongruities between doctrine and practice, and uncertainties over the nature of the divine will. The Qur'an eventually became the canonical source of the prohibition, but a close reading of its pronouncements on wine reveal the injunction to have been neither absolute or unconditional.

The most common word for wine in the Qur'an is *khamr* (which appears six times), while a variety of other words – *sakar, sakra, sukara* and *sakkara* – are repeatedly used to connote intoxicants or the state of drunkenness.[3] From a philological perspective, the large vocabulary suggests a highly nuanced attitude towards wine and its effects. At its worst, wine appears along with gambling, idol-worship, and divination as a Satanic 'abomination'.

> Keep away from them so that you may prosper.
> Satan only wants to create enmity and hatred among you
>   with wine and gambling,
>   and to divert you from the remembrance of God, and from
>   prayer. Will you not abstain?[4]

At its best, wine is the main reward in the Garden of Repose, the ideal state that follows the apocalyptic Day of Judgment. Here, 'rivers of wine' that are 'a joy to those who drink' are promised to the elect while 'a boiling water so hot it cuts the bowels to pieces' is served to the damned.[5] Even when consumed in quantity, this paradisiacal wine leaves no ill effects. Those partaking in their heavenly reward consume 'bowls and decanters' and 'receive no ache from it, nor suffer intoxification'. In paradise, the elect remain undisturbed by earthly ambiguities.[6]

Thus, from a worldly perspective, wine is viewed as ethically corrosive while cosmically it is praised as one of God's gifts to the righteous.[7] Unfortunately, the Qur'an is not always clear in distinguishing between the two states of being. For example, in one passage that obviously refers to the earthly realm, we read

> And in the fruits of . . . the grape-vine
>   you obtain an intoxicant (*sakar*) and good food.
> In this are signs for those who understand.[8]

Here the interpretive key is put in the hands of the consumer who may or may not 'understand' the insights wine can provide.

The Qur'an is supplemented in Islamic belief by the Hadith, a collection of accounts of what Muhammad said or did, approved or disapproved.[9] Unlike the Qur'an, the Hadith is fairly consistent in its condemnation of wine and other intoxicants, although at no point does it explicitly say that the Prophet prohibited wine.[10] On the contrary, it reveals that wine-drinking, even excessive wine-drinking, was commonplace among the people of Mecca and Medina. Thus we hear that Muhammad's companions held frequent drinking parties that led to disruptions in ritual prayer, and that his uncle, Hamzab 'Abd al-Muttalib, mutilated some camels while in an intoxicated state.[11] Moreover, from another text, al-Tabari's monumental *History* (*Ta'rikh*), we learn that despite the prohibitionary atmosphere, 'several Muslims have taken to wine. We asked them about this, but they justified their act by saying, "we have been given a choice, and we have chosen".[12]

Later Muslim scholars sought to reconcile the Qur'an's inconsistencies by arranging its undated remarks on wine in an order that suggests a chronological progression towards a clear condemnation of the drink.[13] By this logic, the sequence would begin with the reference to the grape-vine as 'good food', and end with the passage warning that wine, in the company of gambling and idol-worship, was an abomination of the devil.

The Islamic discourse on wine included poetical texts that extended the imaginative boundaries between the permissible and the forbidden. Drawing upon the rich tradition of *Jahiliya*, or pre-Islamic, verse that glorified wine's unique capacity to induce both physical pleasure and psychic pain, poets of the Abbasid (post-Muhammad) period created the independent genre known as the *Khamriya*, or wine ode.[14]

The finest expression of this genre is the *Rubáiyát* of the Persian polymath, Omar Khayyam (1048–1131). Khayyam praises wine throughout the work, and in many dimensions. On one level, wine offers an escape from the harshness of the real world:

> Drink wine, to make thee unaware
> Of all the griefs that vex the mind,
> And bring thy foeman, who designed
> Thy utmost ruin, to despair.[15]

In some quatrains, an attitude of *carpe diem* prevails:

Drink wine, my friend; for many a moon
When our short span is shuffled through
Shall turn from sickle unto new,
From new to sickle, all too soon.[16]

While in others it offers an alternative to intellectual and spiritual
pursuits:

Tonight I will make a tun of wine,
Set myself up with two bowls of it;
First I will divorce absolutely reason and religion,
Then take to wife the daughter of the vine.

Drink wine, this is life eternal .
This, all that youth will give you;
It is the season for wine, roses and friends drinking together,
Be happy for this moment – it is all life is.

The secular imagery Khayyam evokes constitutes a protest
against the prohibition of wine, a voice of dissent, in effect, against the
strictures of the Qur'an and Hadith. The same attitude is endorsed in
the writings of the Persian philosopher Avicenna (980–1037), who
even went so far as to recommend drinking as one worked. 'At night I
return home,' he wrote in his autobiography, 'and occupy muself with
reading and writing. Whenever I felt drowsy or weak I would turn aside
to drink a cup of wine to regain my strength, and then go back to my
reading.'[17] Later Persian poets wrote positively about wine as well, with
Hafiz of Shiraz (1320–1391) devoting one of his most lyrical works to
the classical theme of 'Love and Wine'. The first stanza begins:

Fill, fill the cup with sparkling wine,
Deep let me drink the juice divine,
To soothe my tortured heart;
For Love, who seem'd at first so mild,
So gently look'd, so gaily smil'd,
Here deep has plung'd his dart.[18]

Although the visual record is rather spare, Persian painters sometimes left traces of early wine culture in their depictions of courtly

scenes or illustrations of the *Khamriya*. Shah Abbas II's palace of
Chehel Soton in Isfahan is decorated, for example, with frescoes that
show the Shah offering cups of wine to his guests or portraying his
courtiers enjoying a glass or two of wine in a bucolic landscape setting. From an iconographical perspective, this seventeenth-century
picture is remarkable in its resemblance both to earlier works of the
Italian Renaissance (illus. 53) and later ones of the French Impres-
sionists (illus. 92) and Fauvists (illus. 98), but the celebration of wine
in Islamic art was to remain a rarity.[19] The illustrations of Hafiz's verses
tend to come from later periods and be quite tame in comparison to
his impassioned poetical expressions.[20]

On a more mystical level, Sufi poets of the thirteenth century
expressed their love of God through the language of intoxication. The
paradigm is found in the work of Ibn al-Farid (1181–1235) and Jalal
al-Din Rumi (1207–1273). In one of his most famous verses, *Dīwān*,
Ibn al-Farid uses the metaphor of wine and intoxication to signal the
transcendental power of Divine Love. For him, the ideal wine is an
ineffable substance, 'pure, but not water; subtle, but not as the air;

103 Chehel Soton
Palace, Isfahan, fresco in
Great Hall, 17th century.

luminous, but not as fire; spirit, but not embodied'. The capacity of this unearthly drink to work miracles is truly mystifying: it can raise the dead, heal the sick and disabled, cause one to regain the sense of smell, keep a wanderer on the right path, protect against snakebite, ward off madness, and resolve doubt. Rather than disrupting the cosmic order, this wine is considered a tool for restoring nature's irregularities to an ideal state. The poem concludes with the lines:

> Joyless in this world is he that lives sober,
> And he that dies not drunk will miss the path of wisdom.
> Let him weep for himself – whose life is wasted
>   without part or lot in wine.[21]

Like Ibn al-Farid, Rumi contrasts material and immaterial existence while relating the experience of earthly drunkenness to ecstatic effects of Divine Love. To clarify the contrast between the worldly and unworldly, he distinguishes between the two kinds of wine:

> Know that in this world the drunkenness of sensuality
>   is despicable compared to the angels' intoxication.
> Their intoxication dwarfs this intoxication –
>   how should they pay any regard to sensuality?
> Until you have drunk fresh water, briny water is as sweet to you
>   as light in the eyes.
> A single drop of heaven's wine will tear your spirit away
>   from all these wines and sakis.[22]

If wine in the Qur'an and Hadith symbolizes the paradisiacal reward, the Sufi poetic tradition allowed an imaginary or mystical intoxication to be experienced in the here and now.[23] Needless to say, it was the injunctions against wine's liberating effects that made it such a compelling metaphor for divine transcendence. Wine in the early Islamic world may not have been prized as it was in the West, but precisely because of the proscription levied against it, it made the perfect totem for imagining the unknowable, and if only with words, having a taste of heaven on earth.

references

Introduction

1 Roger Scruton, *I Drink Therefore I Am: A Philosopher's Guide to Wine* (London, 2009), pp. 38, 52 and 81. Scruton's book, I should say at the outset, is the most intelligent text I have read about wine. His intentions are very different from my own, but he is provocative and immensely well-infomed throughout. No true wine lover should be without it.
2 Nowhere has this been more apparent than in early Islam, where the most extreme and creative interpretive strategies were used to reconcile the use of alcohol with the divine will.
3 Scruton, *I Drink*, 137.
4 Tim Unwin, *Wine and the Vine: An Historical Geography of Viticulture and the Wine Trade* (London and New York, 1991), pp. 29–31.
5 This is the theme of James George Frazer's seminal work, *The Golden Bough: A Study in Magic and Religion* (New York, 1922), esp. chap. xliii.
6 The *urtext* of notions of wine and truthfulness appear in a poem by Alcaeus from about 600 BC (Wolfgang Rosler, 'Wine and Truth in the Greek Symposium', in *In Vino Veritas*, ed. O Murray and M. Tecuşan (Rome, 1995), pp. 106–12).
7 Charles W. Bamforth, *Grape vs. Grain: A Historical, Technological, and Social Comparison of Wine and Beer* (New York, 2008).
8 Originally, the mutual toast was believed to guarantee that the wine had not been poisoned.
9 According to Arthur L. Klatsky, 'Wine, Alcohol and Cardiovascular Diseases', in *Wine: A Scientific Exploration*, ed. M. Sandler and R. Pinder (New York, 2003), p. 125, 'Hypothetical considerations about a possible benefit from the anti-anxiety or stress-reducing effects of alcohol have no good supporting data.'
10 William James, *The Varieties of Religious Experience: A Study in Human Nature* (New York, 1902), p. 297.
11 Scruton, 'The Philosophy of Wine', in *Questions of Taste*: *The Philosophy of Wine*, ed. Barry Smith (Oxford, 2007), pp. 12–13.
12 And wine's story continues to expand: in 2008 it was reported in the news that Prince Charles had converted his stable of automobiles to run on biofuel made from surplus wine (CNN, 2 July 2008).

one: The Origins of Wine

1 Patrick E. McGovern, author of *Ancient Wine: The Search for the Origins of Viniculture* (Princeton, NJ, 2003), has been the key investigator in this fascinating field of study, and this chapter has been substantially informed by his work. His most recent discoveries may be found on the numerous websites he maintains at the University of Pennsylvania. For a more succinct account, see the entry on 'Origins of Viticulture' by Hanneke Wilson in *The Oxford Companion to Wine*, ed. Jancis Robinson, 3rd edn (New York, 2006), pp. 499–500.

2 See Julian Reade, 'The Royal Tombs at Ur', in *Art of the First Cities: The Third Millennium BC from the Mediterranean to the Indus*, ed. Joan Arum with Ronald Falafels, exh. cat., Metropolitan Museum of Art (New York, 2003), pp. 93–119, esp. cat. 60, for the most recent discussion of the seals.

3 Marvin Powell, 'Wine and the Vine in Ancient Mesopotamia: The Cuneiform Evidence', in *The Origins and Ancient History of Wine*, ed. P. E. McGovern, S. J. Fleming and S. H. Katz (Luxembourg, 1996), pp. 97–122, esp. 121; in the same volume, Richard L. Zettler and Naomi F. Miller, 'Searching for Wine in the Archaeological Record of Ancient Mesopotamia in the Third and Second Millenia BC', pp. 123–31, esp. 131 conclude that 'with the possible exception of archaeobotanical remains from Kurban Höyök, [there is] no conclusive evidence for the production and consumption of wine [in ancient Mesopotamia]'.

4 Ronald L. Gorny, 'Viticulture in Ancient Anatolia', in *The Origins and Ancient History of Wine*, pp. 133–74, esp. 151–2.

5 Mu-Chou Poo, *Wine and Wine Offering in the Religion of Ancient Egypt* (London, 1995), p. 68.

6 Ibid., p. 159.

7 See Leonard H. Lesko, *King Tut's Wine Cellar* (Berkeley, CA, 1977), and his later essay 'Egyptian Wine Production During the New Kingdom', in *The Origins and Ancient History of Wine*, pp. 215–30, esp. 221–3. Interestingly, 23 of the jars contained wine from the fourth, fifth and ninth years of his nine-year reign, clearly the best vintages of the time.

8 Ibid., p. 230.

9 Poo, *Wine and Wine Offering*, pp. 151–8.

10 Tim Unwin, *Wine and the Vine: An Historical Geography of Viticulture and the Wine Trade* (London, 1991), pp. 78–9.

11 Françoise Dunand and Christiane Zivie-Coche, *Gods and Men in Egypt: 3000 BCE to 395 CE* (Ithaca, NY, 2004), pp. 241–2, citing Herodotus, *Histories*, Book 2, chap. 42.

12 Salvatore P. Lucia, *A History of Wine as Therapy* (Philadelphia, PA, 1963), chap. 2. See also Lesko, 'Egyptian Wine Production', pp. 229–30.

13 See Max Nelson, *The Barbarian's Beverage: A History of Beer in Ancient Europe* (London, 2005), esp. chap. 3, 'The Greek Prejudice Against Beer'.

14 I have used the third edition of *The New Oxford Annotated Bible* (2001) for the quotations that follow.

15 William Ryan and Walter Pitman, *Noah's Flood: The New Scientific Discoveries about the Event that Changed History* (New York, 1998).

16 For the fascinating historiography of the debate, see Norman Cohn, *Noah's Flood in Western Thought* (New Haven, CT, 1996), esp. chap. 10 for more

recent arguments regarding the plausibility of the Genesis narrative.

17 Numbers 13.23.

18 For a thorough study of ancient wine culture in Israel, see Carey E. Walsh, *The Fruit of the Vine: Viticulture in Ancient Israel*, Harvard Semitic Monographs, no. 60 (Winona Lake, IN, 2000). The exhibition catalogue published in 1999 by the Israel Museum, Jerusalem, also treats Jewish customs (M. Dayagi-Mendels, *Drink and Be Merry, Wine and Beer in Ancient Times*).

19 Ibid., p. 97.

20 The entry on wine in *Eerdman's Dictionary of the Bible*, ed. D. N. Freedman (Grand Rapids, MI, 2000), pp. 1379–80, is a useful source for the various meanings wine had in early religions.

21 Dayagi-Mendels, *Drink and Be Merry*, pp. 110–11.

22 Ibid., p. 111.

two: Wine in Ancient Greece

1 See Max Nelson, *The Barbarian's Beverage: A History of Beer in Ancient Europe* (London, 2005), esp. chap. 3, 'The Greek Prejudice Against Beer'.

2 Mnesitheus wrote in the fourth century BC. For a discussion of the wines available in ancient Greece, see James Davidson, *Courtesans and Fishcakes: The Consuming Passions of Classical Athens* (New York, 1999), pp. 40–43.

3 Ibid., p. 46.

4 See John Chadwick, *The Mycenaean World* (New York, 1976), pp. 99ff. For an account of the later myths of Dionysus, see Walter O. Otto, *Dionysus: Myth and Cult,* trans. R. B. Palmer (Bloomington, IN, 1965).

5 The Third Hymn to Dionysus names Dracanum, Icarus, Naxos, Arcadia, Thebes and Nysa as places where the deity may have been born.

6 In addition to the text by Otto cited above, I have found the essay by Albert Henrichs, 'Greek and Roman Glimpses of Dionysus', in *Dionysus and his Circle: Ancient through Modern*, ed. Caroline Houser (Cambridge, MA, 1979), pp. 1–11; Thomas Carpenter, *Dionysian Imagery in Fifth-Century Athens* (New York, 1997), Richard Seaford, *Dionysus* (New York, 2006); and Renate Schlesier and Agnes Schwarzmaier, eds, *Dionysus: Verwandlung und Ekstase* (Berlin, 2008), to be particularly useful in sorting out the deity's diverse personalities.

7 Juvenilization, however, was not unique to Dionysus, for other gods like Apollo and Hermes also became younger and more effeminate over time.

8 Otto, *Dionysus, Myth and Cult*, p. 117.

9 See Donna Kurtz and John Boardman, *Greek Burial Customs* (Ithaca, NY, 1971), as indexed under the heading 'food offerings'. Some vases found in early Greek tombs were lekythoi, slender vessels that held oils and unguents, not wine. Larger vases like hydrias, amphoras and volute kraters often had hollow bases to facilitate the pouring of libations into the grave.

10 The predominance of Dionysian subject matter on vase painting is evident in the lists assembled by John D. Beazley, *Attic Red-Figure Vase Painters* (Oxford, 1963), vol. III, Index II: Mythological Subjects.

11 I have relied upon Thomas Carpenter, *Dionysian Imagery in Archaic Greek Art* (New York, 1986), for much of what follows.

12 Diana Buitron, *Attic Vase Painting in New England Collections*, exh. cat., Fogg Art Museum, (Cambridge, MA, 1972), cat. 17.

13 I have taken the wording of this passage (lines 218–22) from the forthcoming translation by Robert Bagg. I am most grateful to Professor Bagg for furnishing me with this before its publication.

14 *Moralia*, 648b and 291 a–b (Carpenter, *Dionysian Imagery*, pp. 50–51).

15 Randy Westbrooks, *Poisonous Plants of Eastern North America* (Columbia, NY, 1986), p. 126, who while speaking of English ivy (*Hedera helix L.*), notes that the species is native to Europe.

16 *Moralia* 653A (Otto, *Dionysus*, 155)

17 Athenaeus, *The Learned Banqueters*, trans. S. D. Olson (Cambridge, MA, 2006).

18 Euripides, *The Bacchae*, trans. William Arrowsmith (New York, 1974), pp. 167, 1056 and 1123–4.

19 Carpenter, *Dionysian Imagery*, p. 29.

20 Otto, *Dionysus*, p. 100, citing both ancient and modern sources for his reconstruction of the ceremony.

21 Rush Rehm, *Marriage to Death, The Conflation of Wedding and Funeral Rituals in Greek Tragedy* (Princeton, NJ, 1994), esp. chaps 1 and 2.

22 Herodotus, *Histories*, Book II, 78 (trans. Robin Waterfield (New York, 1998). For an incisive study of the relationship between Greek and earlier Egyptian attitudes towards wine and death, see Cristiano Grottanelli, 'Wine and Death—East and West', in *In Vino Veritas*, ed. O. Murray and M. Tecuşan (Rome, 1995), pp. 62–89.

23 For the career of Theognis, who may have been a fictional figure, see Thomas J. Figuera and Gregory Nagy, eds, *Theognis of Megara: Poetry and the Polis* (Baltimore, MD, 1985).

24 James Davies, *Hesiod and Theognis* (Philadelphia, PA, 1873), p. 164.

25 Ibid., p. 139.

26 The lines are from Amphis's play *Women in Power* but the quotation is from Athenaeus, *The Learned Banqueters*, Book VIII, 336c, vol. IV, p. 29.

27 Ibid., Book VIII, 335e–336b, trans. Olson, vol. IV, p. 27.

28 See Iiro Kajanto, 'Balnea vina venus', in *Hommages à Marcel Renard*, II, ed. Jacqueline Bibauw (Brussels, 1969), especially pp. 357–67 with full citations. I am grateful to my colleague Paula Debnar for the translations. Because epitaphs also constituted an independent literary genre, not all appeared on actual tombstones.

29 Women were normally excluded from such gatherings. Hanneke Wilson, *Wine and Words in Classical Antiquity and the Middle Ages* (London, 2003), p. 47, quotes an anecdote from Diogenes Laertius's *Lives of the Philosophers* (third century BC) attesting to the intensity of male disgust at a married woman's presence at a symposium.

30 For further information on symposium entertainments, see Part V, 'The Symposion as Entertainment' in *Sympotica: A Symposium on the 'Symposion'*, ed. O. Murray (New York, 1990).

31 See François Lissarrague, *The Aesthetics of the Greek Banquet: Images of Wine and Ritual* (Princeton, NJ, 1990), chap. 3, 'Manipulations'.

32 Joseph V. Noble, 'Some Trick Greek Vases', *Proceedings of the American Philosophical Society*, CXII (1968), pp. 371–8.

33 Michael Vickers, 'A Dirty Trick Vase', *American Journal of Archaeology*, LXXII

(1975), p. 282.

34 See the essays by Birgitta Bergquist, 'Sympotic Space: A Functional Aspect of Greek Dining-Rooms', and John Boardman, '*Symposion* Furniture', in *Sympotica*, pp. 37–65, as well as Lissarrague, *The Aesthetics of the Greek Banquet*, pp. 19–20.

35 Unpublished paper delivered in 2007 by Professor Rebecca Sinos at Amherst College, 'The Satyr and his Skin: Connections in Plato's *Symposium*', p. 24.

36 As seen, for example, in some of the furniture illustrated by Boardman, '*Symposium* Furniture', pp. 122–31.

37 Jan Bremmer, 'Adolescents, *Symposion*, and Pederasty', in *Sympotica*, pp. 135–48.

38 Walter Hamilton, 'Introduction' to *Plato: The Symposium* (Baltimore, MD, 1971), p. 13.

39 The drawing is after a red figure kylix in the Metropolitan Museum of Art (56.171.61). An actual vase of this type in the Ashmolean Museum, Oxford is published by Beth Cohen, *The Colors of Clay*, exh. cat., J. Paul Getty Museum (Los Angeles 2006), cat. 74.

40 Hubert Martin, *Alcaeus* (New York, 1972), pp. 50–53; Davies, *Hesiod and Theognis*, p. 164; and *Aeschylus*, ed. and trans. Alan Sommerstein (Cambridge, MA, 2008), III, p. 329.

41 Plato, *The Laws,* trans. Trevor J. Saunders (Baltimore, MD, 1975), pp. 104–5. Earlier in the book (chap. 2) Plato offers a lengthy discourse on 'Drinking Parties as an Educational Device'.

42 Plato, *Phaedrus*, 265a–c, trans. A. Nehamas and P. Woodruff (Indianapolis, IN, 1995), p. 63. John F. Moffitt, *Inspiration: Bacchus and the Cultural History of a Creation Myth* (Leiden, 2005), explores the issue from its ancient origins to the present day.

43 Plato, *Phaedrus*, 245a–b, pp. 28–9.

44 Aristotle, *Problems*, XXX, trans. W. S. Hett (Cambridge, MA, 1970–83), pp. 155–81.

45 Patrick E. McGovern, *Ancient Wine: The Search for the Origins of Viniculture* (Princeton, NJ, 2003), p. 205, cites a Syrian text of the Bronze Age describing a banquet in which 'the gods ate and drank, drank wine until sated, new wine until inebriated'. The *rb marzeah*, or overseer of the festivities, drank so much that he collapsed into a state of incontinence and ended up sitting in his own excrement'.

46 Plato, *Symposium*, 212c and 223d. A seventeenth-century print by Pietro Testa (illus. 76) depicts the arrival of Alcibiades.

47 Eubulus, *The Fragments*, trans. R. L. Hunter (New York, 1983), p. 66. The translation given here is adapted from an unattributed one published by Karen MacNeil, *The Wine Bible* (New York, 2001), p. 605.

48 Bergquist, 'Sympotic Space', pp. 37–9 suggests that eleven couches were 'standard' for symposium gatherings although Nancy Bookidis questions the assumption that each couch was occupied by a single symposiast ('Ritual Dining in the Sanctuary of Demeter and Kore at Corinth: Some Questions', *Sympotica*, pp. 91–2).

49 Davidson, *Courtesans and Fishcakes*, pp. 46–7. See also R. L. Hunter's commentary to *The Fragments* of Eubulus, p. 186, n. 1 for further references.

50 See Guy Hedreen, *Silens in Attic Black-Figure Vase Painting: Myth and Performance* (Ann Arbor, MI, 1992).

51 Homer, *The Odyssey*, trans. E. V. Rieu (London, 1977), XXI, p. 323.

52 The pioneering discussion of the subject is found in Salvatore P. Lucia, *A History of Wine as Therapy* (Philadelphia, PA, 1963), esp. chap. 5, 'Prescriptions of the Early Greek Physicians'.

53 Guido Majno, *The Healing Hand: Man and Wound in the Ancient World* (Cambridge, MA, 1975), p. 142.

54 *The Iliad of Homer*, trans. Richmond Lattimore (Chicago, 1951), Book XI, pp. 506–7, 637–9.

55 Plato, *Republic*, trans. Robin Waterfield (New York, 1993), IV, p. 406.

56 Majno, *The Healing Hand*, p. 187.

57 *Hippocrates*, trans. W.H.S. Jones (New York, 1923), VIII, *Ulcers*, p. 1.

58 *Theogony and Works and Days*, trans. C. M. Schlegel and H. Weinfield (Ann Arbor, MI, 2006), p. 75.

59 For a useful general introduction to the subject, see Noga Arikha, *Passions and Tempers: A History of the Humours* (New York, 2007).

60 *Hippocrates*, IV, *Introduction*, XI.

61 *Hippocrates*, IV, *Humours*, chap. XIV.

62 See G.E.R. Lloyd, 'The Hot and the Cold, the Dry and the Wet in Greek Philosophy', *Journal of Hellenic Studies*, LXXXIV (1964), pp. 92–106 for a fuller explanation of these principles.

63 Ibid., p. 102.

64 *Hippocrates*, II, *Regimen*, chap. LII.

65 Pliny, *Natural History*, trans. H. Rackham (Cambridge, MA, 1945), V, p. 157.

three: Roman Wine

1 *Natural History*, trans. H. Rackham (Cambridge, MA, 1945), Book XIV, XIII. Earlier, in the fourth chapter of the same book, Pliny states that 'Democritus, who professed to know all the different kinds of vines in Greece, was alone in thinking it possible for them to be counted . . . but all other writers have stated that there is a countless and infinite number of varieties.' Pliny probably had vines rather than wines in mind here, while the text of Democritus to which he refers has been lost.

2 Ibid., Book XIV, III. For further discussion of the role geography was understood to play in ancient wine and cuisine, see my chapter 'Regional Tastes', in *Tastes and Temptations, Food and Art in Renaissance Italy* (Berkeley, CA, 2009), esp. 41.

3 See Tim Unwin, *Wine and the Vine: An Historical Geography of Viticulture and the Wine Trade* (London, 1991), chap. 4, esp. pp. 101–13.

4 Ilaria Gozzini Giacosa, *A Taste of Ancient Rome*, trans. Anna Herklotz (Chicago, 1992), plates 14 and 15, illustrates both a tavern and a wineshop with a painted pricelist from Pompeii.

5 Two articles by Katherine M. D. Dunbabin treat the actual dining arrangements: 'Triclinium and Stibadium' in *Dining in a Classical Context*, ed. W. Slater (Ann Arbor, MI, 1991), pp. 122–3, and 'Ut Graeco More Biberetur: Greeks and Romans on the Dining Couch', in *Meals in a Social Context: Aspects of the Communal Meal in the Hellenistic and Roman World,* ed. Inge Nielsen and Hanne S. Nielsen (Aarhus, 1998), pp. 81–101.

6 John D'Arms, 'The Roman *Convivium* and the Idea of Equality', in *Sympotica:*

A Symposium on the 'Symposion', ed. O. Murray (New York, 1990), pp. 308–20. On women and children at Roman banquets, see Keith Bradley, 'The Roman Family at Dinner', in *Meals in a Social Context*, p. 38; and Matthew Roller, *Dining Posture in Ancient Rome: Bodies, Values, and Status* (Princeton, NJ, 2006), esp. chaps 2, 'Dining Women', and 3, 'Dining Children'.

7 For funerary banquets, see Hugh Lindsay, 'Eating with the Dead: The Roman Funerary Banquet', in *Meals in a Social Context*, pp. 67–80; and Katherine Dunbabin, *The Roman Banque: Images of Conviviality* (New York, 2003), chap. 4, 'Drinking in the Tomb'. John R. Clark, *Roman Life, 100 BC to AD 200* (New York, 2007), figs 96 and 105, reproduces frescoes from the House of the Chaste Lovers in Pompeii that capture the conviviality of Roman dinner parties. Other images of mixed gatherings can be found on the Art Resource website, www.artres.com under the subject of 'Roman Banquets', as, for example, Art305158, Art305160 and Art204806.

8 Plutarch, *Cato Maior*, 25, 2, as cited by D'Arms, 'The Roman *Convivium*', p. 313.

9 Juvenal, *Satire* 8, 171–76, as cited by D'Arms, 'The Roman *Convivium*', p. 315.

10 Patrick Faas, *Around the Roman Table*, trans. Shaun Whiteside (New York, 2003), pp. 89ff.

11 Pliny, *Natural History*, Book XIV, VIII, pp. 62–3.

12 The passage struck Quintilian as so evocative that he quoted it as an example of the rhetorical technique of *enargeia*, or vivid description (Emily Gowers, *The Loaded Table: Representations of Food in Roman Literature*, New York, 1993, p. 33).

13 André Tchernia, *Le Vin de Italie Romaine* (Rome, 1986), pp. 24–5.

14 The data is from Jancis Robinson, *The Oxford Companion to Wine* (New York, 2006), Appendix 2C, 'Per Capita Wine Consumption by Country'.

15 Stuart J. Fleming, *Vinum: The Story of Roman Wine* (Glen Mills, PA, 2001), p. 59, gives the lower figure, Tchneria, *Le Vin*, p. 26, the higher.

16 This statistic was provided by Alex Conison in his talk 'Risk Allocation in the Ancient Roman Wine Trade', presented at the *In Vino Veritas* conference held at Binghamton University, 24–5 April 2009.

17 Varro, as quoted in Bradley, 'The Roman Family at Dinner', p. 37; Catullus and Marcial are cited in Gowers, *The Loaded Table*, pp. 232 and 252.

18 Pliny, *Natural History*, Book XIV, XXVIII.

19 *Petronius: Satyrica*, trans. R. B. Branham and D. Kinney (Berkeley, CA, 1999), Book XV, Fragment 57.

20 For Aeschylus's remark, see *Aeschylus*, trans. Alan Sommerstein (Cambridge, MA, 2008), III, p. 329. The phrase *in vino veritas* is typically attributed to Pliny, but his actual words were *volgoque veritas iam attributa vino est* (*Natural History*, Book XIV, XXVIII, pp. 141–2).

21 Ibid., pp. 146–8.

22 Propertius, *Elegies*, trans. G. P. Goold (Cambridge, MA, 1990), Book II, XXXIII; *The Satires of Persius*, trans. Guy Lee (Wolfeboro, NH, 1987), pp. 3, 88–106.

23 Horace, *Odes and Epodes*, trans. Niall Rudd (Cambridge, MA, 2004), Book I, 11.

24 For the Herodotean origins of these concepts, see the previous chapter, n. 22.

25 *Petronius: Satyrica*, ed. and trans. R. Bracht Branham and D. Kinney (Berkeley, CA, 1996), chap. 34, 30.

26 On the subject of *larvae convivialis*, see Katherine Dunbabin, 'Sic erimus cuncti . . . The Skeleton in Greco-Roman Art', *Jahrbuch des Deutsches Archäologischen Institutes*, CI (1986), pp. 185–215. Only a single example of a silver *larva* with movable joints is known (illustrated in *Argenti a Pompei*, ed. P. G. Guzzo (Milan, 2006), cat. 41).

27 The phenomenon is known in other cultures as well. To cite but one historical example, a Zapotec jug with skeleton is in the collection of the Museum of Anthropology and History in Mexico City (photo: Art Resource: Art309921). To this day, Mexican 'Day of the Dead' celebrations continue to feature skulls and skeletal figurines.

28 See Iiro Kajanto, 'Balnea vina venus', in *Hommages à Marcel Renard*, ed. Jacqueline Bibauw (Brussels, 1969), II, pp. 357–67.

29 See Dunbabin, *The Roman Banquet*, chap. 4, 'Drinking in the Tomb', esp. pp. 103–4, for the primary sources of the discussion that follows.

30 The Latin is given in Kajanto, 'Balnea vina venus', p. 362.

31 Georges Dumézil, *Archaic Roman Religion*, trans. Philip Krapp (Chicago, 1970), vol. I, pp. 183–5; 271–2; vol. II, p. 472.

32 Ibid., vol. II, pp. 515–16.

33 Mary Beard et al., *Religions of Rome* (New York, 1998), vol. II, pp. 288–92. In a subsequent passage, Livy transcribes the testimony of a woman questioned by the consuls about the rituals. 'At first', she says, 'It was a rite for women . . . [but once] men were admitted . . . absolutely every crime and vice was performed there. The men had more sex with each other than with the women . . . while women in the dress of Bacchus with streaming hair ran down to the Tiber carrying burning torches'.

34 *Philostratus: Imagines; Callistratus: Descriptions*, trans. A. Fairbanks (Cambridge, MA, 1931), pp. 403–7.

35 See Leonard Barkan, *The Gods Made Flesh: Metamorphosis and the Pursuit of Paganism* (New Haven, CT, 1986), esp. pp. 37–41.

36 Ovid, *Metamorphoses*, trans. Rolfe Humphries (Bloomington, IN, 1955), pp. 81–2.

37 Macrobius, *The Saturnalia*, trans. and ed. Percival V. Davies, (New York, 1969), p. 129.

38 K. Lehmann-Hartleben and E. C. Olsen, *Dionysiac Sarcophagi in Baltimore* (New York, 1942), pp. 37ff.

39 Anna M. McCann, *Roman Sarcophagi in the Metropolitan Museum of Art*, exh. cat. (New York, 1978), cat. 17, pp. 94–106.

40 Ibid., p. 97, with references to additional literature.

41 *The Iliad of Homer*, trans. Richmond Lattimore (Chicago, 1951), Book VI, pp. 130–40. See also Walter O. Otto, *Dionysus: Myth and Cult*, trans. R. B. Palmer (Bloomington, IN, 1965), as indexed, and Simon Hornblower and Antony Spawforth, eds, *The Oxford Classical Dictionary* (New York, 2003), p. 628.

42 *The Myths of Hyginus*, trans. Mary Grant (Lawrence, KA, 1960), Fable 132.

43 Pliny, *Natural History*, Book XIV, XXVIII, p. 140. A century earlier, Horace wrote an epistle (Book I, Epistle XIX) in which he singled out poets as particularly prone to wine-drinking contests. The practice itself seems to have originated in Greek Dionysian festivals known as Anthesteria.

44 Christine Kondoleon, 'Mosiacs of Antioch', in *Antioch, The Lost Ancient City*, ed. C. Kondoleon (Princeton, NJ, 2000), esp. 68–9, stresses the message of

moderation in the mosaic. An alternative reading is supported by the contemporary inscriptions scratched into frescoes at the House of the Triclinium in Pompeii (Clark, *Roman Life*, New York, 2007, fig. 110) that transcribe the high-spirited drinking songs that accompanied first-century banquets. Rather comically, another fresco in that same room (ibid., fig. 109) depicts one of the guests vomiting as he lurches towards the door.

45 Pliny, *Natural History*, Book XXIX, XVI who notes that his Roman forefathers lived 'without physicians . . .but not without medicines'.

46 Emma J. Edelstein and L. E. Edelstein, *Asclepius: A Collection and Interpretation of the Testimonies* (Baltimore, MD, 1945), I, pp. 321ff.

47 Pliny, *Natural History*, Book XXIX, XIII.

48 Martial, *Epigrams*, trans. D. R. Shackleton Bailey (Cambridge, MA, 1993), I.30 and VIII.74.

49 Pliny, *Natural History*, Book XXIII, XXXI–XXXII. In his principal chapter on wine (Book XIV), Pliny seems to be a believer himself, singling out a wine that is 'very good for disorders of the bladder', while noting more generally that 'wine has the property of heating the parts of the body inside when it is drunk and of cooling them when poured on the outside'.

50 Salvatore P. Lucia, *A History of Wine as Therapy* (Philadelphia, PA, 1963), p. 57. Because his writings have not survived, our knowledge of Asclepiades has been pieced together from the later accounts of Pliny and others.

51 Celsus's treatise survives with an English translation by W. G. Spencer first published by Harvard University Press in 1935. The remarks that follow are chiefly taken from Lucia, *A History of Wine as Therapy*, pp. 52ff., who does an excellent job in gathering together the author's thoughts on wine.

52 See John M. Riddle, *Dioscorides on Pharmacy and Medicine* (Austin, TX, 1985), esp. chap. 4.

53 Guido Majno, *The Healing Hand: Man and Wound in the Ancient World* (Cambridge, MA, 1975), p. 399.

54 The basic text on this fascinating subject is Gilbert Watson, *Theriac and Mithridatium, A Study in Therapeutics* (London, 1966).

55 Majno, *The Healing Hand*, p. 414.

56 See Watson, *Theriac*, chap. 3, for the later history of the remedy.

four: Wine in the Middle Ages

1 See, for example, the works illustrated in the *Age of Spirituality, Late Antique and Early Christian Art, Third to Seventh Century*, exh. cat., Metropolitan Museum of Art (New York, 1979), cats. 120–32, 134, 136, 172, 216 and 322.

2 John A. North, *Roman Religion* (New York, 2000), p. 68.

3 Stephen Mitchell, *A History of the Later Roman Empire, AD 284–641* (Malden, MA, 2007), pp. 225 and 227.

4 Recent studies of this material include Paul R. Eddy, *The Jesus Legend: A Case for the Historical Reliability of the Synoptic Jesus Tradition* (Grand Rapids, MI, 2007), and James H. Charlesworth, *The Historical Jesus: An Essential Guide* (Nashville, TN, 2008).

5 The Gospel of Thomas is not included in most modern versions of the Bible but may be found on numerous online sites such as www.thenazareneway.com/thomas.

6 For the attendant nomenclature, see *Eerdmans Dictionary of the Bible*, ed. David N. Freedman (Grand Rapids, MI, 2000), pp. 434 and 791–2.

7 See Dennis E. Smith, *From Symposium to Eucharist: The Banquet in the Early Christian World* (Minneapolis, MN, 2003). In his collection of recipes, Christ's contemporary Marcus Apicius gives the secret of making white wine from red (*The Roman Cookery Book*, trans. B. Flower and E. Rosenbaum, London, 1958, p. 47), a transformation as 'magical' as Jesus's turning wine into his blood.

8 A useful introduction to the subject is provided by Paul Corby Finney, *The Invisible God: The Earliest Christians on Art* (New York, 1994), and Robin Margaret Jensen, *Understanding Early Christian Art* (New York, 2000).

9 For this, and much of what follows, I have relied on Thomas F. Mathews, *The Clash of Gods: A Reinterpretation of Early Christian Art* (Princeton, NJ, 1993). Numerous examples of Dionysian imagery from as late as the sixth or seventh centuries are found in the *Age of Spirituality,* cat. nos 120–32, 134, 136, 172, 216, and 322.

10 As espoused, for example, by André Grabar, *Christian Iconography: A Study of its Origins* (Princeton, NJ, 1968), and *Early Christian Art: From the Rise of Christianity to the Death of Theodosius* (New York, 1968).

11 Mathews, *The Clash of Gods*, p. 141.

12 The early textual evidence has been exaggerated in some modern studies such as Martin Hengel, *Studies in Early Christology* (Edinburgh, 1995), which tend to diminish the differences between the two cults.

13 Jensen, *Understanding Christian Art*, p. 125.

14 Mathews, *The Clash of Gods*, pp. 126–7.

15 *Euripides*, trans. William Arrowsmith (New York, 1974), *Bacchae*, Scene 6–7, 491.

16 On the practicality of Dionysus's androgyny, see Froma I. Zeitlin, 'Playing the Other: Theater, Theatricality, and the Feminine in Greek Drama', in *Nothing to Do With Dionysus?*, ed. John J. Winklin and Froma Zeitlin (Princeton, NJ, 1990), pp. 63–96.

17 This point is made by Tim Unwin, *Wine and the Vine, An Historical Geography of Viticulture and the Wine Trade* (London, 1991), p. 141. See also Joseph A. Jungmann, *The Mass of the Roman Rite, its Origins and Development,* trans. Francis A. Brunner (New York, 1951–5), p. 414.

18 Andrew McGowen, *Ascetic Eucharists, Food and Drink in Early Christian Ritual Meals* (New York, 1999), pp. 233ff. See also Henri Cardinal de Lubac, *Corpus Mysticum: The Eucharist and the Church in the Middle Ages*, trans. Gemma Simmonds et al. (South Bend, IN, 2007), especially Part I.

19 See Paul Bradshaw, *Eucharistic Origins* (New York, 2004), chap. 4. The argument for the presence of water over wine was first put forward in the late nineteenth century by the German scholar Adolf von Harnack.

20 Ibid., chap. 6, p. 1.

21 Jungmann, *The Mass of the Roman Rite*, pp. 38–9.

22 What follows is mainly based on Tim Unwin, *Wine and the Vine*, p. 144ff.

23 See Max Nelson, *The Barbarian's Beverage: A History of Beer in Ancient Europe* (London, 2005), esp. chap. 7.

24 Quotations from Gregory of Tours are given in Stuart Fleming, *Vinum: The Story of Roman Wine* (Glen Mills, PA, 2001), pp. 85–7.

25 Hugh Johnson, *The Story of Wine* (London, 1971), p. 14.

26 William Mole, *Gods, Men, and Wine by William Younger* (London, 1966),
p. 234.

27 *Charlemagne's Courtier: The Complete Einhard*, trans. Paul E. Dutton
(Orchard Park, NY, 1988), p. 31.

28 Ibid., pp. 99–100.

29 Henry R. Loyn and John Percival, *The Reign of Charlemagne: Documents on
Carolingian Government and Administration* (New York, 1976), pp. 64–73,
especially items 8, 48, 62 and 68.

30 Unwin, *Wine and the Vine*, pp. 147–8. See also Desmond Seward, *Monks and
Wine* (London, 1979), who according to Unwin gives more credit to the
clergy than is deserved.

31 Fleming, *Vinum*, p. 85.

32 The only English translation of this is Thomas Owen's from 1805–6, which
is available online at www.ancientlibrary.com/geoponica.

33 Salvatore P. Lucia, *A History of Wine as Therapy* (Philadelphia, PA, 1963),
pp. 92ff.

34 A modern translation of the Regimen can be found in *A Critical Edition of Le
Régime Tresutile et Tresproufitable pour Conserver et Garder la Santé du Corps
Humaine*, trans. Patricia W. Cummins (Chapel Hill, NC, 1976).

35 Unwin, *Wine and the Vine*, p. 179.

36 Lucia, *A History of Wine as Therapy*, p. 101.

37 John Henderson, *The Renaissance Hospital* (New Haven, CT, 2006), chap. 1.

38 Ibid., p. 32.

39 Ibid., pp. 55–6.

40 See Robert J. Forbes, *A Short History of Distillation: From the Beginnings up
to the Death of Cellier Blumenthal* (Leiden, 1970).

41 Both poems are from *Wine, Women, and Song: Medieval Latin Students'
Songs*, trans. John Addington Symonds (London, 1884), pp. 144–53.

42 On the characterization of cooks in the Middle Ages, see my *Tastes and
Temptations, Food and Art in Renaissance Italy* (Berkeley, CA, 2009), p. 26.

43 I illustrate and discuss this work in my chapter 'Sacred Suppers' in *Tastes and
Temptations*, fig. 33.

44 Some have speculated that Ham also had sex with his father, since the sight
of nakedness refers to incestuous behaviour in Leviticus 20.17, but Michael
Coogan, *The New Oxford Annotated Bible*, 3rd edn, ed. Michael Coogan
(New York, 2001), notes to Genesis 9:22–23, thinks this unlikely.

45 See Jack Lewis, *A Study in the Interpretation of Noah and the Flood in Jewish
and Christian Literature* (Leiden, 1968), pp. 177–8 and Don C. Allen, *The
Legend of Noah: Renaissance Rationalism in Art, Science, and Letters* (Urbana,
IL, 1959), p. 73.

46 *The 'Summa Theologica' of St Thomas Aquinas, Literally Translated by Fathers
of the English Dominican Province* (London, 1921), vol. xiii, p. 92.

47 The focal point in interpretations of Genesis 9 turns out not to be Noah's
drunkenness, but the prophetic nature of Ham's vilification. In the medieval
imagination Ham became the archetypal 'other', the sinner whose deeds were
held responsible for a variety of disastrous consequences that included anti-
Semitism, sexual perversion and serfdom. After the Middle Ages, this went
on to include indictments of astrology, idolatry, political tyranny, heresy,
blasphemy and, eventually in modern times, justifications for white racism.
See Lewis, *A Study in the Interpretation of Noah*, passim., Benjamin Braude,

'The Sons of Noah and the Construction of Ethnic and Geographical Identities in the Medieval and Early Modern Periods', *William and Mary Quarterly*, LIV (1997), p. 133, and Stephen Haynes, *Noah's Curse: The Biblical Justification of American Slavery* (New York, 2002), esp. chaps 4 and 5.

48 The most useful discussion I have found on this subject is Horst Wenzel, 'The *Logos* in the Press: Christ in the Wine-Press and the Discovery of Printing', in *Visual Culture and the German Middle Ages*, ed. Kathryn Starkey and H. Wenzel (New York, 2005), pp. 223–49.

49 Cited by Wenzel in ibid., p. 229.

50 As seen for example in numerous illustrated calendar pages that depict the harvest season, one example of which is illustrated in Hugh Johnson, *The Story of Wine*, p. 69 and another on the Art Resource website, www.artres.com, Art194526.

51 Columella, Pliny, Varro and others describe mechanical presses in their treatises. For Roman methods of wine making, see J. J. Rossiter, 'Wine and Oil Processing at Roman Farms in Italy', *Phoenix*, XXXV (1981), pp. 345–61.

52 R. J. Forbes, 'Food and Drink', in *A History of Technology*, ed. Charles Singer et al. (Oxford, 1954–84), vol. II, esp. pp. 112–18. Interestingly, the earliest known illustration of *Christ in the Winepress*, the twelfth-century manuscript of Herrad of Landsperg, already depicts the screw press in use (Forbes, fig. 84).

53 The theme enjoyed its most widespread popularity in Germany, as is evident in the many woodcuts reproduced in *German Single-Leaf Woodcuts before 1500: Anonymous Artists. The Illustrated Bartsch*, vol. CLXIII, ed. Richard Field (New York, 1991).

five: Renaissance Wine

1 Fernand Braudel, *Capitalism and Material Life: 1400–1800*, trans. Miriam Kochan (New York, 1975), p. 162.

2 Tim Unwin, *Wine and the Vine: An Historical Geography of Viticulture and the Wine Trade* (London, 1991), esp. chap. 7, 'Wine in the Age of Discovery'.

3 A. Lynn Martin, *Alcohol, Sex and Gender in Late Medieval and Early Modern Europe* (New York, 2001), p. 5. The same author, pp. 29–30, and Table 2.2, also provides figures on the annual per capita consumption of wine in France and Italy between the fourteenth and seventeenth centuries.

4 *Oeuvres de Henri d'Andeli, trouvère normand du XIII siècle* (Rouen, 1880), pp. 23–31. In like fashion, another thirteenth-century author, the Spanish cleric Francesco Eiximenis, compiled a manuscript entitled *Lo Crestia* (*The Christian*), in which a long digression on wine as a temptation to gluttony is included in a discourse on the Seven Deadly Sins. Eiximenis was unashamedly fond of the wines of his native Catalonia, but recognized the virtues of Greek and Italian wines as well: J. E. Jorge Gracia, 'Rules and Regulations for Drinking Wine in Francesco Eiximenis' "Terc del Crestia" (1384)', *Traditio*, XXXII (1976), pp. 369–85.

5 Petrus de Crescentiis, *Ruralia commoda, Das Wissen des vollkommenen Landwirts um 1300,* ed. Will Richter, vol. II, chap. 4, 'De diversis speciebus vitium'. The book was composed around 1305, and after the invention of printing, reissued many times over.

6 Lorenzo de' Medici, *Selected Poems and Prose*, trans. and ed. J. Thiem

(University Park, PA, 1991), p. 40.

7 'Della qualità dei vini', in *Arte della cucina: Libri di recette; testi sopra lo scalco; il trinciante e i vini*, ed. Emilio Faccioli (Milan, 1966), pp. 313–41.

8 I owe these observations to Ken Albala, *The Banquet: Dining in the Great Courts of Renaissance Europe* (Urbana, IL, 2007), pp. 107–8.

9 See the website www.chateauneuf.com.

10 Unwin, *Wine and the Vine*, p. 232, citing the study of M. Lachiver, *Vins, Vignes et Vignerons: Histoire des Vignobles Français* (Paris, 1988).

11 Braudel, *Capitalism and Material Life*, pp. 165–6. For a comprehensive study of the production and consumption of beer in this period, see Richard W. Unger, *Beer in the Middle Ages and the Renaissance* (Philadelphia, PA, 2004).

12 Ibid., p. 68.

13 Peter Partner, *Renaissance Rome: 1500–1559, A Portrait of a Society* (Berkeley, CA, 1976), p. 88.

14 Jean Verdon, *Boire au Moyen Age* (Paris, 2002), pp. 190ff.

15 Braudel, *Capitalism and Material Life*, p. 165.

16 André Chastel, *The Sack of Rome, 1527*, trans. Beth Archer (Princeton, NJ, 1983), p. 36.

17 Waverly Root, *The Food of Italy* (New York, 1992), p. 448; Burton Anderson, *The Wine Atlas of Italy* (London, 1990), p. 133.

18 Joseph A. Jungmann, *The Mass of the Roman Rite, its Origins and Development,* trans. Francis A. Brunner (New York, 1951–5), II, pp. 37–8.

19 John Varriano, 'At Supper with Leonardo', *Gastronomica*, LXXV (2008), pp. 75–9, and for the food served at other Last Suppers, chap. 4, 'Sacred Suppers', in *Tastes and Temptations*.

20 Giorgio Vasari, *The Lives of the Painters, Sculptors and Architects*, trans. William Gaunt (New York, 1963), II, p. 161. The image reproduced on the ArtStor Digital Library (www.artstor.org) seems to have the best resolution for viewing details.

21 All the copies mentioned here are reproduced on the ArtStor site cited above. For more information about the engraving, see Innis Shoemaker and Elizabeth Broun, *The Engravings of Marc'Antonio Raimondi* (Lawrence, KS, 1981), cat. 30.

22 The transcript of the trial has been published in David Chambers and Brian Pullan, *Venice: A Documentary History 1450–1630* (Toronto, 2001), pp. 232–6.

23 Vasari, *Lives*, III, p. 246. The triangular nimbus above Christ's head was added later in the sixteenth century.

24 *Pontormo's Diary*, trans. R. Mayer (New York, 1982), p. 97. The diary dates from 1554–6, the last years of his life.

25 The sketch is reproduced on the website of the Bridgeman Art Library.

26 See Lee Palmer Wandel, *The Eucharist in the Reformation, Incarnation and Liturgy* (New York, 2006), chaps 3, 4 and 5.

27 Ibid., esp. chap. 5, 'The Catholic Eucharist'.

28 John Gower, *Confessio Amantis*, ed. R. A. Peck, trans. A. Galloway (Kalamazoo, MI, 2004), III, pp. 21ff.

29 The poem is from *Parthenopeus*, II, xii, pp. 7–14 and the translation is that of John Nassichuk who distributed it at his talk 'Bacchus in the Elegiac poetry of Giovanni Pontano' at the *In Vino Veritas* conference held at Binghamton University, 24–5 April 2009.

30 *The Major Latin Poems of Jacopo Sannazaro*, trans. and with commentary by Ralph Nash (Detroit, MI, 1996), pp. 132–5.

31   At http://census.de/. Not all these works are known to have survived to the present day.

32   Ronald Lightbown, *Mantegna: With a Complete Catalogue of the Paintings, Drawings, and Prints* (Berkeley, CA, 1986), 485, cat. 193. On early theories of physiognomics, see Elizabeth Evans, *Physiognomics in the Ancient World* (Philadelphia, PA, 1969).

33   Ascanio Condivi, *The Life of Michelangelo*, trans. A. S. Wohl (University Park, PA, 1999), pp. 19–21; Giorgio Vasari, *The Lives*, IV, pp. 113–14.

34   See Leonard Barkan, *Unearthing the Past, Archaeology and Aesthetics in the Making of Renaissance Culture* (New Haven, CT, 1999), pp. 201–5, and Luba Freedman, 'Michelangelo's Reflections on Bacchus', *Artibus et Historiae*, 47 (2003), pp. 121–35.

35   Freedman, 'Michelangelo's Reflections on Bacchus', pp. 122–3, with the reference to Boissard, cited p. 133 n. 9.

36   Barkan, *Unearthing the Past*, pp. 203 and 382 n. 169.

37   Vasari, *The Lives*, p. 114.

38   Freedman, 'Michelangelo's Reflections on Bacchus', p.125.

39   Condivi, *The Life of Michelangelo*, pp. 23–4.

40   Athenaeus, *The Learned Banqueters*, trans. S. D. Olson (Cambridge, MA, 2006), V, 179e.

41   I have drawn from Charles Carman, 'Michelangelo's *Bacchus* and Divine Frenzy', *Source* II/4 (1983), pp. 6–13, for much of what follows in this discussion. John F. Moffitt later explored some of the same ground in *Inspiration: Bacchus and the Cultural History of a Creation Myth* (Boston, 2005), esp. chap. 2, 'Michelangelo's *Bacchus* as a Historical Metaphor'.

42   Giovanni Pico della Marandola, *On the Dignity of Man*, trans. A. Robert Caponigri (Chicago, 1956), p. 15.

43   *Marsilio Ficino's Commentary on Plato's Symposium*, trans. Sears R. Jayne (Columbia, NY, 1944), 7th speech.

44   Frederick Hartt and David Wilkins, *History of Italian Renaissance Art*, 6th edn (Upper Saddle River, NJ, 2006), p. 342.

45   There were sixteenth-century translations of Ovid into English, French, German, Italian and Spanish. A succinct account of this genre is given by Jacqueline De Weever, *Chaucer Name Dictionary* (New York, 1987), pp. 243–6.

46   For a general survey of the subject see Andreas Emmerling-Scala, *Bacchus in der Renaissance*, 2 vols (Hildesheim, 1994). Among the many specialized studies of the chamber are Dana Goodgal, 'The Camerino of Alfonso I d'Este', *Art History*, I (1978), pp. 162–90; Philip Fehl, 'The Worship of Bacchus and Venus in Bellini's and Titian's Bacchanals for Alfonso d'Este', *Studies in the History of Art*, VI (1974), pp. 37–95, and Andrea Bayer, 'Dosso's Public: The Este Court at Ferrara', in *Dosso Dossi, Court Painter in Renaissance Ferrara*, ed. A. Bayer (New York, 1999), esp. pp. 31–40.

47   *Ovid's Fasti: Roman Holidays*, trans. Betty R. Nagle (Bloomington, IN, 1995), Book I, pp. 391–440.

48   Macrobius, *The Saturnalia*, trans. P. V. Davies (New York, 1969), Book I, chap. 18. I have given a fuller account of the relevant portions of Macrobius' text in chap. 3.

49   Paul Holberton, 'The Choice of Texts for the Camerino Pictures', in *Bacchanals by Titian and Rubens: Papers Given at a Symposium in Nationalmuseum, Stockholm*, ed. G. Cavalli-Björkman (Stockholm, 1987), pp. 57–66.

50 Philostratus, *Imagines, Callistratus: Descriptions*, trans. A. Fairbanks (Cambridge, MA, 1931), Book I, p. 25.

51 Dalyne Shinneman, Appendix IV: 'The Canon in Titian's *Andrians*: A Reinterpretation', in Fehl, 'The Worship of Bacchus and Venus', pp. 37–95, esp. 93–5, discusses the sheet of music in the picture.

52 Most recently in a paper by Philippe Morel entitled 'Bacchus and Christ in Italian Renaissance Painting' given at the Clark Art Institute in Williamstown, Massachusetts, on 4 December 2007.

53 I discuss the erotic poetry and some of the visual images it inspired in chap. 8, 'Erotic Appetites', in my book *Tastes and Temptations*. The eating and drinking habits of Renaissance poets and artists is discussed more fully in chap. 1, 'Artists and Cooks', of the same volume.

54 See James Lynch, 'Giovanni Paolo Lomazzo's *Self-portrait* in the Brera', *Gazette des Beaux-Arts*, LXIV (1964), pp. 189–97, and M. V. Cardi's 'Intorno all'autoritratto in veste di Bacco di Giovan Paolo Lomazzo', *Storia dell'arte*, LXXXI (1994), pp. 182–93 for detailed investigations of the picture's iconography.

55 One thinks, for example, of Annibale Carracci's *Bean Eater* (illustrated online at www.artres.com, Art 1552).

56 For a thematic analysis of Italian literature through the sixteenth century, see D. P. Rotunda, *Motif-Index of the Italian Novella in Prose* (Bloomington, IN, 1942), especially pp. 8–14 (deceptions) and 314 (humour based on drunkenness).

57 Piccolpasso, *The Three Books of the Potter's Art*, facsimile trans. and introduced by R. Lightbown and A. Caiger-Smith (London, 1980), I, fol. 6v–7r, II, 23–4.

58 Wendy M. Watson, *Italian Renaissance Ceramics* (Philadelphia, PA, 2001), cat. 88, pp. 173–4.

59 Rudolf E. A. Drey, *Apothecary Jars: Pharmaceutical Pottery and Porcelain in Europe and the East 1150–1850* (London, 1978). The glossary at the end of the book lists more than 1700 different potions whose names are inscribed on surviving jars.

60 For a modern translation, see *Hildegard's Healing Plants*, trans. B. W. Hozeski (Boston, 2001).

61 Martin, *Alcohol, Sex, and Gender* (New York, 2001), p. 43, citing sixteenth-century texts by Tommaso di Silvestro and Andrew Boorde.

62 See Salvator P. Lucia, *A History of Wine as Therapy* (Philadelphia, PA, 1963).

63 Ibid., p. 140.

64 Mitchell Hammond, 'Paracelsus and the Boundaries of Medicine in Early Modern Augsburg', in *Paracelsian Moments: Science, Medicine, and Astrology in Early Modern Europe*, ed. G. S. Williams and C. D. Gunnoe (Kirksville, MO, 2002), pp. 19–33.

65 John Henderson, *The Renaissance Hospital: Healing the Body and Healing the Soul* (New Haven, CT, 2006), p. 206.

66 Ibid., p. 204.

67 For a brilliant analysis of Italian treatises of the time, see Ken Albala, 'To Your Health: Wine as Food and Medicine in Sixteenth-Century Italy', in *Alcohol: A Social and Cultural History,* ed. M. P. Holt (Oxford, 2006), pp. 11–23. The discussion that follows is mainly taken from his reading of eight texts: Giovanni Battista Confalonieri, *De vini natura disputatio* (Venice, 1535); Antonio

Fumanelli, *Commentario de vino, et facultatibus vini* (Venice, 1536); Girolamo Fracastoro, *Opera Omnia* (Venice, 1555); Gugliemo Grataroli, *De vini natura* (Strasbourg, 1565); Giovanni Battista Scarlino, *Nuovo trattato della varietà, e qualità de vini che vengono in Roma* (Rome, 1554); Bartolomeo Taegio, *L'humore* (Milan, 1564); Jacobus Praefectus, *De diversorum vini generum* (Venice, 1559); and Andrea Bacci, *De naturali vinorum historia* (Rome, 1596).

68 Ibid., pp. 12–13, with citations to the passages quoted below.

69 Ibid., pp. 14–20, with citations to the passages quoted below.

70 Ibid., pp. 18 and 21.

71 *The Praise of Folly,* trans. Clarence H. Miller (New Haven, CT, 1979), pp. 25 and 73.

72 Ibid., Introduction, p. x. During Erasmus' lifetime the book appeared in 36 editions published in eleven cities including two in Italy.

73 Dirk Bax, *Hieronymous Bosch: His Picture-Writing Deciphered* (Rotterdam, 1979), makes a valiant effort to explain the artist's iconography. See 'jug, jar, pitcher, pot', as indexed, for a discussion of the wine vessels that appear in his pictures.

74 See Laura D. Gelfand, 'Social Status and Sin: Reading Bosch's Prado *Seven Deadly Sins and Four Last Things Painting*', in *The Seven Deadly Sins: From Communities to Individuals*, ed. R. Newhauser (Leiden, 2007), pp. 229–56.

75 The first quotation is from *Jacob's Well*, a collection of fifteenth-century sermons, and the second from *The Goodman of Paris*, a late fourteenth-century behavioural manual. Both are cited by Susan E. Hill, '"The Ooze of Gluttony": Attitudes Towards Food, Eating, and Excess in the Middle Ages', in *The Seven Deadly Sins*, pp. 57–70, esp. 66.

76 The consumption of beer at the time has been estimated at twelve times that of wine. See Unger, *Beer in the Middle Ages and the Renaissance*, pp. 108, 132.

77 Schoen's print illustrates *Die vier Wunderberlichen Eygenschaft und Würckckung des Weins* (The Four Wonderous Properties of Wine and their Effects), popular verses penned by Hans Sachs, a fellow resident of Nuremberg. The pertinent passages are translated on the State Library of South Australia website www.winelit.slsa.sa.gov.au/wine.

78 Unger, *Beer in the Middle Ages and Renaissance*, p. 229.

79 Sermon taken from Luther's Church Postil of 1525 (*The Complete Sermons of Martin Luther*, ed. and trans. John N. Lenker (Grand Rapids, MI, 1988), pp. 55–69).

80 *The Essays of Michel de Montaigne*, trans. M. A. Screech (London, 1991), pp. 382, 385 and 387.

81 Ernest S. Bates, *Touring in 1600, A Study in the Development of Travel as a Means of Education* (Boston, 1911), p. 242.

82 Gugliemo Gratioli's treatise *De vini natura* (1565) simply affirms the stereotype while *De diversorum vini generum* (1559) by the Sicilian physician Jacobus Praefectus suggests the climatic cause (Albala, 'To Your Health', pp. 16–20).

83 See Mack P. Holt, 'Europe Divided: Wine, Beer, and the Reformation in Sixteenth-Century Europe', in *Alcohol: A Social and Cultural History*, pp. 25–40.

84 Ibid., pp. 32–3 for this and the quote that follows.

85 Ibid., p. 34, and D. F. Wright, ed., *Martin Bucer: Reforming Church and Community* (Cambridge, 1994), especially the chapters by Gottfried Hammann on Bucer in England and Martin Greschat on Bucer's influence on Calvin.

86 *Luther: Letters of Spiritual Counsel*, ed. and trans. Theodore G. Tappert, in *Library of Christian Classics*, vol. XVIII (Philadelphia, PA, 1955), pp. 84–7. The letter is also published in Richard Marius, *Martin Luther* (Cambridge, 1999), pp. 122–3.

87 Ibid., pp. 105–7.

88 Janny de Moor, 'Dutch Cooking and Calvin', in *Oxford Symposium on Food and Cookery, Proceedings of the Oxford Symposium on Food and Cookery*, ed. Harlan Walker (Devon, 1995), p. 97.

89 William J. Bouwsma, *John Calvin: A Sixteenth-Century Portrait* (New York, 1988), p. 136.

90 De Moor, 'Dutch Cooking and Calvin', p. 98.

91 See Christa Grössinger, *Humour and Folly in Secular and Profane Prints of Northern Europe, 1430–1540* (London, 2002), esp. chap. 8, 'Scatology and the Grotesque'. Illustrations of the other three woodcuts by Weiditz may be found in Max Geisberg, *The German Single-Leaf Woodcut: 1500–1550* (New York, 1974), G1510, G1524 and G1515. For an overview of popular moralizing imagery of the time, see R. W. Scribner, *For the Sake of Simple Folk: Popular Propaganda for the German Reformation* (Cambridge, 1981), esp. chap. 4, 'Popular Culture'.

92 *François Rabelais: Gargantua and Pantagruel*, trans. and ed. M. A. Screech (New York, 2006), p. 225. Screech places *Gargantua* after the first two books of *Pantagruel* (and explains why on pages xi–xii of his Introduction), but I have maintained the traditional sequence of placing *Gargantua* first.

93 Ibid., p. 829.

94 Ibid., pp. 205, 226 and 872.

95 Mikhail Bahktin, *Rabelais and his World*, trans. Hélène Iswolsky (Bloomington, IN, 1984), esp. chap. 3, 'Popular Festive Forms and Images in Rabelais'.

96 Bahktin, *Rabelais*, pp. 342–3.

97 François Rabelais, *Gargantua*, pp. 229, 135, 146, 404, 408, and 667. A posthumously published essay attributed to Rabelais, *Traité de bon usage de vin*, further expands on the benefits of wine drinking while warning the reader to avoid the consumption of beer and water. The original manuscript is in the Library of the National Museum of Prague and it has recently been republished in both French and Italian. I consulted the Italian edition, *Trattato sul buon uso del vino*, critical edition with notes by Patrik Ourednik, trans. A. Catalano (Palermo, 2009).

98 Screech catalogues these events in the Chronology that precedes his translation of Rabelais' text.

99 The first view is that of Screech, *François Rabelais*, Introduction, p. xix, and the second is Florence M. Weinberg's in *The Wine and The Will: Rabelais's Bacchic Christianity* (Detroit, MI, 1972), pp. 34 and 45–66. Weinberg is also author of the entry on wine in *The Rabelais Encyclopedia*, ed. Elizabeth C. Zegura (Westport, CT, 2004), pp. 262–3, where she again emphasizes 'Rabelais's preoccupation with wine symbolism'. Donald Frame's review of modern Rabelais scholarship in the introduction to his own translation of the *Complete Works of Rabelais* (Berkeley, CA, 1991), pp. xliv–xlvii, fails to cite Weinberg's contribution.

six: The Seventeenth and Eighteenth Centuries

1 *Bacco in Toscana* is reproduced in Emilio Faccioli, *Arte della Cucina, libri de ricette, testi sopra lo scalco, il trinciante e i vini dal XIV al XIX secolo* (Milan, 1966), II, pp. 209–36. The unflattering comment is from Peter Brand and Lino Pertile, ed., *The Cambridge History of Italian Literature* (New York, 1999), p. 317.

2 I discuss the increased sense of regionalism in seventeenth-century books of cookery in *Tastes and Temptations: Food and Art in Renaissance Italy* (Berkeley, CA, 2009), chap. 3.

3 Hugh Johnson, *The Story of Wine* (London, 2005), p. 107.

4 *The Diary of Samuel Pepys*, ed. Robert Latham and Matthew Williams (Berkeley, CA, 1970), VI, p. 151.

5 Rod Phillips, *A Short History of Wine* (New York, 2002), p. 135.

6 Eleanor S. Godfrey, *The Development of English Glassmaking, 1560–1640* (Oxford, 1975), pp. 229–32.

7 For a discussion of the history of corks and corkscrews, see Jancis Robinson, *The Oxford Companion to Wine* (New York, 2006), pp. 200–2.

8 Phillips, *A Short History of Wine*, p. 137.

9 Thus, for example, the expansion of the paper-making industry to satisfy the needs of the newly invented printing press in the late fifteenth century prompted artists to use the surplus of paper for drawing and printmaking.

10 Giovanni Rebora, *Culture of the Fork: A Brief History of Food in Europe*, trans. A. Sonnenfeld (New York, 1998), pp. 40–41.

11 Robinson, *The Oxford Companion to Wine*, pp. 656–9.

12 Phillips, *A Short History of Wine*, p. 138.

13 Karen MacNeil, *The Wine Bible* (New York, 2001), p. 162.

14 *Journal de la santé du roi Louis XIV de l'année 1647 à l'année 1711* (Paris, 1862), p. 211, and online at http://gallica.bnf.fr.

15 The play was George Etherege's *She Would if She Could* (A. Lynne Martin, *Alcohol, Sex, and Gender in Late Medieval and Early Modern Europe*, New York, 2001, p. 50).

16 Robinson, *The Oxford Companion to Wine*, p. 719. For a full discussion of early efforts at winemaking in the United States, see Thomas Pinney, *A History of Wine in America: From the Beginnings to Prohibition* (Berkeley, CA, 1989), especially Parts I and II.

17 This is one of the few early texts on wine to be reprinted (Sala Bolognese, 1989).

18 A bibliography of some of these is given in Salvatore P. Lucia, *A History of Wine as Therapy* (Philadelphia, PA, 1963), pp. 220–21.

19 William Buchan, *Domestic Medicine, or, A Treatise on the Prevention and Cure of Diseases by Regimen and Simple Medicines* (1769). Buchan's book went through nineteen editions in Europe and America before his death in 1805. The quotations that follow are taken from the first American edition (Fairhaven, VT, 1798).

20 As I have pointed out elsewhere, the Ushak carpet covering the table, the Savonarola chair, and the maiolica pottery can each be compared with known examples from the period (*Caravaggio: The Art of Realism*, University Park, PA, 2006, chap. 8). The expression *tra il sacro e profano* was coined by

Cardinal Ottavio Paravicino in 1603.

21 Howard Hibbard, *Caravaggio* (New York, 1983), p. 352.

22 Cesare Ripa's emblem in his *Iconologia* includes a faun with a bunch of grapes wearing a crown of herbs on his head. Donald Posner, *Annibale Carracci: A Study in the Reform of Italian Painting around 1590* (London, 1971), pp. 314–15.

23 John Florio, *A Worlde of Words, or Most Copious and Exact Dictionarie in Italian and English* (London, 1598), p. 271, where the expression *dare le pesche* is also defined as 'to yield one's bum, or consent to unnatural sinn'. For more on this subject, see Adrienne Von Lates, 'Caravaggio's Peaches and Academic Puns', *Word and Image*, XI (1995), pp. 55–60.

24 The effeminacy of Bacchus originated with Aeschylus and Euripedes, both of whom call him 'womanly' (Otto, *Dionysus, Myth and Cult*, trans. R. B. Palmer, Bloomington, IN, 1965, p. 176).

25 *Philostratus: Imagines; Callistatus: Descriptions*, trans. A. Fairbanks (Cambridge, MA, 1931), pp. 403–7.

26 I discuss Del Monte's collections and the use Caravaggio may have had for them in *Caravaggio: The Art of Realism*, p. 23.

27 For the culture of collecting and viewing at this time, see Francis Haskell, *Patrons and Painters: Art and Society in Baroque Italy* (New York, 1971).

28 Charles Dempsey, *Annibale Carracci: The Farnese Gallery, Rome* (New York, 1995), p. 44.

29 G. P. Bellori, *The Lives of Annibale and Agostino Carracci*, trans. C. Enggass (University Park, PA, 1968), p. 34. John R. Martin, *The Farnese Gallery* (Princeton, NJ, 1965), offers the most erudite of the modern explanations.

30 Charles Dempsey, '*Et nos Cedamus Amori*: Observations on the Farnese Gallery', *Art Bulletin*, I (1968), pp. 363–74. The occasion, Dempsey suggests, may have been the wedding in 1600 of one of the members of the Farnese family.

31 For a thoughtful review of the conflicting literature, see Anthony Hughes, 'What's The Trouble with the Farnese Gallery? An Experiment in Reading Pictures', *Art History*, XI/3 (1988), pp. 335–48.

32 See J. Perez-Sanchez and N. Spinosa, *Jusepe de Ribera 1591–1652* (New York, 1992), p. 187, and C. Felton and W. Jordan, eds, *Jusepe de Ribera: Lo Spagnoletto 1591–1652* (Fort Worth, TX, 1982), pp. 109–11.

33 I am grateful to Giulia Bernardini for furnishing me with a copy of her unpublished MA thesis, 'Intoxication and Excoriation: On the Depiction of Baseness in Jusepe de Ribera's *Drunken Silenus* and *Apollo and Marysas*' (University of Colorado, 2006), whose interpretation I follow.

34 The identifications are based on comparisons with known portraits of the four figures that are currently in museums in Florence, Detroit, Boston and Berlin.

35 Peter C. Sutton, 'Introduction', in *The Age of Rubens*, ed. P. C. Sutton (Boston, 1993), p. 13.

36 José López-Rey, *Velázquez' Work and World* (New York, 1968), p. 52 has called this 'a baroque double-edged parody of the false worlds of the fable and of sinful human ways, and the laugh is made heartier, healthier, and pregnant, as the clowning tosspots vie in their bearing with the loutish nudes of Bacchus'.

37 The basic study of this fascinating group of artists is G. J. Hoogewerff, *De Bentvueghels* (with an English summary) (The Hague, 1952). See also Peter

Schatborn and Judith Verbene, *Drawn to Warmth: 17th-Century Dutch Artists in Italy* (Zwolle, 2001).

38 For these Northern artists, the principal source is David Levine and Ekkehard Mai, *I Bambocciand: Niederländische Malerrebellen im Rom des Barock* (Milan, 1991). Levine's 'The Bentvueghels: 'Bande Academique'' in *IL60: Essays Honoring Irving Lavin on his Sixtieth Birthday* (New York, 1990), pp. 207–26.

39 The classic study of this painting is Dora Panofsky, 'Narcissus and Echo: Notes on Poussin's "Birth of Bacchus" in the Fogg Museum of Art', *Art Bulletin*, XXXI (1949), pp. 112–20. Other illuminating interpretations are Stephen Bann, *The True Vine: On Visual Representation and the Western Tradition* (Cambridge, 1989), pp. 150–56, and Elizabeth Cropper and Charles Dempsey, *Nicholas Poussin: Friendship and the Love of Painting* (Princeton, NJ, 1996), pp. 294–302.

40 My translation is adapted from Cropper and Dempsey, *Nicholas Poussin*, p. 295.

41 Philostratus, *Imagines*, Book I, p. 23.

42 Ibid., p. 302.

43 This particular interpretation was first put forward by Oskar Bätschmann in *Nicholas Poussin: Dialectics of Painting* (cited by Bann, *The True Vine*, p. 153).

44 The remark is from Testa's biographer, Joachim von Sandrart, as quoted by James Clifton, 'Pietro Testa', Oxford Art Online at www.oxfordartonline.com.

45 For a full discussion of the print, see Elizabeth Cropper, *Pietro Testa 1612–1650: Prints and Drawings* (Philadelphia, PA, 1988), cat. 114, pp. 245–9.

46 Elizabeth Cropper, *The Ideal of Painting: Pietro Testa's Düsseldorf Notebook* (Princeton, NJ, 1984).

47 Testa's biography is given by Cropper in *Pietro Testa 1612–1650: Prints and Drawings*, pp. xi–xxxvi.

48 The work, which dates to *c.* 1620–40, is published in Carola Fiocco and Gabriella Gherardi, *Museo del vino di Torgiano: Ceramiche* (Perugia, 1991), cat. 211.

49 I have taken this and the three quotations that follow from Martin, *Alcohol, Sex, and Gender*, pp. 48–9, who gives full citations.

50 Ibid., p. 49.

51 See Varriano, *Caravaggio: The Art of Realism*, pp. 129–35, for a discussion of the artist's epistemological peers.

52 Leonard J. Slatkes and Wayne Franits, *The Paintings of Hendrick ter Brugghen: Catalogue Raisonné* (Philadelphia, PA, 2007), pp. 156–7, cat. a48.

53 *Essaies upon the Five Senses* (London, 1620), pp. 45–57.

54 See Schama's groundbreaking article, 'The Unruly Realm: Appetite and Restraint in Seventeenth-Century Holland', *Daedalus*, CVIII (1979), pp. 103–23.

55 Ibid., p. 112.

56 Simon Schama, *An Embarrassment of Riches: An Interpretation of Dutch Culture in the Golden Age* (New York, 1987).

57 For the role that comedy plays throughout Steen's oeuvre, see Mariët Westermann, *The Amusements of Jan Steen: Comic Painting in the Seventeenth Century* (Zwolle, 1997).

58 David Courtwright, *Forces of Habit: Drugs and the Making of the Modern World* (Cambridge, MA, 2001), pp. 1–5, has called the period after 1500 the age of the 'psycho-active revolution'.

59 For a discussion of damsels, dandies, and the role wine plays in his art, see the essay by Albert Blankert, 'Vermeer's Modern Themes and their Tradition', in *Johannes Vermeer* (Washington, DC, 1995), esp. pp. 34–7.

60 The treatise, by Cornelis de Bie, was published in 1661 (cited by Blankert, 'Vermeer's Modern Themes', p. 33).

61 See Schama, *An Embarrassment of Riches*, especially Part Two, 'Doing and Not Doing', for a discussion of Dutch prosperity and the reactions it provoked.

62 Calvin's views on luxury are collected by William J. Bouwsma, *John Calvin: Sixteenth-Century Portrait* (New York, 1988), esp. pp. 57–8. See also Janny de Moor, 'Dutch Cooking and Calvin', in *Cooks and Other People: Proceedings of the Oxford Symposium on Food and Cookery* (Devon, 1999), pp. 94–105.

63 Mark Morford, *Stoics and Neostoics: Rubens and the Circle of Lipsius* (Princeton, NJ, 1991).

64 For concise discussions of both *memento mori* and *vanitas* in art and literature, see the first two chapters of Kristine Koozin, *The Vanitas Still Lifes of Harmen Steenwyck: Metaphoric Realism* (Lewiston, ME, 1990).

65 According to statistics cited by Jutta-Annette Page, *The Art of Glass: The Toledo Museum of Art*, exh. cat., Toledo Museum of Art (2005), cat. 43, the *roemer* was especially popular in Germany and the Netherlands, with one glasshouse in Amsterdam working twelve hours a day to produce them and only three making beer glasses.

66 One, dated 1643, in the Corning Museum of Glass, represents an Old Testament grape harvest accompanied by the inscription 'Kent u Selven' (Know Thyself) and 'Nota Bene', followed by a verse extolling wine taken in moderation:

> Look, this wine taken with a plan
> Brought joy to many a man
> But if one indulges too much
> Wrong wine creates sorrow as such.

See W. Franz, A. Strauss and J. Sichel, eds, *Glass Drinking Vessels from the Collection of Jerome Strauss*, exh. cat., Corning Museum of Glass (1955), cat. 97. I am grateful to Elisabeth de Bièvre for the translation from Dutch.

67 See the excellent catalogue entry on this picture (cat. 6) in James Welu et al., *Judith Leyster: A Dutch Master and Her World*, exh. cat., Worcester Art Museum (1993).

68 As seen, for example, in works by Hieronymous Bosch and Adrian Brouwer (illustrated by Welu, *Judith Leyster*, figs 6b and 6d).

69 The verse was composed by Samuel Ampzing to accompany an engraving by Jan van de Velde of *Death with an Hourglass,* illustrated in Welu, *Judith Leyster,* fig. 6g.

70 Ibid., pp. 160–61.

71 Ibid., fig. 6e.

72 The website www.playshakespeare.com is especially useful for searches of this kind.

73 'The Act to Repress the Odious and Loathsome Sin of Drunkenness' of 1606 was by no means the first law that attempted to regulate drunkenness in England. For others, see the chapter 'Grids of Order: Regulation', in the

forthcoming *Public Drinking in the Early Modern World: Voices from the Tavern, 1500–1800*, ed. Thomas E. Brennan (London, 2011).

74 *Henry IV, Part II*, IV.iii.103–36.

75 *Macbeth*, II.iii.32–9.

76 One Victorian temperance tract masquerading as a work of scholarship has made this point: Frederick Sherlock, *Shakespeare on Temperance, with Brief Annotations* (1882), reprinted (New York, 1972).

77 Richard Brathwaite, *A Solemn Joviall Disputation, Theoreticke and Practicke: Briefly Shadowing the Law of Drinking* (London, 1617). The fact that the book went through at least four editions before 1627 is an indication of its popularity. For a social history of the English alehouse, see Peter Clark, *The English Alehouse: A Social History 1200–1830* (New York, 1983).

78 Cedric C. Brown, 'Sons of Beer and Sons of Ben: Drink as a Social Marker in Seventeenth-Century England', in *A Pleasing Sinne: Drink and Conviviality in Seventeenth-Century England*, ed. Adam Smyth (Cambridge, 2004), pp. 3–20.

79 *The Poetical Works of Robert Herrick*, ed. L. C. Martin (Oxford, 1956), p. 259.

80 Ibid., p. 187.

81 For this aspect of Herrick's verse, see A. Leigh Deneef, *'This Poetic Liturgie': Robert Herrick's Ceremonial Mode* (Durham, NC, 1974), pp. 167–72.

82 *The Poetical Works*, p. 122.

83 The quotation is from John Toland's contemporary biography, cited in William R. Parker, *Milton: A Biographical Commentary*, 2nd revd edn G. Campbell (Oxford, 1999), vol. II, p. 1096.

84 The lines are from *Paradise Lost*, Book VII, and *Comus*, lines 46–7 respectively.

85 *Samson Agonistes*, lines 1673–89.

86 From the Manchester Ballads, II, 14; as transcribed in Angelica McShane Jones, 'Roaring Royalists and Ranting Brewers: The Politicisation of Drink and Drunkenness in Political Broadside Ballads from 1640 to 1689', in *A Pleasing Sinne*, pp. 69–87, esp. 72. Much of what follows in this discussion is based on her essay.

87 The ballad was called *The Loyal Subject (as is reason) Drinks good sack and is free from Treason* (Jones, 'Roaring Royalists', p. 80).

88 Robinson, *The Oxford Companion to Wine*, pp. 172–3.

89 See Charles Ludington, '"Be Sometimes to your Country True": The Politics of Wine in England, 1660–1714', in *A Pleasing Sinne*, pp. 89–106, for more on this issue.

90 This is the topic of a forthcoming paper by Charles Ludington, 'Politeness, Wine Connoisseurship, and Political Power in Early Eighteenth-Century England'.

91 Phillips, *A Short History of Wine*, pp. 135–6.

92 Jefferson's taste in wines have been extensively written about. Here, I primarily rely upon Jim Gabler, *Passions: The Wines and Travels of Thomas Jefferson* (Baltimore, MD, 1995).

93 Ibid., pp. 289–91.

94 Ibid., especially pp. 3–8.

95 Robinson, *The Oxford Companion to Wine*, p. 719.

96 Franklin's interests in wine are less well known than Jefferson's, but a useful compilation of his thoughts with quotations from *Poor Richard's Almanac* may be found on the website www.wineintro.com/history.

seven: Modern Wine

1 The construction of the French railway system in the third quarter of the nineteenth century made it even easier for wines from nearly every region to become available throughout the country. See Roger Price, *The Economic Modernization of France, 1730–1880* (London, 1975), p. 76.

2 Tim Unwin, *Wine and the Vine, An Historical Geography of Viticulture and the Wine Trade* (London, 1991), p. 280.

3 Ibid., pp. 224–5.

4 Ibid., p. 225.

5 Jancis Robinson, *The Oxford Companion to Wine* (New York, 2006), pp. 123–4, and Thomas Pinney, *A History of Wine in America: From Prohibition to the Present* (Berkeley, CA, 2005), esp. chaps 9–12.

6 Pinney, *A History of Wine in America*, p. 305.

7 Robinson, *The Oxford Companion to Wine*, pp. 543–4; and Unwin, *Wine and the Vine*, pp. 283–4.

8 For an account of the worldwide phylloxera epidemic, see Christy Campbell, *Phylloxera: How Wine was Saved for the World* (New York, 2004).

9 Patrice Debré, *Louis Pasteur*, trans. E. Forster (Baltimore, MD, 1998), p. 231.

10 In a letter dated 6 May 1855 Fenton describes the circumstances under which this posed photograph was taken (*Roger Fenton, Photographer of the Crimean War; His Photographs and his Letters from the Crimea,* with an essay on his life and work by Helmut and Alison Gernsheim, New York, 1973, p. 74).

11 Rod Phillips, *A Short History of Wine* (New York, 2002), p. 294.

12 Ibid., pp. 293–4.

13 The quotation is from the website Herbdata New Zealand at www.herbdatanz.com. under the heading of 'Medicated Wine'.

14 Salvatore P. Lucia, *A History of Wine as Therapy* (Philadelphia, PA, 1963), p. 145.

15 Ibid., pp. 145 and 221.

16 Ibid., p. 147.

17 Roberts Bartholomew, *A Treatise on the Practice of Medicine,* 5th edn (New York, 1883), pp. 895–905.

18 E. Fullerton Cook and Charles H. LaWall, eds, *Remington's Practice of Pharmacy*, 8th edn (Philadelphia, PA, 1936), p. 1018.

19 The rival Pharmacopoeial Convention had deleted all wines and wine-based medicines from its list of approved medications a year earlier. See Joseph P. Remington, *The Practice of Pharmacy: A Treatise*, 6th edn (Philadelphia, PA, 1917), pp. 512–19, which includes 'wine of beef', 'wine of iron' and 'wine of white ash'. Until the United States Pharmacopoeia (founded in 1820) and the National Formulary (founded in 1888) officially merged in 1975, the two publications operated somewhat independently of one another, a fact that explains variations between them.

20 Fran Grace, *Carrie A. Nation: Retelling the Life* (Bloomington, IN, 2001), esp. pp. 123 and 264.

21 Robert C. Fuller, *Religion and Wine: A Cultural History of Wine Drinking in the United States* (Knoxville, TN, 1996), pp. 91–2.

22 For a provocative discussion of the many forces that sustained temperance movements throughout the world at this time, see Steve Charters, *Wine and*

Society: The Social and Cultural Context of a Drink (Boston, 2006), pp. 272–83.

23 Fronia E. Wissman, Oxford Art Online entry on Corot (www.oxfordartonline.com).

24 See Bruce Laughton, *Honoré Daumier* (New Haven, CT, 1996), pp. 42–6.

25 One also thinks of the caricatures of drunken servants made earlier in the century by Louis-Leopold Boilly, especially in his illustrated volume, *Recueil de Grimace* (Susan Siegfried, *The Art of Louis-Leopold Boilly: Modern Life in Napoleonic France* (New Haven, CT, 1995).

26 Robert L. Herbert, *Impressionism: Art, Leisure, and Parisian Society* (New Haven, CT, 1988), p. 65.

27 See also W. Scott Haine, 'Drink, Sociability, and Social Class in France, 1789–1945', in *Alcohol: A Social and Cultural History,* ed. Mack P. Holt (Oxford, 2006), pp. 121–44. The quotation is from Edward King, *My Paris, French Character Sketches* (Boston, 1869) (cited by Herbert, *Impressionism,* p. 65).

28 Phillips, *A Short History of Wine,* p. 241.

29 Ibid., p. 224. This statistic is for the period 1840–82.

30 For a picture of their relationship in this period, see Julia Frey, *Toulouse-Lautrec: A Life* (New York, 1994), especially pp. 227–9.

31 Jean-Charles Sournia, *A History of Alcoholism* (Oxford, 1990), especially chap. 4, 'Magnus Huss and Alcoholism, 1807–1890'.

32 Ibid., pp. 54 and 75–80.

33 Alfred Delvau, *Histoire anecdotique des cafés et cabarets de Paris,* 1862; cited by Herbert, *Impressionism,* p. 74.

34 Gerd Woll, *Edvard Munch: Complete Paintings. Catalogue Raisonné* I, 1880–1897 (London, 2008), cat. 348.

35 Jane Lee, Oxford Art Online entry on Derain (www.oxfordartonline.com).

36 Wine labels should perhaps not be forgotten in this context either. The practice of affixing descriptive paper labels to bottles began in the nineteenth century when pre-bottled wine became common (Robinson, *The Oxford Companion to Wine,* pp. 97 and 385), but in modern times these have tended to become pictorial advertisements for the wines themselves. Old master paintings have occasionally been reproduced, and since 1945, one vineyard, Château Mouton-Rothschild, has commissioned an artist to design the upper register of its label. Distinguished painters like Francis Bacon, Georges Braque, Marc Chagall, Joan Miró, Pablo Picasso and Andy Warhol have contributed to the programme. For the full collection of labels, see www.theartistlabels.com/mouton/.

37 Picasso's Dionysian imagery is the subject of Diane Headley's essay 'Picasso's Response to Classical Art' in *Dionysos and his Circle,* ed. C. Houser (Cambridge, MA, 1979), pp. 94–100.

38 Pablo Picasso, *Vollard Suite* (Madrid, 1993), especially pls 57, 59 and 67.

39 For a history of champagne glasses, see Tom Stevenson, *Christie's World Encyclopedia of Champagne and Sparkling Wine* (Bath, 2002), p. 31.

40 For the Vatican's collection of sacred modern art, see Giovanni Fallani, *Collezione vaticana d'arte religiosa moderna* (Milan, 1974).

41 The information and quotation is from the museum's 2008 wall label (www.tate.org.uk).

42 See Denis McMamara, 'The Dangerous Path: Leonard Porter and the Sincerity of Hope', *The Classicist,* VIII (2009), pp. 118–27.

43 Private communication from the artist.

44 In an interview printed in the catalogue of his most recent exhibition (2007), Ligare uses the terms 'altar-like spaces' and 'metaphysical' realism to describe his work, but it is clear that formal values rather than iconography are his principal concern (www.davidligare.com/interview.html).

45 Private communication from the artist.

46 Robert Louis Stevenson, *The Strange Case of Dr Jekyll and Mr Hyde* (Peterborough, OH, 2005), p. 28.

47 Robert Louis Stevenson, *The Silverado Squatters* (New York, 1923), p. 25.

48 *Don Juan*, Canto Two, verse 178, in *The Complete Poetical Works of Lord Byron,* ed. Jerome J. McGann (New York, 1980–93), p. 144.

49 Ibid., Canto Four, verse 24, p. 819.

50 Ibid., Canto Four, verse 25, p. 211.

51 *The Collected Poems of W. B. Yeats* (New York, 1956), p. 92.

52 'Ode to a Nightingale', in *The Complete Poetry and Selected Prose of John Keats*, ed. H. E. Briggs (New York, 1951), p. 291.

53 See Everett Carter, *Wine and Poetry*, Chapbook 5 (Davis, CA, 1976), pp. 15–16, for a fuller interpretation of the meaning of wine in the poem.

54 Joanna Richardson, *Baudelaire* (New York, 1994), pp. 232–7.

55 Charles Pierre Baudelaire, trans. Roy Campbell (London, 1952), p. 141.

56 Robert Browning, 'Aristophanes' Apology', in *The Complete Poetic and Dramatic Works of Robert Browning* (Boston, 1895), p. 644.

57 Browning, 'Apollo and the Fates', in *The Complete Poetic and Dramatic Works*, p. 950.

58 Letter to Thomas Higginson, July 1862 (*The Letters of Emily Dickinson*, ed. Thomas H. Johnson (Cambridge, MA, 1958), p. 411.

59 *A Concordance to the Poems of Emily Dickinson*, ed. S. P. Rosenbaum (Ithaca, NY, 1964), pp. 837, 446–67 and 749.

60 *The Poems of Emily Dickinson*, ed. R. W. Franklin (Cambridge, MA, 1999), p. 400.

61 Ibid., p. 65.

62 Jack Capps, *Emily Dickinson's Reading, 1836–86* (Cambridge, MA, 1966), pp. 48 and 157, who, noting biblical analogies, writes 'the poem is a statement of one of the basic tenets of Christian stewardship'.

63 Pablo Neruda, *Elemental Odes*, trans. Margaret S. Peden (London, 1991), p. 165.

64 For their relationship, see Matilde Urrutia, *My Life with Pablo Neruda* (Stanford, CA, 2004).

65 *The Collected Poems of Tennessee Williams*, ed. D. Roessel and N. Moschovakis (New York, 2002), p. 113.

66 Christopher Conlon, '"Fox-Teeth in Your Heart": Sexual Self-Portraiture in the Poetry of Tennessee Williams', *The Tennessee Williams Annual Review*, no. 4 (2001), p. 1, online at www.tennesseewilliamsstudies.org.

67 Suzanne Daley, 'Williams Choked to Death on a Bottle Cap', *New York Times*, 27 February 1983.

68 The transcription is from the editor's introduction, 'Planting the Vines: An Introduction', in *Wine and Philosophy: A Symposium on Thinking and Drinking*, ed. F. Allhoff (Oxford, 2007), pp. 2–3.

69 See ibid. for a fuller discussion of the role wine plays in the film.

70 Guido Majno, *The Healing Hand: Man and Wound in the Ancient World*

(Cambridge, MA, 1975), p. 187.

71 Ibid., pp. 188 and 498, n. 261. Majno reports that the first experiment was conducted by Dr D. Kekessy of the Institut d'Hygiène at the University of Geneva, and the second, by M. Draczynski, was published in the journal *Wein und Rebe* in 1951.

72 M. E. Weisse and R. S. Moore, 'Antimicrobial Effects of Wine', in *Wine: A Scientific Exploration*, ed. M. Sandler and R. Pinder (New York, 2003), pp. 299–313.

73 Ibid., p. 306.

74 Majno, *The Healing Hand*, pp. 188 and 498, n. 265.

75 The key assumption in most discussions of wine's benefits is *moderation*. For a clear-headed study of the dangers of over-consumption, see Frederick Adolf Paola, '*In Vino Sanitas*', in *Wine and Philosophy*, pp. 63–78.

76 Giorgio Ricci et al., 'Alcohol Consumption and Coronary Heart-Disease', *The Lancet*, CCCXIII/8131 (1979), 1404.

77 The programme was presented in America by Morley Safer on CBS's *60 Minutes*.

78 Mitch Frank, 'Harnessing Wine's Healing Powers', *The Wine Spectator*, 31 May 2009, pp. 54–58.

79 Arthur L. Klatsky, 'Wine, Alcohol and Cardiovascular Diseases', in *Wine: A Scientific Exploration*, p. 125, wrote 'Hypothetical considerations about a possible benefit from the anti-anxiety or stress-reducing effects of alcohol have no good supporting data.' To my knowledge, the only publication to suggest that 'on the psychic level [wine] increases cerebral activity in a euphoric way' is the semi-scientific work of E. A. Maury, *Wine is the Best Medicine* (Kansas City, KS, 1977).

80 Dr David Sinclair at the Harvard Medical School has been at the forefront of such studies.

81 Some of these points are made by Klatsky in the article cited above, p. 108.

82 M. Bobak and M. Marmot, 'Wine and Heart Disease: A Statistical Approach', in *Wine: A Scientific Exploration*, pp. 92–107.

83 Mathilde Cathiard-Thomas, one of the organizers of the centers and owner of a company in the cosmetics business, has co-authored with Corinne Pezard a little book entitled *La santé par le raisin et la vinothérapie* which ostensibly covers the history of medicinal wines but ends with a lengthy discourse on the benefits of the products her company manufactures. It was originally published in France in 1998, but I consulted the Italian translation, *Vinoterapia: In salute con il vino e con la vite* (Rome, 2007).

eight: Outside the Western Tradition

1 See Patricia Berger, *The Art of Wine in East Asia* (San Francisco, CA, 1986).

2 My discussion of these texts is greatly indebted to Kathryn Kueny, *The Rhetoric of Sobriety: Wine in Early Islam* (Albany, NY, 2001). Her work, in turn, acknowledges the fundamental studies of Ignaz Goldziher and A. J. Wensinck, whose relevant publications are cited in her bibliography.

3 Ibid. pp. 4–5.

4 Sura 5: 90–91 (al-Ma'ida), as quoted in Keuny, *The Rhetoric*., p. 6.

5 Sura 47:15 (Muhammad), as quoted in Kueny, *The Rhetoric*, p. 14.

6 Sura 56:18–19 (al-Wāqi'a) , as quoted in Kueny, *The Rhetoric*, p. 15.

7 Ibid., p. 3.

8 Ibid., p. 10.

9 Ibid., p. 25.

10 Ibid., p. 26.

11 Sura 16: 67 (al-Nahl), as quoted in Kueny, *The Rhetoric*, p. 65.

12 *The History of al-Tabari*, vol. XIII, *The Conquest of Iraq, South Western Persia, and Egypt*, trans. G.H.A. Juynboll (Albany, NY, 1989) pp. 151–4, as quoted by Kueny, *The Rhetoric*, p. 155, n. 4.

13 Kueny, *The Rhetoric*, p. 65, who also points out on p. 127, n. 321 the uncertain dating of the Qur'an itself.

14 M. M. Badawi, 'Abbasid Poetry and its Antecedents', in 'Abbasid Belles-Lettres', vol. II of *Cambridge History of Arabic Literature*, ed. J. Ashtiany et al. (Cambridge, 1990), p. 154 (cited by Kueny, *The Rhetoric*, p. 102).

15 *Omar Khayyam: A New Version Based upon Recent Discoveries*, ed. Arthur J. Arberry (London, 1952), stanza 203, 116.

16 Ibid., stanza 136, 94.

17 Avicenna, as quoted in Roger Scruton, *I Drink, Therefore I Am* (London, 2009), p. 109.

18 *Persian Poems: An Anthology of Verse Translations*, ed. A. J. Arberry (London, 1954), pp. 62–3.

19 Sussan Babaie, 'Shah 'Abbas II, the Conquest of Quandahar, the Chihil Sutun, and Its Wall Paintings', in *Muqarnas*, II (1994), pp. 125–42.

20 See for example the miniature from *c.* 1830 on the Art Resource website, www.artres.com, Art184010.

21 R. A. Nicholson, *Studies in Islamic Mysticism* (Cambridge, 1921), p. 186.

22 William C. Chittick, *The Sufi Path of Love* (Albany, NY, 1983), p. 312; quoted by Kueny, *The Rhetoric*, p. 112.

23 Ibid., p. 114.

bibliography

Accetto, Torquato, *Della dissimulazione onesta*, ed. Silvano Nigro (Turin, 1997)

Aeschylus, ed., and trans. Alan Sommerstein (Cambridge, MA, 2008)

Albala, Ken, *The Banquet: Dining in the Great Courts of Renaissance Europe* (Urbana, IL, 2007)

—, 'To Your Health: Wine as Food and Medicine in Sixteenth-Century Italy', in *Alcohol: A Social and Cultural History*, ed. M. P. Holt (Oxford, 2006)

Allen, Don C., *The Legend of Noah: Renaissance Rationalism in Art, Science, and Letters* (Urbana, IL, 1959)

Allhoff, Fritz, 'Planting the Vines: An Introduction', in *Wine and Philosophy: A Symposium on Thinking and Drinking*, ed. Fritz Allhoff (Oxford, 2007)

Anderson, Burton, *The Wine Atlas of Italy* (London, 1990)

Apicius, Marcus, *The Roman Cookery Book*, trans. B. Flower and E. Rosenbaum (London, 1958)

Arberry, Arthur J., ed., *Omar Khayyam: A New Version Based upon Recent Discoveries* (London, 1952)

—, ed., *Persian Poems: An Anthology of Verse Translations* (Cambridge, 2008)

Arikha, Noga, *Passions and Tempers: A History of the Humours* (New York, 2007)

Aristotle, *Problems*, trans. W. S. Hett (Cambridge, MA, 1970–83)

Art Resource, Inc. website, at www.artres.com

Ashtiany, Julia, T. M. Johnstone, J. D. Latham and R. B. Serjeant, eds, 'Abbāsid Belles-Lettres', *Cambridge History of Arabic Literature*, vol. II (Cambridge, 1990)

Athanassakis, Apostolos N., *The Homeric Hymns*, 2nd edn (Baltimore, MD, 2004)

Athenaeus, *The Learned Banqueters*, trans. S. D. Olson (Cambridge, MA, 2006)

Badawi, M. M., ed., 'Abbasid Poetry and its Antecedents', in *Modern Arabic Literature* (Cambridge, 1992)

Bahktin, Mikhail, 'Popular Festive Forms and Images in Rabelais', in *Rabelais and his World*, trans. Hélène Iswolsky (Bloomington, IN, 1984)

Bann, Stephen, *The True Vine: On Visual Representation and the Western Tradition* (Cambridge, 1989)

Barkan, Leonard, *The Gods Made Flesh: Metamorphosis and the Pursuit of Paganism* (New Haven, CT, 1986)

—, *Unearthing the Past: Archaeology and Aesthetics in the Making of Renaissance Culture* (New Haven, CT, 1999)

Bartholomew, Roberts, *A Treatise on the Practice of Medicine*, 5th edn (New York, 1883)

Bates, Ernest S., *Touring in 1600, A Study in the Development of Travel as a Means of Education* (Boston, 1911)

Baudelaire, Charles Pierre, *Poems of Baudelaire*, trans. Roy Campbell (London, 1952)

Bayer, Andrea, 'Dosso's Public: The Este Court at Ferrara', in *Dosso Dossi, Court Painter in Renaissance Ferrara*, ed. A. Bayer (New York, 1999)

Bax, Dirk, *Hieronymous Bosch: His Picture-Writing Deciphered*, trans. N. A. Bax-Botha (Rotterdam, 1979)

Beard, Mary, J. North, and S. Price, *Religions of Rome* (Cambridge, 1998)

Beazley, John D., *Attic Red-Figure Vase Painters* (Oxford, 1968)

Bellori, Giovanni Pietro, *The Lives of Annibale and Agostino Carracci*, trans. C. Enggass (University Park, PA, 1968)

Berger, Patricia, *The Art of Wine in East Asia* (San Francisco, CA, 1986)

Bergquist, Birgitta, 'Sympotic Space: A Functional Aspect of Greek Dining-Rooms', in *Sympotica: A Symposium on the 'Symposion'*, ed. Oswyn Murray (New York, 1990), pp. 37–65

Bernardini, Giulia, 'Intoxication and Excoriation: On the Depiction of Baseness in Jusepe de Ribera's *Drunken Silenus* and *Apollo and Marysas*', MA thesis, University of Colorado, Boulder (2006)

Blankert, Albert, 'Vermeer's Modern Themes and their Tradition', in *Johannes Vermeer* (Washington, DC, 1995)

Boardman, John, 'Symposion Furniture', in *Sympotica: A Symposium on the 'Symposion'*, ed. Oswyn Murray (New York, 1990), pp. 122–31

Bobak, M., and M. Marmot, 'Wine and Heart Disease: A Statistical Approach', in *Wine: A Scientific Exploration* (London, 2003), pp. 99–107

Bookidis, Nancy, 'Ritual Dining in the Sanctuary of Demeter and Kore at Corinth: Some Questions', in *Sympotica: A Symposium on the 'Symposion'*, ed. Oswyn Murray (New York, 1995), pp. 86–94

Bouwsma, William J., *John Calvin: A Sixteenth-Century Portrait* (New York, 1988)

Bradshaw, Paul, *Eucharistic Origins* (New York, 2004)

Brand, Peter, and Lino Pertile, *The Cambridge History of Italian Literature* (New York, 1999)

Brathwaite, Richard, *A Solemn Joviall Disputation, Theoreticke and Practicke: Briefly Shadowing the Law of Drinking* (London, 1617)

Braude, Benjamin, 'The Sons of Noah and the Construction of Ethnic and Geographical Identities in the Medieval and Early Modern Periods', *William and Mary Quarterly*, LIV (1997), pp. 103–42

Braudel, Fernand, *Capitalism and Material Life: 1400–1800*, trans. Miriam Kochan (New York, 1975)

Bremmer, Jan, 'Adolescents, *Symposion*, and Pederasty', in *Sympotica: A Symposium on the Symposion*, ed. Oswyn Murray (New York, 1995), pp. 135–48

Brennan, Thomas E., ed., 'Grids of Order: Regulation', in *Public Drinking in the Early Modern World: Voices from the Tavern, 1500–1800* (London, 2011)

Brown, Cedric C., 'Sons of Beer and Sons of Ben: Drink as a Social Marker in Seventeenth-Century England', in *A Pleasing Sinne: Drink and Conviviality in Seventeenth-Century England*, ed. Adam Smyth (Cambridge, 2004), pp. 3–20

Browning, Robert, *The Complete Poetic and Dramatic Works of Robert Browning* (Boston, 1895)

Bucer, Martin, *Martin Bucer: Reforming Church and Community*, ed. D. F. Wright (Cambridge, 1994)

Buchan, William, *Domestic Medicine, or, A Treatise on the Prevention and Cure of Diseases by Regimen and Simple Medicines* (Fairhaven, VT, 1798)

Buitron, Diana, *Attic Vase Painting in New England Collections*, exh. cat., Fogg Art Museum, (Cambridge, MA, 1972)

Byron, *The Complete Poetical Works of Lord Byron: Don Juan*, ed. Jerome J. McGann (New York, 1980)

Camiz, Franca T., 'The Castrato Singer: From Informal to Formal Portraiture', *Artibus et Historiae*, IX/18 (1988), pp. 171–86

Campbell, Christy, *Phylloxera: How Wine was Saved for the World* (New York, 2004)

Capps, Jack, *Emily Dickinson's Reading, 1836–86* (Cambridge, MA, 1966)

Cardi, Maria V., 'Intorno all'autoritratto in veste di Bacco di Giovan Paolo Lomazzo', *Storia dell'arte*, LXXXI (1994), pp. 182–93

Carman, Charles, 'Michelangelo's *Bacchus* and Divine Frenzy', *Source*, II/4 (1983), pp. 6–13

Carpenter, Thomas, *Dionysian Imagery in Archaic Greek Art* (New York, 1986)

—, *Dionysian Imagery in Fifth Century Athens*, Oxford Monographs on Classical Archaeology (New York, 1997)

Carter, Everett, *Wine and Poetry* (Davis, CA, 1976)

Cathiard-Thomas, Mathilde, and Corinne Pezard, *Vinoterapia: In salute con il vino e con la vite* (Rome, 2007)

Chadwick, John, *The Mycenaean World* (New York, 1976)

Chambers, David, and Brian Pullan, *Venice: A Documentary History 1450–1630* (Toronto, 2001)

Chapman, H. Perry, W. T. Kloek and A. K. Wheelock Jr, eds, *Jan Steen: Painter and Storyteller* (Washington, DC, 1996)

Charlesworth, James H., *The Historical Jesus: An Essential Guide* (Nashville, TN, 2008)

Charters, Steve, *Wine and Society: The Social and Cultural Context of a Drink* (Boston, 2006)

Chastel, André, *The Sack of Rome*, trans. Beth Archer (Princeton, NJ, 1983)

Chittick, William C., *The Sufi Path of Love* (Albany, NY, 1983)

Clark, John, *Roman Life, 100 BC to AD 200* (New York, 2007)

Clark, Peter, *The English Alehouse: A Social History 1200–1830* (New York, 1983)

Cohen, Beth, *The Colors of Clay*, exh. cat, J. Paul Getty Museum (Los Angeles, 2006)

Courtwright, David, *Forces of Habit: Drugs and the Making of the Modern World* (Cambridge, 2001)

Condivi, Ascanio, *The Life of Michelangelo*, trans. A. S. Wohl (University Park, PA, 1999)

Conlon, Christopher, '"Fox-Teeth in Your Heart": Sexual Self-Portraiture in the Poetry of Tennessee Williams', *The Tennessee Williams Annual Review*, no. 4 (2001)

Coogan, Michael. *The New Oxford Annotated Bible* (New York, 2007)

Cook, E. F., and C. H. LaWall, *Remington's Practice of Pharmacy*, 8th edn (Philadelphia, PA, 1936)

Cropper, Elizabeth, *Pietro Testa 1612–1650: Prints and Drawings* (Philadelphia, PA, 1988)

—, *The Ideal of Painting: Pietro Testa's Düsseldorf Notebook* (Princeton, NJ, 1984)

—, and C. Dempsey, *Nicholas Poussin: Friendship and the Love of Painting* (Princeton, NJ, 1996)

Crescentiis, Petrus de, 'De Diversis Speciebus Vitium', in *Das Wissen Des Vollkommenen Landwirts Um 1300*, trans Will Richter, 2 vols (Heidelberg, 1995–2002)

Cummins, Patricia W., trans., *A Critical Edition of Le Regime Tresutile et Tresproufitable pour Conserver et Garder la Santé du Corps Humaine* (Chapel Hill, NC, 1976)

Daley, Suzanne, 'Williams Choked to Death on a Bottle Cap', *New York Times*, 27 February 1983

D'Andeli, Henri, 'Trouvère Normand du XIII Siècle', in *Oeuvres* (Rouen, 1880), pp. 23–31

D'Arms, John, 'The Roman *Convivium* and the Idea of Equality', in *Sympotica: A Symposium on the Symposion*, ed. Oswyn Murray (New York, 1990), pp. 308–20

Davidson, James, *Courtesans and Fishcakes: The Consuming Passions of Classical Athens* (New York, 1999)

Davies, James, *Hesiod and Theognis* (Philadelphia, 1873)

Dayagi-Mendels, M., *Drink and Be Merry, Wine and Beer in Ancient Times* (Jerusalem, 2000)

Debré, Patrice, *Louis Pasteur*, trans. E. Forster (Baltimore, MD, 1998)

De Moor, Janny, 'Dutch Cooking and Calvin', *Oxford Symposium on Food and Cookery, Proceedings of the Oxford Symposium on Food and Cookery*, ed. Harlan Walker (Devon, 1995), pp. 94–105

Dempsey, Charles. *Annibale Carracci: The Farnese Gallery, Rome* (New York, 1995)

—, '*Et nos Cedamus Amori*: Observations on the Farnese Gallery', *Art Bulletin*, L (1968), pp. 363–74

Deneef, A. Leigh, '*This Poetic Liturgie*': Robert Herrick's Ceremonial Mode (Durham, NC, 1974)

Dickinson, Emily, *The Poems of Emily Dickinson*, ed. R. W. Franklin (Cambridge, MA, 2005)

Drey, E. A., *Apothecary Jars: Pharmaceutical Pottery and Porcelain in Europe and the East 1150–1850* (London, 1978)

Dumézil, Georges. *Archaic Roman Religion* (Baltimore, MD, 1996)

Dunand, Françoise, and C. Zivie-Coche, *Gods and Men in Egypt: 3000 BCE to 395 CE. Histories* (Ithaca, NY, 2004)

Dunbabin, Katherine M. D., *The Roman Banquet: Images of Conviviality* (New York, 2003)

—, 'Sic erimus cuncti . . .The Skeleton in Graeco-Roman Art', *Jahrbuch des Deutschen Archaeologischen Instituts*, 101 (1986), pp. 185–55

—, "Ut Graeco more biberetur: Greeks and Romans on the Dining Couch', in *Meals in a Social Context: Aspects of the Communal Meal in the Hellenistic and Roman World*, ed. I. Nielsen and H. S. Nielsen (Aarthus, 1998), pp. 81–101

—, 'Triclinium and Stibadium', in *Dining in a Classical Context*, ed. W. Slater (Ann Arbor, MI, 1991), pp. 121–48

Dutton, Paul E., *Charlemagne's Courtier: The Complete Einhard* (Orchard Park, NY, 1998)

Eddy, Paul R., *The Jesus Legend: A Case for the Historical Reliability of the Synoptic Jesus Tradition* (Grand Rapids, MI, 2007)

Edelstein, E. J., and L. E. Edelstein, *Asclepius: A Collection and Interpretation of the Testimonies* (Baltimore, MD, 1945)

Emmerling-Scala, Andreas, *Bacchus in Der Renaissance*, 2 vols (Hildesheim, 1994)

Erasmus, Desiderius, *The Praise of Folly*, trans. Clarence H. Miller (New Haven, CT, 1979)

Eubulus, *The Fragments*, trans. R. L. Hunter (New York, 1983)

Euripedes, *Alcestis*, trans. William Arrowsmith (New York, 1974)

—, *Bacchae*, trans. William Arrowsmith (Chicago, 1978)

Evans, Elizabeth, *Physiognomics in the Ancient World* (Philadelphia, PA, 1969)

Faas, Patrick, *Around the Roman Table: Food and Feasting in Ancient Rome*, trans. Shaun Whiteside (Chicago, 2005)

Faccioli, Emilio, 'Della qualità dei Vini', in *Arte Della Cucina: Libri di Recette*, ed. Emilio Faccioli (Milan, 1966)

Fallani, Giovanni, *Collezione vaticana d'arte religiosa moderna* (Milan, 1974)

Fehl, Philip, 'The Worship of Bacchus and Venus in Bellini's and Titian's Bacchanals for Alfonso d'Este', *Studies in the History of Art*, VI (1974), pp. 37–95

Felton, Craig, and W. Jordan, eds, *Jusepe de Ribera: Lo Spagnoletto 1591–1652* (Fort Worth, TX, 1982)

Ficino, Marsilio, 'Commentary on Plato's Symposium', trans. Sears R. Jayne (Columbia, NC, 1944)

Fiocco, Carola, and G. Gherardi, *Museo del vino di Torgiano: Ceramiche* (Perugia, 1991)

Figuera, Thomas J., and Gregory Nagy, eds, *Theognis of Megara: Poetry and the Polis* (Baltimore, MD, 1985)

Finney, Paul Corby, *The Invisible God: The Earliest Christians on Art* (New York, 1994)

Fleming, Stuart, *Vinum: The Story of Roman Wine* (Glen Mills, PA, 2001)

Florio, John, *A Worlde of Words, or Most Copious and Exact Dictionarie in Italian and English* (London, 1598)

Forbes, R. J., 'Food and Drink', in *A History of Technology*, ed. Charles Singer et al., 8 vols (Oxford, 1954–84)

Frame, Donald, *Complete Works of Rabelais* (Berkeley, CA, 1991)

Frank, Mitch, 'Harnessing Wine's Healing Powers', *The Wine Spectator*, 31 May 2009

Franz, W., A. Strauss and J. Sichel, *Glass Drinking Vessels from the Collection of Jerome Strauss*, exh. cat., Corning Museum of Glass (Corning, NY, 1955)

Frazer, James George, *The Golden Bough: A Study in Magic and Religion* (New York, 1922)

Freedman, Luba, 'Michelangelo's Reflections on Bacchus', *Artibus et Historiae*, XLVII (2003), pp. 121–35

Frey, Julia, *Toulouse-Lautrec: A Life* (New York, 1994)

Fuller, Robert C., *Religion and Wine: A Cultural History of Wine Drinking in the United States* (Knoxville, TN, 1996)

Gabler, Jim, *Passions: The Wines and Travels of Thomas Jefferson* (Baltimore, MD, 1995)

Geisberg, Max, *The German Single-Leaf Woodcut: 1500–1550*, revd and ed. Walter Strauss (New York, 1974)

Gelfand, Laura D., 'Social Status and Sin: Reading Bosch's Prado *Seven Deadly Sins* and *Four Last Things* Paintings', in *The Seven Deadly Sins: From Communities to Individuals*, ed. R. Newhauser (Leiden, 2007)

Gernsheim, Helmut, and A. Gernsheim, *Roger Fenton: Photographer of the Crimean War; His Photographs and his Letters from the Crimea* (New York, 1973)

Giacosa, Ilaria Gozzini, *A Taste of Ancient Rome* (Chicago, 1992)

Godfrey, Eleanor S., *The Development of English Glassmaking, 1560–1640* (Oxford, 1975)

Goodgal, Dana, 'The Camerino of Alfonso I d'Este', *Art History*, I (1978), pp. 162–90

Gorny, Ronald L., 'Viticulture in Ancient Anatolia', in *The Origins and Ancient History of Wine*, ed. P. E. McGovern, S. J. Fleming and S. H. Katz (Luxembourg, 1996)

Gower, John, *Confessio Amantis*, trans. A. Galloway, ed. R. A. Peck, vol. III (Kalamazoo, 2004)

Gowers, Emily, *The Loaded Table: Representations of Food in Roman Literature* (New York, 1997)

Grabar, André, *Christian Iconography: A Study of its Origins* (Princeton, NJ, 1968)

—, *Early Christian Art: From the Rise of Christianity to the Death of Theodosius* (New York, 1968)

Grace, Fran, *Carry A. Nation: Retelling the Life* (Bloomington, IN, 2001)

Gracia, J. E. Jorge, 'Rules and Regulations for Drinking Wine in Francesco Eiximenis' "Terc del Crestia" (1384)', *Traditio*, XXXII (1976), pp. 369–85

Green, Robert M., *A Translation of Galen's Hygiene* (Springfield, IL, 1951)

Grössinger, Christa. *Humour and Folly in Secular and Profane Prints of Northern Europe, 1430–1540* (London, 2002)

Grottanelli, Christiano, 'Wine and Death–East and West', in *In Vino Veritas*, ed. Oswyn Murray and Manuela Teçusan (Rome, 1995), pp. 62–89

Haine, W. Scott, 'Drink, Sociability, and Social Class in France, 1789–1945', in *Alcohol: A Social and Cultural History*, ed. Mack P. Holt (Oxford, 2006), pp. 121–44.

Hamilton, Walter, 'Introduction' to *Plato: The Symposium* (Baltimore, MD, 1971)

Hammond, Mitchell, 'Paracelsus and the Boundaries of Medicine in Early Modern Augsburg', in *Paracelsian Moments: Science, Medicine, and Astrology in Early Modern Europe*, ed. G. S. Williams, C. D. Gunnoe (Kirksville, MO, 2002), pp. 19–33

Hartt, Frederick, and David Wilkins, *History of Italian Renaissance Art*, 6th edn (Upper Saddle River, NJ, 2006)

Haskell, Francis, *Patrons and Painters: Art and Society in Baroque Italy* (New York, 1971)

Haynes, Stephen R., *Noah's Curse: The Biblical Justification of American Slavery* (New York, 2007)

Headley, Diane, 'Picasso's Response to Classical Art', *Dionysos and his Circle*, ed. C. Houser (Cambridge, MA, 1979)

Hedreen, Guy, *Silens in Attic Black-Figure Vase Painting: Myth and Performance* (Ann Arbor, MI, 1992)

Henderson, John, *The Renaissance Hospital: Healing the Body and Healing the Soul* (New Haven, CT, 2006)

Hengel, Martin, *Studies in Early Christology* (Edinburgh, 1995)

Henrichs, Albert, 'Greek and Roman Glimpses of Dionysus', in *Dionysus and his Circle: Ancient through Modern*, ed. Caroline Houser (Cambridge, MA, 1979)

Herbert, Robert L., *Impressionism: Art, Leisure, and Parisian Society* (New Haven, CT, 1988)

Herbdata New Zealand, Ltd. 2002–8, at www.herbdatanz.com

Herrick, Robert, *The Poetical Works of Robert Herrick*, ed. L. C. Martin (Oxford, 1956)

Herodotus, *The Histories*. trans. Robin Waterfield (New York, 1998)

Hibbard, Howard, *Caravaggio* (New York, 1983)

Hildegard von Bingen, *Hildegard's Healing Plants: From Her Medieval Classic Physica*, trans. B. W. Hozeski (Boston, MA, 2001)

Hill, Susan E., '"The Ooze of Gluttony": Attitudes Towards Food, Eating, and Excess in the Middle Ages', in *The Seven Deadly Sins: From Communities to Individuals*, ed. R. Newhauser (Leiden, 2007), pp. 57–70

Hippocrates. Humours and Ulcers, trans. W.H.S. Jones (New York, 1923)

Holberton, Paul, 'The Choice of Texts for the Camerino Pictures', in *Bacchanals by Titian and Rubens: Papers Given at a Symposium in Nationalmuseum, Stockholm, March 18–19 1987*, ed. G. Cavalli-Björkman (Stockholm, 1987), pp. 57–66

Holt, Mack P., 'Europe Divided: Wine, Beer, and the Reformation in Sixteenth-Century Europe', in *Alcohol: A Social and Cultural History* (New York, 2006), pp. 25–40

Homer, *The Iliad of Homer*, trans. Richmond Lattimore (Chicago, 1951)

—, *The Odyssey*, trans. E. V. Rieu (London, 1977)

Hoogewerff, G. J., *De Bentvueghels* (The Hague, 1952)

Hubert, Martin, *Alcaeus* (New York, 1972)

Hughes, Anthony, 'What's The Trouble with the Farnese Gallery? An Experiment in Reading Pictures', *Art History*, XI/3 (1988), pp. 335–48

Jensen, Robin M., *Understanding Christian Art* (New York, 2000)

Johnson, Hugh, *The Story of Wine* (London, 2005)

Johnson, Thomas H., ed., *The Letters of Emily Dickinson* (Cambridge, MA, 1958)

Jones, Angelica M., 'Roaring Royalists and Ranting Brewers: The Politicisation of Drink and Drunkenness in Political Broadside Ballads from 1640 to 1689', in *A Pleasing Sinne: Drink and Conviviality in Seventeenth-Century England*, ed. A. Smyth (Cambridge, MA, 2004), pp. 69–87

Jungmann, Joseph A., *The Mass of the Roman Rite, its Origins and Development*, trans. Francis A. Brunner, 2 vols (New York, 1951–5)

Juynboll, G.H.A., *The History of al-Tabari*, vol. XIII, *The Conquest of Iraq, South Western Persia, and Egypt*, trans. G.H.A. Juynboll (Albany, NY, 1989), pp. 151–4

Kajanto, Iiro, 'Balnea vina venus', in *Hommages à Marcel Renard*, ed. Jacqueline Bibauw (Brussels, 1969), II, pp. 357–67

Keats, John, 'Ode to a Nightingale', in *The Complete Poetry and Selected Prose of John Keats*, ed. H. E. Briggs (New York, 1951)

King, Edward, *My Paris: French Character Sketches* (Boston, 1869)

Klatsky, Arthur L., 'Wine, Alcohol and Cardiovascular Diseases', in *Wine: A Scientific Exploration*, ed. M. Sandler and R. Pinder (New York, 2003), pp. 108–39

Kondoleon, Christine, 'Mosiacs of Antioch', in *Antioch: The Lost Ancient City* (Princeton, NJ, 2000)

Koozin, Kristine, *The Vanitas Still Lifes of Harmen Steenwyck: Metaphoric Realism* (Lewiston, ME, 1990)

Kueny, Kathryn, *The Rhetoric of Sobriety: Wine in Early Islam* (Albany, NY, 2001)

Kurtz, Donna C., and John Boardman, *Greek Burial Customs* (Ithaca, NY, 1971)

Laertius, Diogenes, ed., *Lives of Eminent Philosophers*, trans. R. D. Hicks (Cambridge, MA, 1966)

Laughton, Bruce, *Honoré Daumier* (New Haven, CT, 1996)

Lehmann-Hartleben, K., and E. C. Olson, *Dionysiac Sarcophagi in Baltimore* (New York and Baltimore, 1942)

Lesko, Leonard H., 'Egyptian Wine Production During the New Kingdom', in *The Origins and Ancient History of Wine*, ed. P. E. McGovern, S. J. Fleming and S. H. Katz (Luxembourg, 1996), pp. 215–30

—, *King Tut's Wine Cellar* (Berkeley, CA, 1977)

Levine, David, and E. Mai, *I Bamboccianti: Niederländische Malerrebellen im Rom des Barock* (Milan, 1991)

—, 'The Bentvueghels: "Bande Academique"', *IL60: Essays Honoring Irving Lavin on his Sixtieth Birthday* (New York, 1990), pp. 207–26

Lewis, Jack, *A Study in the Interpretation of Noah and the Flood in Jewish and Christian Literature* (Leiden, 1978)

Lightbrown, Ronald, *Mantegna: With a Complete Catalogue of the Paintings, Drawings, and Prints* (Berkeley, CA, 1986)

Lissarrague, François, *The Aesthetics of the Greek Banquet: Images of Wine and Ritual* (Princeton, NJ, 1990)

Lloyd, G.E.R, 'The Hot and the Cold, the Dry and the Wet in Greek Philosophy', *Journal of Hellenic Studies*, LXXXIV (1964), pp. 92–106

López-Rey, José, *Velázquez' Work and World* (Greenwich, NY, 1968)

Loyn, H. R., and J. Percival, *The Reign of Charlemagne: Documents on Carolingian Government and Administration* (New York, 1975)

Lubac, Henri (Cardinal) de, *Corpus Mysticum: The Eucharist and the Church in the Middle Ages*, trans. Gemma Simmonds et al. (South Bend, IN, 2007)

Lucia, Salvatore P., *A History of Wine as Therapy* (Philadelphia, PA, 1963)

Ludington, Charles, '"Be sometimes to your country true": The Politics of Wine in England, 1660–1714', in *A Pleasing Sinne*, ed. A. Smyth (Cambridge, 2004), pp. 89–106

Luther, Martin, *The Complete Sermons of Martin Luther*, trans. and ed. John N. Lenker (Grand Rapids, MI, 1988)

—, *Letters of Spiritual Counsel*, ed., and trans. Theodore G. Tappert, *Library of Christian Classics*, vol. XVIII (Philadelphia, PA, 1955)

Lynch, James, 'Giovanni Paolo Lomazzo's *Self-portrait* in the Brera', *Gazette des beaux arts*, LXIV (1964), pp. 189–97

McCann, Anna M., *Roman Sarcophagi in the Metropolitan Museum of Art*, exh. cat. (New York, 1978)

McGovern, Patrick E., *Ancient Wine: The Search for the Origins of Viniculture* (Princeton, NJ, 2003)

—, W. J. Fleming, and S. Katz, eds, *The Origins and Ancient History of Wine* (Luxembourg, 1996)

McGowen, Andrew, *Ascetic Eucharists: Food and Drink in Early Christian Ritual Meals* (New York, 1999)

McNamara, Denis, 'The Dangerous Path: Leonard Porter and the Sincerity of Hope', *The Classicist*, VIII (2009), pp. 118–27

MacNeil, Karen, *The Wine Bible* (New York, 2001)

Macrobius, *The Saturnalia*, trans. P. V. Davies (New York, 1969)

Majano, Guido, *The Healing Hand: Man and Wound in the Ancient World* (Cambridge, MA, 1975)

Marius, Richard, *Martin Luther: Letters of Spiritual Counsel* (Cambridge, MA, 1999)

Martial, *Epigrams*, trans. D. R. Shackleton Bailey (Cambridge, MA, 1933)

Martin, John R., *The Farnese Gallery* (Princeton, NJ, 1965)

Martin, Lynn A., *Alcohol, Sex and Gender in Late Medieval and Early Modern Europe* (New York, 2001)

Mathews, Thomas F., *The Clash of the Gods: A Reinterpretation of Early Christian Art* (Princeton, NJ, 1993)

Maury, E. A., *Wine is the Best Medicine* (Kansas City, KS, 1977)

Mayer, Rosemary, *Pontormo's Diary* (London, 1982)

Medici, Lorenzo, *Selected Poems and Prose*. trans. J. Thiem (University Park, PA, 1991)

Mitchell, Stephen, *A History of the Later Roman Empire, AD 284–641* (Malden, MA, 2007)

Moffitt, John F., *Inspiration: Bacchus and the Cultural History of a Creation Myth* (Boston, 2005)

Mole, William, *Gods, Men and Wine by William Younger* (London, 1966)

Montaigne, Michel de, *The Essays of Michel de Montaigne*, trans. M.A. Screech (London, 1991)

Morford, Mark, *Stoics and Neostoics: Rubens and the Circle of Lipsius* (Princeton, NJ, 1991)

Murray, Oswyn, 'The Symposion as Entertainment' in *Sympotica: A Symposium on the 'Symposion'*, ed. Oswyn Murray (New York, 1990)

Myers, Allen C., *Eerdmans Dictionary of the Bible*, 1st edn (Grand Rapids, MI, 2000)

Nelson, Max, *The Barbarian's Beverage: A History of Beer in Ancient Europe* (London, 2005)

Neruda, Pablo, *Elemental Odes*. trans. Margaret S. Peden (London, 1991)

Nicholson, R. A., *Studies in Islamic Mysticism* (Cambridge, 1921)

Nielsen, Hanne S., and I. Nielsen, *Meals in a Social Context: Aspects of the Communal Meal in the Hellenistic and Roman World* (Aarhus, 1998)

Noble, Joseph V., 'Some Trick Greek Vases', *Proceedings of the American Philosophical Society*, CXII (1968), pp. 371–8

Otto, Walter F., *Dionysus, Myth and Cult, Myth and Cult,* trans. R. B. Palmer (Bloomington, IN, 1965)

Ovid, *Ovid's Fasti: Roman Holidays*, trans. Betty R. Nagle (Bloomington, IN, 1995)

—, *Metamorphoses*, trans. R. Humphries (Bloomington, IN, 1960)

Page, Jutta-Annette, *The Art of Glass: The Toledo Museum of Art* (Toledo, 2005)

Panofsky, Dora, 'Narcissus and Echo: Notes on Poussin's 'Birth of Bacchus' in the Fogg Museum of Art', *Art Bulletin*, XXXI (1949), pp. 112–20

Paola, Frederick A., 'In Vino Sanitas', in *Wine and Philosophy: A Symposium on Thinking and Drinking*, ed. F. Allhoff (Oxford, 2009)

Paracelsus, *The Hermetical and Alchemical Writings of Paracelsus*, trans. Arthur E. Waite (London, 1894)

Parker, William R., and G. Campbell, *Milton: A Biographical Commentary*, 2nd edn (Oxford, 1999)

Partner, Peter, *Renaissance Rome 1500–1559: A Portrait of Society* (Berkeley, CA, 1976)

Pepys, Samuel, *The Diary of Samuel Pepys*, ed. Robert Latham and Matthew Williams (Berkeley, CA, 1970)

Perez-Sanchez, J., and N. Spinosa, *Jusepe de Ribera 1591–1652* (New York, 1992)

Petronius, *Satyricon, Petronius: Satyrica*, trans. R. B. Branham and D. Kinney (Berkeley, CA, 1999)

Phillips, Rod, *A Short History of Wine* (New York, 2002)

Philostratus the Younger, *Philostratus: Imagines; Callistatus: Descriptions*, trans.

A. Fairbanks (Cambridge, MA, 1931)

Picasso, Pablo, *Vollard Suite* (Madrid, 1993)

Piccolpasso, Cipriano, *The Three Books of the Potter's Art*. trans. R. Lightbown and A. Caiger-Smith (London, 1980)

Pinney, Thomas, *A History of Wine in America: From the Beginnings to Prohibition* (Berkeley, CA, 1989)

Plato, *Phaedrus*, trans. A. Nehamas and P. Woodruff (Indianapolis, IN, 1995)

—, *The Symposium*, trans. Walter Hamilton (Baltimore, MD, 1971)

—, *The Laws,* trans. Trevor J. Saunders (Baltimore, 1975)

Pliny, *Pliny: Natural History*, vol. IV trans. by Arthur Rackham, vol. VIII trans. W. S. Jones (Cambridge, MA, 1962)

Poo, Mu-Chou, *Wine and Wine Offering in the Religion of Ancient Egypt* (London, 1995)

Posner, Donald, *Annibale Carracci: A Study in the Reform of Italian Painting around 1590* (London, 1971)

Powell, Marvin, 'Wine and the Vine in Ancient Mesopotamia: The Cuneiform Evidence', in *The Origins and Ancient History of Wine*, ed. P. E. McGovern, S. J. Fleming and S. Katz (Luxembourg, 1996)

Price, Roger, *The Economic Modernization of France, 1730–1880* (London, 1975)

Rabelais, *François Rabelais: Gargantua and Pantagruel*, trans. and ed. M. A. Screech (New York, 2006)

—, *Trattato sul buon uso del vino*, ed. Patrik Ourednik, trans. A. Catalano (Palermo, 2009)

Rebora, Giovanni, *Culture of the Fork: A Brief History of Food in Europe*, trans. A. Sonnenfeld (New York, 1998)

Rehm, Rush, *Marriage to Death: The Conflation of Wedding and Funeral Rituals in Greek Tragedy* (Princeton, NJ, 1994)

Remington, Joseph P., *The Practice of Pharmacy: A Treatise*, 6th edn (Philadelphia, PA, 1917)

Ricci, Giorgio, et al., 'Alcohol Consumption and Coronary Heart-Disease', *The Lancet* CCCXIII/8131 (1979), p. 1404

Richardson, Joanna, *Baudelaire* (New York, 1994)

Riddle, John M., *Dioscorides on Pharmacy and Medicine* (Austin, TX, 1985)

Robinson, Jancis, *The Oxford Companion to Wine*, 3rd edn (New York, 2006)

Root, Waverly, *The Food of Italy* (New York, 1992)

Rosenbaum, Stanford P., ed., *A Concordance to the Poems of Emily Dickinson* (Ithaca, NY, 1964)

Rossiter, J. J., 'Wine and Oil Processing at Roman Farms in Italy', *Phoenix*, XXXV (1981), pp. 345–61

Rotunda, D. P., *Motif-Index of the Italian Novella in Prose* (Bloomington, IN, 1942)

Ryan, William, and Walter Pitman, *Noah's Flood: The New Scientific Discoveries about the Event that Changed History* (New York, 1998)

Sannazaro, Jacopo, *The Major Latin Poems of Jacopo Sannazaro*, ed. Ralph Nash (Detroit, MI, 1996)

Schama, Simon, *An Embarrassment of Riches: An Interpretation of Dutch Culture in the Golden Age* (New York, 1987)

—, 'The Unruly Realm: Appetite and Restraint in Seventeenth-Century Holland', *Daedalus*, CVIII (1979), pp. 103–23

Schatborn, Peter, and J. Verbene, *Drawn to Warmth: 17th-Century Dutch Artists in Italy* (Zwolle, 2001)

Schlesier, Renate, and Agnes Schwarzmaier, eds, *Dionysus: Verwandlung und Ekstase* (Regensburg, 2008)

Scribner, R. W., 'Popular Culture', in *For the Sake of Simple Folk: Popular Propaganda for the German Reformation* (Cambridge, 1981), chap. 4.

Scruton, Roger, 'The Philosophy of Wine', in *Questions of Taste: The Philosophy of Wine*, ed. B. C. Smith (New York, 2007)

—, *I Drink Therefore I Am* (London, 2009)

Seaford, Richard, *Dionysos* (New York, 2006)

Shakespeare, William, *The Complete Works*, ed. G. B. Harrison (New York, 1952)

Sherlock, Frederick, *Shakespeare on Temperance, with Brief Annotations* [1882] (New York, 1972)

Shinneman, Dalyne, Appendix IV: 'The Canon in Titian's *Andrians*: A Reinterpretation', in Philip Fehl, 'The Worship of Bacchus and Venus', *Studies in the History of Art*, VI (1974), pp. 37–95

Shoemaker, Innis, and Elizabeth Broun, *The Engravings of Marc'Antonio Raimondi* (Lawrence, KS, 1981)

Siegfried, Susan, *The Art of Louis-Leopold Boilly: Modern Life in Napoleonic France* (New Haven, CT, 1995)

Sinos, Rebecca, 'The Satyr and his Skin: Connections in Plato's Symposium', lecture at Amherst College, Amherst, MA (2007)

Slatkes, Leonard J., and W. Franits, *The Paintings of Hendrick ter Brugghen: Catalogue Raisonné* (Philadelphia, PA, 2007)

Smith, Dennis E., *From Symposium to Eucharist: The Banquet in the Early Christian World* (Minneapolis, MN, 2003)

Sournia, Jean-Charles, *A History of Alcoholism* (Oxford, 1990)

Squire, Michael, 'Offerings: A New History', in David Ligare, *Offerings: A New History* (London, 2005)

Stevenson, Robert Louis, *The Strange Case of Dr Jekyll and Mr Hyde* (Peterborough, OH, 2005)

—, *The Silverado Squatters* (New York, 1923)

Stevenson, Tom, *Christie's World Encyclopedia of Champagne and Sparkling Wine* (Bath, 2002)

Sutton, Peter C., 'Introduction', in *The Age of Rubens*, ed. P. C. Sutton (Boston, 1993)

Symonds, John Addington, trans., *Wine, Women, and Song: Medieval Latin Students' Songs* (London, 1884)

Taylor, Gary, *Castration, An Abbreviated History of Western Manhood* (New York, 2000)

Tchernia, André, *Le Vin de Italie Romaine* (Rome, 1986)

Theogony and Works and Days, trans. C. M. Schlegel and H. Weinfield (Ann Arbor, MI, 2006)

Unger, Richard W., *Beer in the Middle Ages and the Renaissance* (Philadelphia, PA, 2004)

Unwin, Tim, *Wine and the Vine: An Historical Geography of Viticulture and the Wine Trade* (London, 1991)

Urrutia, Matilde, *My Life with Pablo Neruda* (Stanford, CA, 2004)

Vallot, Antoine, *Journal de la santé du roi Louis XIV de l'année 1647 à l'année 1711* (Paris, 1862), p. 211, and online at http://gallica.bnf.fr

Varriano, John, *Tastes and Temptations: Food and Art in Renaissance Italy* (Berkeley, CA, 2009)

—, *Caravaggio: The Art of Realism* (University Park, PA, 2006)

—, 'At Supper with Leonard', *Gastronomica, The Journal of Food and Culture*, v/4 (2005), pp. 8–14

Vasari, Giorgio, *The Lives of the Painters, Sculptors and Architects*, trans. A. B. Hinds, ed. William Gaunt (New York, 1970)

Verdon, Jean, *Boire Au Moyen Age* (Paris, 2002)

Vermeer, exh. cat. National Gallery of Art, Washington, DC; Royal Cabinet of Paintings Mauritshuis (1995)

Vickers, Michael, 'A Dirty Trick Vase', *American Journal of Archaeology*, LXXIX (1975), p. 282

Von Lates, Adrienne, 'Caravaggio's Peaches and Academic Puns', *Word and Image*, XI (1995), pp. 55–60

Wandel, Lee Palmer, *The Eucharist in the Reformation, Incarnation and Liturgy* (New York, 2006)

Watson, Gilbert, *Theriac and mithridatium: A Study in Therapeutics* (London, 1966)

Watson, Wendy M., *Italian Renaissance Ceramics* (Philadelphia, PA, 2001)

Weisse, M. E., and R. S. Moore, 'Antimicrobial Effects of Wine', in *Wine: A Scientific Exploration*, ed. M. Sandler and R. Pinder (New York, 2003), pp. 299–313

Weinberg, Florence M., *The Wine and The Will: Rabelais's Bacchic Christianity* (Detroit, MI, 1972)

Welu, James, et al., *Judith Leyster: A Dutch Master and Her World* (Worcester, MA, 1993)

Westbrook, Randy, *Poisonous Plants of Eastern North America* (Columbia, NC, 1986)

Wenzel, Horst, 'The *Logos* in the Press: Christ in the Wine-Press and the Discovery of Printing', in *Visual Culture and the German Middle Ages*, ed. K. Starkey and H. Wenzel (London, 2005)

Westermann, Mariët, *The Amusements of Jan Steen: Comic Painting in the Seventeenth Century* (Zwolle, 1997)

De Weever, Jacqueline, *Chaucer Name Dictionary* (New York, 1987)

Williams, T., *The Collected Poems of Tennessee Williams*, ed. D. Roessel and N. Moschovakis (New York, 2002)

Wilson, Hanneke, *Wine and Words in Classical Antiquity and the Middle Ages* (London, 2003)

Winklin, John J., and F. Zeitlin, eds, *Nothing to Do With Dionysus? Athenian Drama in Its Social Context* (Princeton, NJ, 1990)

Woll, Gerd, *Edvard Munch: Complete Paintings. Catalogue Raisonné I, 1880–1897* (London, 2008)

Yeats, William Butler, *The Collected Poems of W. B. Yeats* (New York, 1956)

Younger, William, *Gods, Men and Wine* (Cleveland, OH, 1966)

Zegura, Elizabeth C., 'Rabelais's Preoccupation with Wine Symbolism', in *The Rabelais Encyclopedia* (Westport, CT, 2004)

Zeitlin, Froma I., 'Playing the Other: Theatre, Theatricality, and the Feminine in Greek Drama', in *Nothing to Do With Dionysus*, ed. John J. Winklin and Froma Zeitlin (Princeton, NJ, 1990), pp. 63–96

Zettler, Richard L., and Naomi F. Miller, 'Searching for Wine in the Archaeological Record of Ancient Mesopotamia in the Third and Second Millenia BC', in *The Origins and Ancient History of Wine*, ed. P. E. McGovern, S. J. Fleming and S. Katz (Luxembourg, 1996), pp. 123–31

acknowledgements

Countless friends and colleagues have expressed encouraging words or offered useful references that have led to the enrichment of my text. Many of these were bestowed over a glass or two of wine, and I apologize to those whose names may have descended into the realm of forgotten revelry, but I recall with gratitude the contributions of Valerie Andrews, Martin Antonetti, John Arthur, Bob Bagg, Kenneth Bendiner, Bettina Bergmann, Alex Conison, Paula Debnar, Joe Ellis, Fred Fierst, Barringer Fifield, Patrick Healey, Patrick Hunt, Elise Kenney, Jennifer King, Lee Lalonde, Nora Lambert, Brad Leithauser, Jonathan Lipman, Michael Marlais, Thomas Mathews, Fred McGinness, Georgeann Murphy, John Nassichuk, Ann Pemberton, David Porter, Leonard Porter, Mary Jo Salter, Monika Schmitter, Rebecca Sinos, David Sofield, Geoffrey Sumi, Carolyn and Joseph Topor, Jennifer Vorbach, Erica Walch, and Clovis Whitfield. I also would like to thank Laura Weston for having prepared the bibliography and taken many of the photographs, Martha Jay for her meticulous editorial contributions, Helen Kemp for her proofreading and Joan Davis for compiling the index. Karen-Edis Barzman deserves special mention for having organized the splendid *In Vino Veritas* conference at Binghamton University in April 2009 where I was introduced to many texts and ideas from outside my own field of art history.

Michael Leaman, publisher of Reaktion Books, was a master of efficiency and diplomacy in overseeing the design and publication of the manuscript as well as in coordinating its release with the fall 2010 opening of the exhibition 'Wine and Spirit: Rituals, Remedies, and Revelry' at the Mount Holyoke College Art Museum. There, in the sylvan hills of western Massachusetts, three lissome women, Marianne Doezema, the museum's director, Wendy Watson, its curator, and Rachel Beaupre, Curatorial Assistant, attended to this joint venture with the zealous possession of maenads conducting the rituals of Dionysus. Exchanging wine for coffee, and the *thyrsus* for computers, they danced between the discrete needs of book and exhibition, tempering their frenzy with a seemingly effortless *sprezzatura*. For all the practical, tactical, and spiritual support they offered as these words evolved into print, I raise a dedicatory glass in tribute.

list of illustrations

Frontispiece: Detail from 66: David Ryckaert III, *Temptation of St Anthony*, 1649, oil on copper. Mount Holyoke College Art Museum, South Hadley, MA (purchased with the Warbeke Art Museum Fund, 2009.2.2; photo Petegorsky/Gipe).

1 Neolithic Wine Jar from Hajji Firuz Tepe, *c.* 5400–5000 BC, clay. University of Pennsylvania Museum, Philadelphia, PA (photo courtesy of the University of Pennsylvania Museum).

2 Mesopotamian *Banquet Scene*, lapis lazuli cylinder seal and cast of seal from the 'Queen's Grave' at Ur, *c.* 2600 BC. British Museum, London (photo © The Trustees of The British Museum/Art Resource, NY).

3 *Men making wine, plucking poultry, and bringing offerings to the dead*, detail of Egyptian 18th dynasty (16th–14th century BC) wall painting in the tomb of Nakht, Thebes. Photo © François Guenet/Art Resource, NY.

4 *Ram-headed Situla from the Midas Mound at Gordion*, 8th century BC, University of Pennsylvania Museum, Philadelphia, PA (photo courtesy of the University of Pennsylvania Museum); the original artefact is in the Museum of Anatolian Civilization, Ankara.

5 *Red-figure kylix of Youth in a Wineshop*, attributed to Douris, *c.* 480 BC. Private collection, London (photo courtesy of Sotheby's, Inc.).

6 *Dionysus and his Entourage*, detail from the François Vase, *c.* 570 BC, from Furtwängler, *Griechische Vasenmalerei*. Museo Archeologico Nazionale, Florence.

7 *Dionysus and his Entourage* black-figure amphora by the Rycroft Painter, *c.* 530–520 BC. Worcester Art Museum, Worcester, MA.

8 Side view of red-figure kylix with *Dancing Maenad*, attributed to Oltos, *c.* 525–500 BC. Mount Holyoke College Art Museum, South Hadley, MA (purchased with the Nancy Everett Dwight Fund, 1967.11.B.SII; photo Petegorsky/Gipe).

9 Black-figure skyphos with Herakles, Athena and Hermes, attributed to the Theseus Painter, *c.* 500 BC. Mount Holyoke College Art Museum, South Hadley, MA (purchased with the Nancy Everett Dwight Fund, 1925.3.B.SII; photo Petegorsky/Gipe).

10 *Dancing Maenad*, interior of a red-figure kylix attributed to Oltos,

525–500 BC. Mount Holyoke College Art Museum, South Hadley, MA (purchased with the Nancy Everett Dwight Fund, 1967.11.B.SII; photo Petegorsky/Gipe).

11 *Dionysus Sailing the Sea*, black-figure kylix by Exekias, 540 BC. Staatliche Antikensammlung, Munich (photo Preussischer Kulturbesitz/Art Resource, NY).

12 *Gigantomachia*, red-figure amphora by the Suessula Painter, *c.* 410–400 BC. Musée du Louvre, Paris (photo Réunion des Musées Nationaux/Art Resource, NY).

13 *Dionysus and his Entourage*, red-figure hydria in the manner of the Meidias Painter, *c.* 400 BC–390 BC. Harvard Art Museum, Arthur M. Sackler Museum (bequest of David M. Robinson, 1960.347; photo © President and Fellows of Harvard College).

14 *Women Ladling Wine before Dionysus*, red-figure stamnos by the Dinos Painter, late 5th century BC. Museo Archeologico Nazionale, Naples (photo courtesy of Scala/Art Resource, NY).

15 *Reveller*, red-figure kylix attributed to Douris, *c.* 480 BC. Museum of Fine Arts, Boston (Henry Lillie Pierce Fund, 98.930; photo © 2010 Museum of Fine Arts, Boston).

16 *A Symposium*, black-figure amphora attributed to the circle of the Affecter Painter, *c.* 550–525 BC. Mead Art Museum, Amherst College, Amherst, MA (Museum Purchase, AC 1950.59).

17 *A Symposium*, red-figure kylix attributed to Makron, signed by Hieronas potter, *c.* 480 BC. The Metropolitan Museum of Art, New York, NY (photo © The Metropolitan Museum of Art/Art Resource, NY).

18 *Erotic Scene*, red-figure kylix attributed to Douris, *c.* 480 BC. Museum of Fine Art, Boston (gift of Landon T. Clay, 1970.233; photo © 2010 Museum of Fine Arts, Boston).

19 *Two Youths at a Symposium*, red-figure kylix by the Colmar Painter, *c.* 500–490 BC. Musée du Louvre, Paris (photo courtesy Réunion des Musées Nationaux/Art Resource, NY).

20 Drawing of a detail of a *Symposium* vase with a woman drinking from a phallic-footed kylix, *c.* 510 BC; after Lissargue, *The Aesthetics of the Greek Banquet* (Princeton, NJ: Princeton University Press, 1991).

21 *Seated Silenus*, terracotta vase, 4th century BC. The Metropolitan Museum of Art, New York (photo © The Metropolitan Museum of Art/Art Resource, NY).

22 *Drunken Silenus on a Lion Skin*, bronze, 270–250 BC, found in the Villa of the Pisoni, Herculaneum. Museo Archeologico Nazionale, Naples (photo courtesy Erich Lessing/Art Resource, NY).

23 Wine merchant's sign in Pompeii, 1st century AD. Photo courtesy of Werner Forman/Art Resource, NY.

24 Silver goblet with skeletons, from the Treasure of Boscoreale, late 1st century BC–1st century AD. Musée du Louvre, Paris (photo courtesy of Réunion des Musées Nationaux/Art Resource, NY).

25 *Mosaic skeleton* from Pompeii, 1st century AD. Museo Archeologico

Bible, *c.* 1320–30. British Library, London (photo © HIP/Art Resource, NY).

44 *Christ in the Winepress*, woodcut, 15th century. Staatsbibliothek, Munich. Photo Mount Holyoke College Art Museum, South Hadley, MA.

45 Zanino di Pietro, *The Last Supper*, 1466, fresco in Chiesa di S. Giorgio, San Polo di Piave. Photo courtesy of Cameraphoto Arte, Venice/Art Resource, NY.

46 Leonardo da Vinci, *The Last Supper*, fresco in Santa Maria delle Grazie, Milan, *c.* 1495–8. Photo courtesy of Erich Lessing/Art Resource, NY.

47 Paolo Veronese, *The Feast in the House of Levi*, 1573, oil on canvas. Galleria dell'Accademia di Venezia, Venice (photo courtesy of Alinari/Art Resource, NY).

48 Jacopo Pontormo, *Supper at Emmaus*, 1525, oil on canvas. Galleria degli Uffizi, Florence (photo courtesy of Scala/Ministero per i Beni e le Attività culturali/Art Resource, NY).

49 Michelangelo Buonarroti, *The Drunkenness of Noah*, *c.* 1508–1512, fresco in Sistine Chapel, Rome. Photo courtesy of Erich Lessing/Art Resource, NY.

50 Hieronymus Wierix, *Christ in the Mystical Winepress*, before 1619, engraving. Mount Holyoke College Art Museum, South Hadley, MA.

51 Andrea Mantegna, *Bacchanal with Silenus*, 2nd half of 15th century, etching. Musée du Louvre, Paris (photo courtesy of Réunion des Musées Nationaux/Art Resource, NY).

52 Michelangelo Buonarroti, *Bacchus*, 1496–7, marble. Museo Nazionale del Bargello, Florence (photo © Alinari/Art Resource, NY).

53 Giovanni Bellini and Titian, *Feast of the Gods*, 1514/29, oil on canvas. National Gallery of Art, Washington, DC (Widener Collection, 1942.9.1.(597)/PA; image courtesy of the Board of Trustees, National Gallery of Art).

54 Titian, *Meeting of Bacchus and Ariadne*, 1520–23, oil on canvas. National Gallery, London (photo © National Gallery/Art Resource, NY).

55 Titian, *Bacchanal of the Andrians*, 1518–19, oil on canvas. Museo del Prado, Madrid (photo courtesy of Scala/Art Resource, NY).

56 Giovanni Paolo Lomazzo, *Self-Portrait*, 1568, oil on canvas. Pinacoteca di Brera, Milan (photo courtesy of Scala/Art Resource, NY).

57 Maiolica puzzle jug, late 16th–early 17th century. Philadelphia Museum of Art, Philadelphia (1998.176.8).

58 Pieter Coecke van Aelst, *Prodigal Son*, *c.* 1530, oil on panel. Museo Correr, Venice (photo © Cameraphoto Arte, Venice/Art Resource, NY).

59 Jan van Hemessen, *Loose Company*, 1543, oil on panel. Wadsworth Atheneum, Hartford, CT (The Ella Gallup Sumner and Mary Catlin Sumner Collection Fund, 1941.233; photo courtesy of Wadsworth Atheneum Museum of Art/Art Resource, NY).

60 Hieronymus Bosch, *Allegory of Intemperance*, *c.* 1495–1500, oil on panel. Yale University Art Gallery, New Haven (gift of Hannah D. and Louis M. Rabinowitz, 1959.15.22).

61 Erhard Schoen, *Four Properties of Wine*, 1528, woodcut. Photo Mount Holyoke College Art Museum, South Hadley, MA.

79 Hendrick Terbrugghen, *Young Man with Wineglass by Candlelight*, 1623, oil on canvas. Private collection (image © Sterling and Francine Clark Institute, Williamstown, Massachusetts).

80 Jan Steen, *Merry Company* ('As the Old Sing, so Pipe the Young'), 1663, oil on canvas. Royal Cabinet of Paintings 'Mauritshuis', The Hague (photo courtesy of Scala/Art Resource, NY).

81 David Teniers the Younger, *Tavern Scene*, 1680, oil on canvas. The Memorial Art Gallery of the University of Rochester, Rochester, NY (Bertha Buswell Bequest, 55.70).

82 Jan Vermeer, *Officer and Laughing Girl*, c. 1657, oil on canvas. The Frick Collection, New York.

83 Gerard Terborch, *The Gallant Officer*, 1662–3, oil on canvas. Musée du Louvre, Paris (photo courtesy of Réunion des Musées Nationaux/Art Resource, NY).

84 Pieter Claesz., *Still-life with Roemer*, 1647, oil on panel. Private collection (photo: Petegorsky/Gipe).

85 Judith Leyster, *The Last Drop*, c. 1639, oil on canvas. Philadelphia Museum of Art, Philadelphia, PA (John G. Johnson Collection, 1917; photo © The Philadelphia Museum of Art/Art Resource, NY).

86 'The Lawes of Drinking', frontispiece from Richard Brathwaite, *The Solemn Jovial Disputation...* (London, 1617). Photo Houghton Library, Harvard University, Cambridge, MA.

87 Circle of William Hogarth, *Mr Woodbridge and Captain Holland*, 1730, oil on canvas. Private collection (photo © Agnew's, London, courtesy of The Bridgeman Art Library).

88 Thomas Rowlandson, *The Brilliants*, 1801, lithograph. Photo courtesy of The Bridgeman Art Library.

89 Roger Fenton, *The Wounded Zouave*, 1856, salt print photograph. Mount Holyoke College Art Museum, South Hadley, MA (purchased with the Abbie Bosworth Williams (Class of 1927) Fund, 2009.11; photo Petegorsky/Gipe).

90 Jean-Baptiste-Camille Corot, *Bacchanal at the Spring*, 1872, oil on canvas. Museum of Fine Arts, Boston (Robert Dawson Evans Collection, 17.3234; photo © 2010 Museum of Fine Arts, Boston).

91 Honoré Daumier, *The Drinking Song*, 1860–63, pencil, watercolour, conté crayon, and pen and ink on laid paper. Sterling and Francine Clark Art Institute, Williamstown, MA, 1955.1504 (image © Sterling and Francine Clark Art Institute).

92 Edouard Manet, *Déjeuner sur l'herbe* ('Luncheon on the Grass'), 1863, oil on canvas. Musée d'Orsay, Paris (photo courtesy of Erich Lessing/Art Resource, NY).

93 Claude Monet, *Déjeuner sur l'herbe* ('Luncheon on the Grass'), 1865–6, oil on canvas. State Pushkin Museum of Fine Arts, Moscow (photo courtesy of Scala/Art Resource, NY).

94 Pierre Auguste Renoir, *Luncheon of the Boating Party*, 1881, oil on canvas. Phillips Collection, Washington, DC (photo courtesy of The Bridgeman Art

index